AFRICAN CIVILISATIONS
IN THE NEW WORLD

AFRICAN CIVILISATIONS IN THE NEW WORLD

by
ROGER BASTIDE

Translated from the French by
PETER GREEN

With a Foreword by
GEOFFREY PARRINDER

HARPER TORCHBOOKS
Harper & Row, Publishers
New York, Evanston, San Francisco, London

PREFACE

A myth of the American Negro past has been that there was no past, that all marks of culture were lost in the terrible uprooting from the African homelands whence Negroes were taken physically and spiritually naked to America, so that they came to accept an alien civilisation without hindrance. A modification of this notion was that nasty or irrational things survived or were invented, such as Voodoo, to prove that Negro mentality remained African and could not be assimilated into the social and technical patterns of the New World. Then the idea of *négritude* arose as a reaction against assimilation, often adopting an uncritical enthusiasm for the African heritage. Even the best intentions could be turned to support the conviction that Negroes were at once innocent arrivals in America and also that they could not be integrated because they did not change, either in the past or the present.

Amid these and other theories Roger Bastide has sought for many years, with great learning and skill, to discover and present the facts. A professor at the Sorbonne in Paris, with a profound knowledge of American Negro religions, especially southern and central, and also of the African background, it is surprising that none of his books has hitherto been translated into English.

The choice of the present work as an introduction to a wider public is doubly fortunate. It presents his picture of the whole of Negro America, and it shows how widely his references range through French, English, Spanish, Portuguese and other languages, some of which are unknown or not available to the general reader. The opening chapters sketch the facts of immigration through the slave trade and the kind of societies that were established. It is worth while reading these chapters carefully as they, with the illustrative tables, give the framework to the whole picture. But Bastide has an especial interest in Negro religions and the long chapters that follow compose the central sections of his book. His expert description of the original African religions, which survive in some forms in Africa – Fanti-Ashanti, Calabar, Yoruba and others – is thoroughly trustworthy. These are based on first hand investigations in Africa, which African specialists will know to be fully reliable, but which need to be taken into account by a wider public and particularly that which is concerned with American Negro religions. Against this outline the study of Voodoo, in its varieties and changes, is given far more clearly, sympathetically yet scientifically, than in the great majority of writings on Voodoo. Just as important is the further chapter on the mixtures of African religion with Christianity apart from Voodoo, with special attention to the different expressions which have appeared in Roman Catholic and Protestant parts of America. In a brief conclusion Bastide surveys a changing world, with its new social, technical and urban problems, in which Afroamerican culture neither continues unchanged nor disappears. In fact he sees this culture spreading to Europeans in a new integration, and the whole pattern of culture-contact takes on larger dimensions. His book, however, is scientific rather than speculative, it always looks from theories back to facts, and it is a major contribution to racial understanding whose appearance in English dress will be welcomed by lovers of African and Afroamerican cultures.

University of London

GEOFFREY PARRINDER

CONTENTS

INTRODUCTION

The current vogue for the study of African civilisations in America is a comparatively recent phenomenon. Before the abolition of slavery such a thing was inconceivable, since up till then the Negro had simply been regarded as a source of labour, not as the bearer of a culture. The study of institutions, or particular methods of production – their historical origins, development, and economic value – was a pursuit reserved for philosophers and scholars. But when the Negro became a citizen, a question of some urgency arose concerning him. Could he, or could he not, be integrated into the population as a whole? Was he assimilable, was he capable of becoming completely 'Latin' or 'Anglo-Saxon'? Or did he possess an alien culture of his own, with quite different *mores* and modes of thought, that would prevent (or at the very least seriously hamper) his absorption into Western society? This is what led one of the pioneer investigators in the field, Nina Rodrigues of Brazil, to study the religion of the Negroes in his country, where – amid a flourishing Portuguese civilisation, and under a surface camouflage of Catholicism – what he termed 'fetichistic animism' was still extremely active. His final verdict proved a negative one. He spoke of 'the illusion of catechesis': according to him, the Brazilian Negro belonged to a wholly alien world, and remained impervious to modern ideas.[1] Fernando Ortiz came to very similar conclusions when investigating the African population of Cuba, which he described as a *Lumpenproletariat*, living on the margins of society.[2] The same is true of Haiti, where the urban *élite* (consisting largely of mulattos) shows bitter hostility to the Voodoo cult of the rural masses (these being for the most part Negroes), arguing that it constitutes the biggest obstacle to the island's social and economic development.

Yet it was in Haiti that the concept of *négritude*, of 'black culture', first arose: though the recognition of Voodoo as a cultural reality (rather than a mere tissue of superstitions) had to wait until the island was occupied by North Americans. It was, indeed, this occupation which awoke a sense of nationalism among the *élite*, made them aware that all Haitians shared a common cultural heritage, and finally, through Price-Mars, produced an enthusiastic reassessment of their African past.[3] Yet in both cases, as this survey makes clear, the problem of Negro civilisation in the Americas was approached from a political rather than a scientific viewpoint. From the very beginning, science was trapped in a web of propaganda (both pro and con), and used to serve primarily ideological ends.

It has taken a long time (and then only during the past few decades) for science to sever its connections with ideology. No man has contributed more to the process of severance than Melville J. Herskovits. His most praiseworthy achievement has been to apply the principles and methods of cultural anthropology to the study of African survivals in Black America. He also deserves credit for the way in which, during the course of his enquiries, he progressively refined and improved his research technique. To begin with, modestly enough, he applied the functional theory (then current among British and American anthropologists) simply to isolate the existence of any such survivals. If whole areas of culture had resisted the appalling pressures put upon them by slavery, that meant that such African customs served a purpose, were useful, fulfilled some function that was indispensable to the survival of the Negro group concerned. From here Herskovits back-tracked along the chain of causality, probing African civilisations for the origins of those cultural traits he had met with among American Negroes, using comparative and historical methods in conjunction. Finally, under the influence of the so-called 'Culture and Personality' school, and basing himself on the idea that cultures are always acquired, never innate, he seems to have become increasingly preoccupied, until his death, with investigating those psychological mechanisms by means of which the American Negro adapted himself to a new milieu through the intermediary assistance of his African heritage.[4]

Yet have the links between science and ideology in fact been wholly severed? In a period such as ours, when the problem of racial integration faces the whole of America (and sometimes, as in the United States, provokes violent reactions), while

Europe, no less than Africa and Asia, is grappling with the problem of decolonisation – can we possibly hope for absolute impartiality? Even the most honest scholar, for all his determination to remain objective, is almost sure to be swayed, despite himself, by certain background assumptions, the more insidious since he is unconscious of them. The sociology of knowledge has accustomed us to make allowances for such subjective distortions, on the student's part, in the object of his researches. And even if the description he gives us is accurate, may it not still have repercussions on the *praxis* of those racial groups in active ferment today? Truth is not a mere copy of reality: it is always dynamic, involved in action. For example, when Herskovits launched his famous notion of 'reinterpretation', what else was he doing, in fact, but giving a modern twist to the old North American segregationist theory? By maintaining, in effect, that the Negro, when forced to adjust to a new environment, always does so in his own way, reinterpreting the West in African terms, does not Herskovits tacitly admit that the African mentality never changes? And by so doing, does he not (no doubt quite unintentionally) lend support to those who maintain that the Negro is non-assimilable? At all events, black sociologists such as Frazier have clearly perceived the danger which Herskovits' theory constitutes for their people's cause, and have reacted violently against it.[5] As they see it, slavery utterly destroyed Negro culture – at least in the United States – and left nothing but a gaping void in its place. When they talk of the assimilation of the American Negro, they are not referring to a change-over between African and Anglo-Saxon cultures. For them the transition is from white-imposed anarchy to a reorganisation of the Negro group along lines suggested by its social environment. Thus the Herskovits–Frazier debate is something more than a straightforward clash between scholars. Behind it – colouring its arguments and expressions, perhaps even the root cause of dissension – we glimpse the grim drama of racial integration. Yet cannot integration itself be seen as a kind of betrayal, the most terrible form which Negro alienation could assume? The idea of *négritude* was born in the West Indies, and its ideological aim is to bring the American Negro back to the roots of his ancestral culture. Here Herskovits, who laid such emphasis on the Negro's fidelity to his past, scores heavily. Any scholar who sets out to study Afroamerican problems, then, finds himself involved, willy-nilly, in an agonised debate – and one on the outcome of which the whole future of America depends. He must keep a close eye on his conclusions, not as a means of disguising what he regards as reality, but in order to conduct a special kind of research-within-research, on himself: a species of intellectual-cum-psychological self-analysis (whether he is black or white makes no odds). For here we stand at the very heart of the alienated world, where any scholar – despite his best intentions – is alienated too.

REFERENCES

1. Nina Rodrigues, *L'animisme fétichiste des nègres de Bahia*, Bahia, 1900.
2. Fernando Ortiz, *Hampa Afro-cubana: Los Negros Brujos*, Madrid, n.d.
3. L. Price-Mars, *Ainsi parla l'oncle*, Compiègne, 1923.
4. *The Myth of the Negro Past*, New York, 1941, rev. ed. 1958; 'Problem, method and theory in Afroamerican studies', *Afroamerica* I, 1 and 2 (1945); 'Some psychological implications of Afroamerican studies', *Selected Papers of the XXIXth Int. Congress of Americanists*, Chicago, 1952.
5. E. Franklin Frazier, *The Negro in the United States*, New York, 1949.

CHAPTER I

SOME BASIC FACTS

Neither a historical survey, properly considered, nor a study of slavery as a means of production is called for here. All we need is to sketch in any facts from the American colonial period which may have some influence on the survival – or, *per contra*, the disappearance – of African cultural patterns amongst American Negroes. From this viewpoint, the first important fact to be borne in mind is the volume and continuity of the slave trade. Unfortunately we have a lack of reliable evidence on this problem, since large numbers of documents have either disappeared or still remain buried in archives. As a result, statistics vary quite remarkably according to which source one consults. The *Encyclopédie catholique* estimates the number of slaves transported from Africa to the New World at 12,000,000; according to Helps, the total figure was not more than 5–6,000,000. The trouble is that the criteria employed to calculate the traffic in slaves vary from author to author. Some simply work out their statistics on the basis of the dues or taxes paid by the slave dealers (or their customers): but this ignores all clandestine traffic – something which always existed, to a greater or lesser extent. Others base their figures on the known range of products (both agricultural and mineral), the productivity rate of a slave *per annum*, his length of service (seven years was the average): but all these factors remain to some extent arbitrary. Other scholars, again, start from the number of ships chartered for the slave-trade, their individual tonnage, and the length of the voyages they undertook (discounting the months they spent in port). It has been calculated that on the so-called 'three-cornered run' – Africa–America–Europe–Africa – a Spanish or Portuguese vessel only shipped a cargo of slaves once every eighteen months.[1] Any figures we may reach, then, will be the merest approximations. Here are those given in the *Negro Year Book* for 1931–2:[2]

1666–1776:	Slaves imported exclusively by the English for the English, French and Spanish colonies	3,000,000
1680–1786:	Slaves imported for the English colonies of America	2,130,000
1716–1756:	Slaves imported into the other New World colonies, at the rate of about 70,000 *per annum*	3,500,000
1752–1762:	Jamaica receives 71,000 slaves	
1759–1765:	Guadeloupe receives 40,000 slaves	
1776–1800:	Average imports *per annum*: English, 38,000; Portuguese, 10,000; Dutch, 4,000; French, 20,000; Danes, 2,000; total, 74,000, reaching a cumulative total of	1,850,000

We may note, however, that several of these figures contradict one another, and, above all, that no information is given for the nineteenth century – though this was the period when the slave-trade reached its peak, and is of the greatest importance for anyone attempting to understand contemporary Afroamerican cultural patterns.

In the United States, for instance, the northern states never had a Negro population of more than 5 per cent. Agriculture in this area was handled through smallholdings or medium-sized farms; the population consisted largely of religious dissenters, craftsmen and factory workers, engaged in activities which presupposed an ideology of freedom. It is true that in the south, the home of the great plantations, slavery expanded considerably from the eighteenth century onwards: in 1756 Virginia had 120,156 Negroes against 173,316 whites, in 1742 Maryland had 140,000 Negroes and only 100,000 whites, while in 1765 the figures for both Carolinas were 90,000 Negroes, 40,000 whites. Nevertheless, it was only after the invention of the machine-loom and the consequent boom in cotton production at the beginning of the nineteenth century that the slave-trade really reached its peak. During this period some 80,000 Negroes were imported annually. Similarly in Brazil: it was the expansion of the coffee industry that sent nineteenth-century slave imports soaring. In 1798, of a total population of 3,250,000 inhabitants, 1,582,000 were slaves and 406,000 free Negroes: by 1817, when the over-all total had risen to 3,817,000, the slaves numbered 1,930,000, and the free Negroes 585,000.

It should be noted that the coloured population did not increase solely as a result of the slave-trade. Other contributory factors were a birth-rate that exceeded the number of deaths, and a more equitable ratio between the sexes. In Cuba, for example, it was only after the abolition of the slave-trade that the black population began to rise. This phenomenon came about quite spontaneously, through the elimination of the unmarried surplus (more male than female workers were purchased in Africa), and the progressive equalisation of the sexes at birth. In Jamaica, on the other hand, the steady increase of colour among the population during the nineteenth century was due to the departure of the white landowners after slavery was abolished. In 1830 there were 324,000 coloured persons to 20,000 whites (that is, one white to every sixteen mulattos or blacks): in 1890, 620,000 against 15,000 (a ratio of one to forty-one). Thus little by little certain parts of America began to 'go black'.

However, as an aid to explaining the survival of ancient traditions, it is less important to ascertain the actual numbers of Africans imported than to identify their ethnic origin. This is a problem which has greatly interested Afroamerican ethnologists,[3] and concerning which certain observations need to be made. To begin with, the sources tapped for slaves vary from one country to another. Negroes imported into English colonies came mostly from what used to be known as the Gold Coast, while Spanish territories drew largely on Angola and the Congo. Even within the same area there was liable to be a change of source from time to time. Bahia in Brazil offers a good example. During the sixteenth century its trade was with the Guinea Coast (using that term in its broadest sense); during the seventeenth, with Angola; during the eighteenth, with the Côte de Mina. Finally, during the nineteenth century, when the traffic became illegal and clandestine, we find that the distribution was of a less regular pattern: between 1803 and 1810 twenty ships arrived from the Côte de Mina, bringing 47,114 Sudanese, and thirty-one from Angola, with 11,494 Bantus.[4] It is clear that such cultural traits as were imported during the seventeenth and eighteenth centuries have been lost, and that present-day Afroamerican societies go back only to the very end of the slave-trade; which explains why, in Bahia, the Bantu civilisation has been eclipsed by that from the Côte de Mina.

Secondly, though evidence as to ethnic origin may be of great interest historically speaking, it offers little of value to the ethnologist. It seems clear that a slave was given a Christian name (if he had been baptised), or a first name from mythology if he was a *bossale*:[5] but in either case his surname would indicate his ethnic origin. Consequently the nominal rolls of plantations provide us with interesting information concerning their workers' tribal and geographic distribution. Nevertheless, such evidence does not take us very far, since surnames were not chosen by the Negroes themselves, but picked for them by their white masters. The result tended to be names that were far too generalised for the ethnologist. He could do very little, for instance, with a name like 'John Congo'. When we consider the bewildering variety of Congolese ethnic groups, and the heterogeneous nature of their cultural patterns (e.g. some patrilinear, others matrilinear), it becomes immediately apparent that the plantation rolls can be of very little use to us. To confuse matters further, a slave was often given, not the name of his own ethnic region, but that of the port from which he embarked. For example, anyone shipped from the fort of El Mina, be he Ashanti, Ewe or Yoruba, was known indiscriminately as 'Mina'. Above all, when we catalogue all the tribal names that occur in the inventories (as, e.g., Beltram has done for Mexico and Escalante for Colombia), we find that there is hardly a single African tribe that failed to provide a contingent for the New World. Wolof, Manding, Bambara, Bissago, Agni: the list is interminable. Yet these Negroes, for the most part, have left no surviving trace of their original native cultures. It follows that the best method of investigating Afroamerican social groups is not to start in Africa, and see how much of what we find there survives across the Atlantic, but rather to study Afroamerican cultural patterns as they exist today, and then work gradually back from them towards Africa. The most profitable line of approach, in other words, is precisely the opposite of that pursued by historians.[6]

The last important observation to be made on this topic is that America offers us a most extraordinary instance of schism between ethnic origins and cultural patterns. In the beginning, as is well known, urban slaves and 'free blacks' were formed into 'nations', with their own 'kings' and 'governors'. There are two possible explanations of such a phenomenon. It may have been deliberate policy on the part of the governing classes, designed to prevent the slaves from acquiring the notion that they were an exploited group, and operating through the old formula of 'divide and rule'. Moreover, such a policy paid off, since every plot was betrayed in advance to the white bosses by slaves of another tribe or group. Alternatively, we may have here a genuinely spontaneous process of association, especially amongst those Negroes who followed a trade or craft. Fellow-countrymen wanted an opportunity to meet one another; they also sought some way of celebrating their customary feast days together, and of keeping up – under a top-dressing of Catholicism – their own religious traditions.

These 'nations' were organised with most admirable efficiency, and numerous examples of them are on record, ranging from the United States (where, in the north at least, the Negroes elected their own governors) down as far as the Argentine. In Rio de la Plata we find four 'nations', Conga, Mandingo, Ardra and Congo, the more important being subdivided into 'provinces'. In Montevideo, similarly, the Congo 'nation' was composed of no less than six 'provinces': Cunga, Guanda, Angola, Munjolo, Basundi and Boma.[7] In Peru, according to Ricardo Palma, 'the Angolans, Caravelis, Mozambiquians, Congos, Chalas and Terranovans bought houses in the outer suburbs [of Lima] and there established their so-called Fraternity Houses', also known as *cabildos*, complete with kings, queens, ladies-in-waiting and orchestras.[8] Fernando Ortiz has written an excellent monograph on the *cabildos* of Cuba and their masked dancers, known as *diablitos*. Here, again, we find various 'nations': Ganga, Lucumi, Carabali, Congo, and so on.[9] In Brazil, the division into 'nations' operated at several different levels and in various institutions. To begin with, there was the army, where coloured troops formed four separate battalions, known as Minas, Ardras, Angolans and creoles. There were the Catholic religious fraternities: in Bahia, for instance, that of Our Lady of the Rosary had only Angolan members, while Yorubas met in a down-town church. Finally, there were the cult-groups and mutual-aid societies, with their fraternity houses in the suburbs. It was here, in private, that genuine African religious ceremonies took place, and armed rebellions were planned.

But after the suppression, first of the slave-trade, and then of slavery itself, these 'nations', in so far as they were ethnically-based groups, soon vanished. We need only establish some Negro genealogies to see that ethnic fusion became the rule: what emerged everywhere was a generalised 'Negro type', of highly mixed origins. When Frazier visited Brazil he was struck by this phenomenon;[10] it was quite liable, for instance, to produce a pattern of miscegenation such as the following:

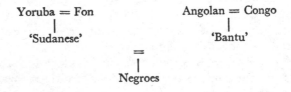

However, while such inter-marriages dissolved the old ethnic groupings, the 'nations' continued to flourish as centres of traditional culture, in the form of such institutions as *santaria*, *candomblés*, or *Vaudous*. In Brazil, for example, we find a whole variety of *candomblés*: Nago (Yoruba), Ewe, Quetu (a town in Dahomey), Oyo (a town in Nigeria), Ijesha (a district of Nigeria), Angola, Congo, and so on. In other words, these civilisations became detached from the ethnic group which imported them, and took on a life of their own. They were capable of attracting not only mulattos and Indian half-breeds, but also a number of Europeans; we hear of certain 'daughters of God' who were French or Spanish by origin, doubtless white-skinned, but nevertheless regarded as 'African' on account of their wholehearted participation in a cultural pattern brought over from Africa itself.[11] In Cuba there existed a secret society among the Calabar Negroes (Efik or Efor, known as *Ñañigos*); side by side with this there sprang up a white society of the same name, founded by a French half-breed. It borrowed the Negroes' rites and beliefs; the only difference lay in its being more of a political pressure-group (somewhat akin to free-masonry) than a purely religious brotherhood dedicated to the quest for immortality.[12]

In these conditions it is easy to see how students can speak of a double *diaspora*: that of African cultural traits, which transcend ethnic groupings, and that of the Negroes themselves, who have lost their original African characteristics through interbreeding, and have been absorbed by their social environment – English, Spanish, French, or Portuguese.

When we examine the first of these two phenomena, one fact strikes us immediately. In any given area there is a dominant African culture; *but the predominance of that culture (whichever it may be) bears no direct relation to the preponderance of such-and-such an ethnic group in the slave-shipments to the area concerned.* To judge from the record, one might suppose that, once slavery had been abolished and inter-marriage was the rule, a bitter struggle developed between the 'nations' (now purely cultural associations without any ethnic basis), and that this struggle culminated in the triumph of one culture over the rest. For instance, in Bahia (Brazil), though we still find Nago (Yoruba), Gêgê (Dahomean), Angolan and Congo *candomblés*, nevertheless it is the Nago *candomblé* alone which has inspired all the rest with their theology (through a system of correspondences between the gods of the various ethnic groups), their ceremonial ritual, and their basic festivals. In Haiti the various nations have been transformed into 'mysteries', or, in other words, have become divinities: Congo Mayombé, Congo Mandragues, Mandragues Gé-Rouge, Ibo, Caplaou, Badagri, Maki, Bambara, Conga. Caught up in the movement towards syncretism, they have come under the sway of the dominant Dahomean religion, so that today the various cultural patterns they represent are no more than integrated and subordinated elements of Fon culture.[13] Examples could be multiplied. It is, then, possible to chart the geographical distribution of the various dominant cultures from Africa, each of which (to put the matter briefly) has set the tone for one (and only one) region of America.

In the United States we have to take note of two main centres. The first, that of the Gullah Islands and Virginia, seems to have been occupied by a cultural group which originated in the former Gold Coast, now Ghana. The types of drum found in Virginia during the mid-eighteenth century (and now on display in the British Museum), together with the practice of naming children after their birthday, both provide clear cultural links with the Fanti–Ashanti civilisation. The second centre spreads out from New Orleans towards the southern states, and testifies to the existence, in Louisiana, of a double-level culture, Dahomean in religion (*Vaudou* cult) and Bantu as regards its folklore (the *calenda* dance). In Central America we find an Afroamerican cultural zone of a highly unusual type, that of the Black Caribs. Here the African and Indian elements have undergone so close a process of syncretisation that it is virtually impossible to distinguish between them. Yoruba culture is predominant in Cuba and Trinidad, in north-east Brazil (Alagoas, Recife, Bahia), and in southern Brazil (from Porto Alegre to Pelotas). In these various regions one also finds nuclei of different cultural groupings (Carabali, Congo, etc.), but without the determining influence of Yoruba culture, which dominates all the rest. On Haiti, and in northern Brazil (S. Luiz do Maranhão), it is Dahomean, and more particularly Fon, culture which leads the field. The predominant cultural pattern on Jamaica is that of the Gold Coast Kromantis, both in the religious sphere and as regards names and folklore (e.g. the tales about Miss Nancy, i.e. *Anansi*, or the spider). Kromanti would also appear to be the main dominant influence (though to a less pronounced degree) in all the other English colonies throughout the West Indies – e.g. Barbados (the game of *wari*, *yam*-festival) and St Lucia (*yam*-festival, *apinti* drum). But it is above all among the Bush Negroes of Dutch and French Guiana that we find Fanti–Ashanti Gold Coast culture in its purest form. This is not to say that it has not incorporated certain alien elements – the Dahomean *Vodous*, for instance, and certain Bantu spirits such as the Loanga Winti; but when it does so, they have become integral elements of Fanti–Ashanti culture. Thus we can already construct a provisional map of black America, indicating the dominant African civilisations. This map (I repeat) bears no necessary relation to any original *ethnic* predominance.

However, these African civilisations have in the course of time undergone greater or lesser modifications, and in some cases have finally disappeared altogether. As a result there is another chart we can draw up, indicating the comparative prevalence of African survivals, according to their degree of retention. Herskovits has worked out this table, (see page 14), using the following symbols:

a = pure African
b = strongly African
c = fairly African
d = slightly African
e = faint traces, or none, of African customs
? = no traces[14]

It is obvious that such survivals will to a large extent depend on the density of the black population in certain areas. Undoubtedly there are other factors involved beside the demographic one, and we shall return to them later in the course of this book. To begin with, however, I should like to concentrate on the unequal distribution of Negroes throughout the American continent, and attempt to chart its pattern. People commonly talk of three Americas: white America, which includes both the northern parts of the continent (Canada, a proportion of the U.S.A.) and the extreme south (Uruguay, Chile, the Argentine): Indian America (Central and part of South America): and lastly Black America, the only category with which we are here concerned. It would seem, then, on the face of it, that to draw up a racial-distribution map for the New World is a simple enough task: and so it is, if we are prepared to accept a loose approximation. If, on the other hand, we try to produce relatively precise statistics, we run into difficulties.

The first snag is that none of these countries takes either race or colour into account in its census returns. This is particularly true of the Latin American countries, which regard themselves as 'democracies', i.e. as régimes in which all citizens possess equal rights. Ministry officials feel that to introduce categories of race or colour into their census returns would be a mark of discrimination – something they are anxious to avoid at all costs. It follows that we have no more than approximate estimates, sometimes based on sampling, more often merely impressionistic.

For those countries which *do* indicate their citizens' ethnic origins in such returns, by far the biggest problem is the existence of a mixed-blood population, including every shade of colour from deep black to pale brown. No one really knows

[HERSKOVITS]	Technology	Economic Life	Social Organisation	Institutions	Religion	Magic	Art	Folklore	Masks	Languages
Guiana (bush)	b	b	a	a	a	a	b	a	a	b
(Paramaribo)	c	c	b	c	a	a	c	a	a	c
Haiti (rural)	a	b	b	c	a	b	d	a	a	c
Haiti (towns)	a	d	c	c	b	b	e	a	a	c
Brazil (Bahia)	d	d	b	d	a	a	b	a	a	a
Brazil (Porto Alegre)	e	e	c	d	a	a	e	?	a	c
N. Brazil (towns)	e	d	c	e	a	b	e	d	a	b
N. Brazil (rural)	c	c	b	e	c	b	e	b	b	d
Jamaica (marrono)	c	c	b	b	b	a	e	a	b	c
Jamaica (gen.)	e	d	d	d	c	b	e	b	b	d
Trinidad (Toco)	a	d	c	b	c	b	e	b	a	d
Trinidad (Port of Spain)	e	d	c	b	a	a	e	b	a	c
Cuba	e	d	c	b	a	a	b	b	a	a
Virgin Isles	e	d	c	d	e	c	?	b	?	d
Gullah Isles	c	c	c	d	e	b	e	a	b	b
United States (rural south)	d	e	c	d	c	c	e	c	b	e
U.S. (north)	e	e	c	d	c	c	e	d	b	e

Note: If we are to obtain a reasonably precise geographic picture of the distribution of African cultural traits in America, we must study these two charts (indicating dominant cultures and degrees of survival) simultaneously.

how to classify such a group. Every nation has its own racial ideology, and the census rolls will tend to express this ideological pattern rather than hard demographic facts. Thus in the U.S.A. any person who has a drop of Negro blood in his veins is regarded as 'coloured'. In Brazil, on the other hand, any person who has a drop of white blood in his veins, especially if he enjoys a certain social status, will be treated as a white, or at the very least placed in the 'mulatto' category. But there is more to it than that. In Brazil, each individual fills in his own return, and it is obvious that the coloured person – living as he does in a white-dominated society – will tend to make himself out to be somewhat paler skinned than in fact he is. (This is exactly parallel to a phenomenon we may note in the United States: when people there are questioned about their social position, they all tend to identify themselves as middle-class.) When a citizen is illiterate, the task of deciding on his colour falls to the census clerk, and this is there personal prejudice may creep in. One striking example happened in 1950, when it was found that the black population of Brazil had undergone a sudden increase, while the number of mulattos had dropped off. This ran directly counter to the prevailing trend, which had witnessed a progressive diminution of the 'black' group, and a steady proportional increase of 'whiteness' among the population as a whole. It is clear that on this occasion the census officials had classified dark-skinned mulattos as black, and had only placed those with pale skins in the 'mulatto' category. In Brazil there is also one further difficulty we should take note of: no distinction is drawn between the mulatto and the half-breed or mestizo. In point of fact the *pardos* category includes every variety of mixed blood, and therefore needs to be studied in relation to its environmental context. In the Amazon region, for instance, where there is a tiny proportion of blacks in the population, it is clear that the *pardos* are mostly Indian mestizos: in Bahia, on the other hand, which has a predominantly Negro population, the same term refers largely to mulattos.

Working from census returns and all other possible sources of information, Frank Tannenbaum has worked out statistics (see page 16), to show the numbers of Negroes and mulattos in the various countries of America for the year 1940.

[FRANK TANNENBAUM]

NORTH AMERICA	Negroes	Per-centage	Mulattos	Per-centage	Total population
Alaska	150	0·21	Included		72,961
Canada	20,559	1·80	with		11,422,000
United States	13,455,988	12·01	Negroes		131,669,275
	13,476,697	9·42			143,181,636
MEXICO, ANTILLES, CENTRAL AMERICA					
Mexico	80,000	0·41	40,000	2·04	19,446,015
Antilles	5,500,000	39·29	3,000,000	21·43	14,000,000
Guatemala	4,011	0·12	2,000	0·06	3,284,269
British Honduras	15,000	25·55	20,000	34·03	58,759
Honduras	55,275	4·99	10,000	0·90	1,107,859
S. Salvador	100	0·0001	100	0·0001	1,744,535
Nicaragua	90,000	6·52	40,000	2·28	1,380,287
Costa Rica	26,900	4·09	20,000	0·14	656,129
	5,854,157	13·84	3,403,308	8·04	42,309,452
SOUTH AMERICA					
Colombia	405,076	4·50	2,205,382	24·32	9,205,283
Venezuela	100,000	2·79	1,000,000	27·93	3,580,000
British Guiana	100,000	29·30	80,000	23·44	341,237
Dutch Guiana	17,000	9·55	20,000	11·23	177,980
French Guiana	1,000	0·25	1,000	0·25	40,000
Ecuador	50,000	2·00	150,000	6·00	2,500,000
Peru	29,054	0·41	80,000	0·71	7,023,110
Bolivia	7,800	0·26	5,000	0·15	3,300,000
Brazil	5,789,924	14·00	8,276,321	20·01	41,356,605
Paraguay	5,000	0·52	5,000	0·52	960,000
Uruguay	10,000	0·46	50,000	2·30	2,145,545
Chile	1,000	0·02	3,000	0·06	5,023,539
Argentine	5,000	0·038	10,000	0·076	13,129,723
	6,520,854	7·34	11,885,703	13·38	88,784,023
	25,851,708	9·42	15,289,011	5·56	274,275,111

However, the distribution figures which he gives refer to whole countries or vast areas, and still furnish us with no more than an approximate picture of the actual distribution of Negroes throughout America. The point is that the black population is not evenly distributed among the over-all population of each country: it tends to concentrate in clearly defined areas, which are, for the most part, those where slavery reached its highest peak. Consequently we have both to locate the central points of these 'coloured areas', and to delimit their outer boundaries.

Though slavery once existed there, Canada has never had a large Negro population. What Negro slaves there were tended to be domestic servants. However, the Abolitionist movement in the United States, followed by the War between the States, drove many Negroes to seek refuge in Canada. It has been calculated that in 1860 about 50,000 of them crossed the frontier. By 1900 the annual figure had fallen to 17,000, though it subsequently rose once more, with an influx of immigrants both from the United States and the British dependencies in the West Indies, in search of a higher standard of living. These groups are mainly to be found in Ontario, and in the provinces of Nova Scotia, New Brunswick, and Quebec.

In the United States, the vast majority of all African immigrants' descendants are still concentrated in the rural southern states, which were the slave states *par excellence*, and today account for no less than four-fifths of North America's entire coloured population. One curious historical fact is that the Negroes took no part in the great drive to the west. If we except the states of Texas, Oklahoma, Louisiana, Arkansas and Missouri, which belong more to the south than to the west, we find that in 1940 no more than 2·2 per cent of the over-all American Negro population was domiciled west of the Mississippi. Even in Texas and Oklahoma the Negroes constituted no more than 12·5 per cent of the population. On the other hand there has been (especially during and after the First World War) a large-scale movement of Negroes to the major northern cities. We can explain this movement in terms of the extraordinary industrial development then taking place throughout the north, which produced a virtually unlimited demand for labour. It was also due to the coloured man's desire for any kind of change from his wretched life as a depressed agricultural worker, and the hope that in an area of the U.S.A. which was reputedly free of racialism he might contrive to raise his standard of living. The 1929 Depression and the Second World War produced further waves of immigrants. But while in the south the slaves' descendants were predominantly (78·8 per cent) country dwellers, and as such dispersed over a wide area, those who went north concentrated exclusively in the towns. In 1940 the north had no more than 300,000 Negroes domiciled in rural areas.

This 'Great Migration', as it is now known, has been the subject of an outstanding study by Edward E. Lewis (*The Mobility of the Negro*, New York, 1931). Lewis also emphasises the importance of the crisis in the cotton industry, over and above the industrialisation of the north, as a contributory attraction for would-be immigrants. At all events, in 1910 there were only 1,025,674 Negroes in the north, and no more than 10,000 southern immigrants arriving annually. Between 1916 and 1925 over a million Negroes moved north, and the coloured population in Chicago rose from 44,103 to 109,458. In Cleveland, between 1910 and 1920, we can observe a similar increase, from 8,448 to 34,451; in New York, from 91,709 to 152,467; in Detroit, from 5,741 to 40,838; in Philadelphia, from 84,459 to 134,359. In contrast, during the same period, we find Mississippi losing 15,000 men in a few months, Alabama 50,000, and South Carolina 65,000, with the result that, in the last-named state, the majority of the population became white rather than black. To sum up, then, we find, in the south, a still heavily concentrated Negro population, with percentages varying from a quarter to a half of the total inhabitants (Mississippi, South Carolina, Georgia, Alabama, Louisiana, North Carolina); and in the north, coloured urban agglomerations in large cities as New York, Chicago and Detroit, but few or no Negroes in the rural areas.

Following Tannenbaum's example, I have given one inclusive figure for the West Indies. It is clear that this figure may well convey an erroneous impression, and that here too we need to specify the density of the Negro population in each individual island. Take Cuba, for example: in 1840 the Negro population outnumbered the whites, but since then their proportion has steadily dwindled, and today the official figures are 75 per cent whites, 24 per cent Negroes and mulattos, 1 per cent Chinese. In contrast to this picture, the 3,111,917 inhabitants of Haiti (according to the 1950 census returns) are all, or nearly all, of African descent. The neighbouring Dominican Republic has a population consisting of 13 per cent whites, 68 per cent mulattos, and 19 per cent so-called 'pure' Negroes. In Puerto Rico the figures are 73 per cent whites, a mere 4 per cent Negroes, and 23 per cent mulattos. Jamaica, like Haiti, is almost 100 per cent black; 68 per cent pure Negroes,

28·3 per cent mulattos. The same is true of the Bahamas or Lucayes (85 per cent coloured), Barbados (70 per cent pure Negroes and only 7 per cent white), and, generally speaking, of all the minor British dependencies in the Antilles, such as Dominica and St Lucia. However, after the abolition of slavery, numbers of workers were imported from India, with the result that in some of these islands – Trinidad, for example – we are liable to find a sizeable minority of Indian immigrants. The six small islands that compose the Dutch West Indies also have a predominantly Negro population. When we turn to the French Antilles (the islands of Martinique and Guadeloupe) we once more find the coloured population in the ascendant. In 1959 Dr Jean Benoist estimated the population of Martinique as follows: 1,760 whites, 245,000 Negroes or mestizos, 6,000 Indians and Chinese, making a grand total of 260,000 inhabitants. We have no comparable figures available for Guadeloupe; but on the eve of Abolition there were 12,000 whites (of whom a good three-quarters were in the army or militia) against 93,000 slaves.

It is plain, then, that we have to distinguish between the various islands of the West Indies, since some – such as Cuba and Puerto Rico – are practically white (at least for official purposes), while others, including Jamaica and the Republic of Haiti, are virtually all black, and others again, the Dominican Republic for example, occupy an intermediate position. Similarly with Brazil, a country the size of Europe without Russia, which cannot be treated as a single indivisible *bloc*. We have to distinguish between three different Brazils, – white, black and Indian, or *caboclo*. Here too, as we have done above in the case of the U.S.A., we must distinguish between the various states of the Union: the break-down which follows is based on the 1940 census returns.

State	Negroes and Mestizos	Percentage of State population	Percentage of the total pop. of Brazil
NORTH			
Acre	36,200	45·37	0·24
Amazonia	306,100	68·72	2·07
Para	521,800	55·24	3·53

However, we should note that cross-breeding in this area was almost entirely with the Indian population, and thus it is more

useful, in this particular case, to compare the 'whites' (W) with
the 'blacks', (N) which gives us the following set of statistics
(M = Mestizo):

Acre	43,308 W	11,296 N	24,774 M
Amazonia	274,811 W	63,349 N	540,914 M
Para	420,887 W	89,942 N	430,653 M

State	Negroes and Mestizos	Percentage of State population	Percentage of the total pop. of Brazil
NORTH-EAST			
Maranhão	656,000	53·11	4·43
Piaui	447,100	54·68	3·02
Ceara	987,500	47·23	6·67
Rio Grande (N.)	433,800	56·49	2·93
Parahyba	656,600	46·16	4·44
Pernambuco	1,121,800	45·45	8·25
Alagoas	410,900	43·20	2·78
Total	4,813,700	48·26	32·52
EAST			
Sergipe	288,500	53·19	1·95
Bahia	2,790,900	71·23	18·85
Minas Gerais	2,614,020	38·55	17·66
Espirito Santo	293,020	37·96	1·98
Rio de Janeiro	739,000	40·01	4·99
Former federal district	505,900	28·68	3·42
Total	7,231,900	46·28	48·85

These two regions, then, constitute what we may truly term
'Black Brazil'. When we move on to the south or west we reach
either White Brazil (south) or Indian Brazil (west):

State	Negroes and Mestizos	Percentage of State population	Percentage of the total pop. of Brazil
São Paulo	864,400	12·02	5·84
Parana	151,900	12·29	1·02
Santa Catarina	65,400	5·55	0·44
Rio Grande (S.)	374,200	11·27	2·53
Total	1,455,900	11·26	9·83

This is not to say that the coloured population did not
formerly attain very high proportions in certain areas of the
south, such as the old coffee-growing belt of São Paulo and the

coastal strip of the southern Rio Grande. But since this is the part of Brazil with a temperate climate, it has tended (ever since the end of the Empire) to become a privileged enclave for European immigrants – Italian, German, Swiss, Spanish, Portuguese and, latterly, in the São Paulo area, Japanese. Thus the once-important Negro group has gradually dwindled into an ever-decreasing minority percentage of the population as a whole.

WEST-CENTRAL

Matto Grosso	209,300	48·42	1·41
Goiaz	229,600	27·78	1·55
Total	438,900	34·87	2·96

Here again, as for the north, if we want to get some idea of the Negro's true position, and to avoid confusing mestizos with mulattos, we will do better to make a distinction between the three colours:

Matto Grosso:	219,706 W	36,567 N	172,628 M
Goiaz:	595,890 W	140,040 N	89,311 M

Thus it becomes clear that the distribution of coloured Brazilians varies enormously from one region to another, forming seven-tenths of the population in Bahia, two-fifths at Minas, roughly half in Pernambuco, Ceara, Parahyba and Maranhão, a shade over one-tenth in the southern states, and no more than 5 per cent at Santa Catarina. A more detailed analysis would, of course, reveal further divergencies in the sub-areas of each individual state. In Santa Catarina, Negroes are virtually restricted to the capital and its environs. In the east and north-east, they are mostly found along the coastal littoral, a region previously occupied by plantations that depended on slave-labour. The coloured population rapidly thins out as one moves into the interior, the *sertão*, a cattle-grazing region which has never required a large labour force.

Similar observations can be made concerning those countries of Spanish America which still contain remnants of their original Negro populations. No Negro can stand the high altitudes encountered in the Andes, and thus the only coloured population in Peru is to be found on the Pacific coast. If we look at the over-all population figures there, the incidence of Negroes and mulattos is a mere 0·47 per cent. If, on the other hand, we make a separate examination of the three major zones into which Peru is divided, we find a somewhat different picture. Along the coastal belt, the coloured population rises to 4·18 per cent (figure for Ica), while it drops to 0·04 per cent in the mountains (Cuzco), and 0·02 per cent in the Amazon forest. In Colombia, Bolivia and Ecuador, Negroes are only found in coastal provinces or the valleys of the interior; above a height of 10,000 ft. they vanish altogether and only the Indians remain. When we turn to Venezuela, we find that the coloured population is concentrated in those areas which were formerly strongholds of plantation slavery and fades out as one moves further inland. Here it is not so much the altitude which creates a frontier as the primeval forest, the domain of the Indian.

REFERENCES

1. José Antonio Saco, *Historia de la esclavitud de la raza africana en el Nuevo Mundo*, 4 vols., rev. ed., Havana, 1938; Frank Tannenbaum, *Slave and Citizen: the Negro in America*, New York, 1947; Mauricio Goulard, *Escravidão africana ao Brasil*, 2nd ed., S. Paulo, 1950.

2. E. D. Morel, *Negro Year Book*, 1931–2, p. 305.

3. Herskovits, *The Myth of the Negro Past*; Gonzalo-Aguirre Beltran, *La poblacion negra de Mexico* (1519–1810), Mexico, 1946; A. Ramos, *As culturas negras no novo mundo*, S. Paulo, 1946; and *O Negro Brasileiro*, S. Paulo, 2nd ed., 1940; Aquiles Escalante, *El Negro en Colombia*, Bogota, 1964; etc.

4. Luiz Vianna, filho, *O Negro na Bahia*, Rio de Janeiro, 1946.

5. A term used to designate a Negro freshly arrived from Africa – synonymous with 'savage'.

6. Nina Rodrigues, *Os Africanos no Brasil*, 2nd ed., S. Paulo, 1935.

7. Cf. the textural citations from ancient writers in Carvalho Neto, *El Negro Uruguayo*, Quito, 1965.

8. *Tradiciones Peruanas*, T.I., Barcelona, 1893.

9. *Los Cabildos Afrocubanos*, Habana, 1923.

10. 'The Negro Family in Bahia', *Amer. Sociol. Rev.* VII, 4 (1942), pp. 465–78.

11. R. Bastide, *Les réligions africaines au Brésil*, Paris, 1961.

12. Lydia Cabrera, *La Sociedad Secreta Abakuá*, La Habana, 1958

13. Alfred Métraux, *Le Vaudou haïtien*, Paris, 1958.

14. The actual table (p. 14) is reproduced from Herskovits, *Man and his Works*, New York.

CHAPTER II

AFRICAN SOCIETIES AND/OR
NEGRO SOCIETIES

The slave-ships carried not only men, women and children, but also their gods, beliefs, and traditional folklore. They maintained a stubborn resistance against their white oppressors, who were determined to tear them loose, by force if need be, from their own cultural patterns, and acclimatise them to those of the West. Such resistance was most successful in the towns, where the Negroes could meet at night and reorganise their primitive communities more easily than they could out in the countryside. No doubt the revolts they engineered bore witness to their determination to escape the economic exploitation of which they were the victims, and hideous working conditions; but this was by no means their only motive. Such rebellions also hint at their struggle against being dominated and swallowed up by an alien culture. It should come, then, as no surprise that in America we find whole enclaves of African civilisation surviving intact, or at least to a very substantial extent.

On the other hand, slavery tended, little by little, to destroy these cultural imports from the Dark Continent. The process began at once, with the actual immigrants (*bossales*). Under a slave economy members of the same family were liable to be dispersed, and thus to keep up the old traditional way of life, based on tribe and kinship, was quite impossible. This new, artificial régime, with its disproportionate ratio between the sexes (not to mention the white man's concupiscence) led to a completely new pattern of sexual relationships, a kind of enforced promiscuity, which bore no resemblance to previous African *mores*. Later, in the second generation, that of the so-called creoles, the Negroes came to realise that slavery, for all its harshness, left open a number of loopholes for those who wanted to climb the social ladder. This process could be effected both inside and outside the framework of slavery itself. In the former case, it meant advance from field-work to domestic service for the women, and for the men, from manual labour to an overseer's job. In the latter, the *entrée* to society as a whole lay through enfranchisement and admission to the class of 'Free Negroes'. But such loopholes were only available to those who embraced Christianity and Western values, which meant renouncing their own ancestral customs and beliefs. As a result, the various original African civilisations finally became extinct. Yet these 'white-souled Negroes', as they were sometimes termed, always remained in the very lowest strata of society, even after their enfranchisement, separate from, and ignored by, the white community. As a result, they tended everywhere to form relatively isolated communities, within a nation which accorded them no more than second-class status. The social rules which such communities worked out for themselves had very little connection either with the tribal lore of Africa (now finally lost), or with the institutions of the whites, who persisted in denying them integration. However, when discussing these Negro communities, we should not presume either a total absence or a disintegration of culture. To make life possible for themselves they hammered out a new cultural pattern of their own, shaping it in response to the demands of their new environment. Thus, in addition to African or Afro-american cultures, we can distinguish a third category, which we may term 'Negro'.

The great danger is of confusing them, through a desire to find African cultural survivals everywhere (though in fact these have long since vanished). Alternatively, we find the tendency to deny African influence altogether, and see nothing but 'the Negro' everywhere. Every instance needs to be studied in isolation and subjected to the most meticulous analysis. In this field, any generalisation runs the risk of camouflaging some underlying truth, and of revealing (as I said in my introduction) little more than the writer's own ideological assumptions. Obviously one cannot here examine each separate case, or survey all the numerous controversial problems with which the subject is rife; the best one can do is select a few examples. Such an approach should at least indicate the complexity of the situation which we are investigating, the confusion that surrounds such terms as *négritude* or *Africanitude;* it should also provide us with distinguishing criteria, and – as I believe – with a more adequate conceptual terminology for digesting the widespread evidence at our disposal in America (whether our approach is by way of cultural groupings, or, again, through a study of the predominantly coloured régimes).

Until very recent years the student's main sphere of interest has lain in the *non-European* aspects of this cultural field; being soaked in our own culture, we are more liable to notice those elements which diverge from it. We are better acquainted with the Bush Negro than with his urban counterpart. The Negro who belongs to a mystery-cult and goes in for ecstatic trances we know; but what about those who are good Catholics, good Protestants, or agnostics? Pursuing the same line of thought a little further, we find that comparatively few studies have been devoted to the various aspects of day-to-day life, whereas an immense bibliography has accumulated round such topics as religion and folklore – in other words, those features which appear most exotic or picturesque, what ethnologists call the peak points of a culture. Yet between such peak points ordinary life goes on, and merits our attention no less.[1] In previous studies, and on the basis of my own experience, I have set forth, for the benefit of those research workers concerned with marginal human societies, what I term the 'principle of dissociation [*principe de coupure*]'.[2] This principle, in fact, operates in our own culture; we do not find the same individual invariably performing the same role in the various groups to which he belongs. Nevertheless, it has an especial importance for the member of a marginal society, since it allows him to avoid precisely those tensions which are caused by cultural clashes and conflicting demands on the individual psyche. A Brazilian Negro can take part in Brazil's economic and political life, while at the same time remaining a faithful member of various African religious fraternities, and feel no sense of contradiction between the two separate worlds in which he moves. Similarly, it is possible that the 'peak points' of an Afroamerican society may always be African in origin, whereas the same Negro who subscribes to it belongs (as far as his day-today life is concerned) to a culture which is not African but Negro – something very different. At present there is still a lack of studies in depth on specific communities of American Negroes, and as a result we shall not be able to establish proper objective and scientific distinctions between the two types of 'civilisation' to which this chapter is devoted. Nevertheless, we possess a sufficient number of incomplete or fragmentary surveys to draw certain firm conclusions from them.

The first topic I propose to examine is that of the economy prevalent in rural Negro communities and in South America generally, since this is a field which has provoked the least amount of heated partisanship among scholars. Even Herskovits, with his known insistence on the importance of African survivals, remarks that the tools and agricultural methods (apart from certain special processes for growing rice) are of European origin. But one characteristic of European peasant society is the possession of land; and this affective attachment does not occur among Americans of African descent. Edith Clarke concluded from this that 'the peasant theory of land-ownership (among the Caribs) reflected the principles of Africans from West Africa'; her analysis, however, demonstrates that land-ownership of this type is the result of a functional adjustment by Negroes to certain clearly determined circumstances, and under the pressure of ascertainable conditions, such as the migration of workers from one place to another, an increase in the coloured population, whether a husband predeceases his wife or vice versa, and so on. In these conditions it may be true that the Black Caribs practise a form of family landownership which differs considerably from the European variety, and possibly shows some similarity with the principles governing family landownership in West Africa – but does this give us the right to assume that we are dealing with a survival of some African 'model'? Would we not be more correct to diagnose it as the result of special local demographic conditions? Such, at any rate, is M. G. Smith's opinion.[3] On this point, which I shall discuss further when dealing with the family, I entirely agree with Smith. Slavery brought about a complete break with African traditions and customs, and persisted too long to allow any renewal of them. From the time of his emancipation, the Negro was forced to accept the laws of the country in which he lived, and, in consequence, certain new forms of ownership. At the same time various new kinds of links with the soil were imposed on him – *métayage*, tenant farming, work as an agricultural labourer – which he could not refuse or evade. Thus when we come across new types of 'family property', different from those prescribed under European legislation, we should not attribute such phenomena to impossible 'survivals', but see them as genuine, and original, 'cultural creations', produced in response to new conditions of life. Here we are squarely within the compass of what we have labelled 'Negro civilisations'. Does this mean that no genuinely African type of ownership is to be found elsewhere? As we have already stated, all generalisations are dangerous. The religious fraternity houses of Bahia may, legally speaking, belong to some individual person (though this is not always the case); but in fact they are the joint property of some African sect, whose religious leaders simply hold them in trust. Just as in Africa the elders (*qua* heads of families) share out the profits of any collective work among the younger members of the tribe and their womenfolk, so here the religious leaders share out the benefits of any joint enterprise among all their followers.

Yet the problem – still in this same sector of the economy – becomes even harder to untangle when we turn from individual to co-operative labour. The latter is found in the bush in Dutch Guiana, and recalls the economic practices of ancient Ghana, the original home of the Bush Negroes. Other such practices, however, like the use of markets and the utilisation of cowrie-shells for money, are no longer found. Co-operative labour also exists on Haiti, where it is known as *combite*, in Jamaica and Trinidad (the name there is *gavap*), in the French Antilles, and more or less everywhere in Central and South America where the coloured population is in the majority.[4] But we also find it in multiracial societies such as that of Brazil, where it appears amongst Indian mestizos, white peasants, and – uniformly – throughout the Negro population; the name for it here is *mutirão*.[5] It is also to be found in the traditional peasant societies of Europe, and often in very similar forms – which leads one legitimately to wonder whether co-operative labour of this sort was imported from Africa or from Europe.

Is it the result of formative pressure exerted by a new environment? In that case we must treat it as a feature of 'Negro civilisation'. Or is it a survival? If so, it belongs to 'African civilisation'. Finally, could it possibly be due to the convergence and fusion of two somewhat similar traditions? Then we must group it as part of an 'Afroamerican civilisation'.

I propose to restrict myself here to the example of Haiti. It is the best known, and has also been that most generally connected with Africa, since the *combite* continues the tradition of the Dahomean *dokpwe*.[6] In the first place, we should observe the marked variety of forms which such collective labour takes. We have the *rôn* (i.e. *la ronde*), a series of small *combites*, whose members take turns to work for each other, generally putting in half a day's work two or three times a week. Then there is the *association*: this involves a larger number of people, and substitutes payment in cash or foodstuffs for a mutual exchange of labour. With the *rôn*, we have a straightforward bartering process, one job against another, for the general benefit of all those involved. The *association* or 'society' produces a group of semi-professional peasants, with their own special organisation (I shall return to this later), who hire themselves out to any landowner in need of a large labour force to get some specific job done quickly. In addition to these two main groups (which are *functionally* distinct from one another) we find a number of others, differing for the most part only in the number of persons they involve. There is the *journée*, a few people who work for smallholders in return for a good meal; the *vanjou*, a team of between fifteen and twenty labourers; and the *corvée*, which can include anything up to a hundred members, and breeds its own cheerfully festive atmosphere. But in none of these, as opposed to the *rôn*, is there any reciprocity of labour. What we have instead is the hiring of an organised labour force for some collective undertaking, on behalf of one particular landowner, with food, dancing, and music thrown in. Undoubtedly Africa, Dahomey in particular, can offer parallels – and just as wide a variety of approach. But a sociologist cannot be content with mere resemblances; to clinch his case he has to establish 'continuity' between African and Haitian institutions, since it is generally agreed that life on Haiti has changed a great deal, and is still changing. What seems fairly certain is that, originally, collective labour was closely bound up with the extended 'big house' family, known under the name of *laku* ('court'), and that during this period it had a genuine historical affiliation with the concept of feudal or extended-family labour. However, with the transformation which domestic society subsequently underwent – the emergence of small individual family units, the parcelling out of hitherto indivisible property – this type of collective labour was similarly modified. It split up into the *rôn* (exchange of services between relatives) and the *corvée* (a group composed of poor peasants or younger sons from comparatively well-off families, who hired themselves out to those who had need of them). In other words, co-operative familial labour, controlled by the patriarch, was replaced by *professional* co-operative labour under a president. Now we find a very similar development taking place in Africa, during the course of colonisation; but this does not entitle us to talk of historical continuity, merely of parallel evolution – by no means the same thing. We may note that since the *corvées* cost a great deal of money – they involve feeding a large labour force, and stinginess is frowned on – the poorer areas of Haiti have largely ceased to employ them.

These 'societies' have a name, a banner (which serves as their titular symbol), an orchestra, and a highly complex hierarchy. Africans have a passion for titles, and it has been noted that those who possessed them commonly lorded it over the rank and file. We find a president (honorary), a consul (who organises labour and is responsible for discipline), a *'Gouverneur La-place'* (in charge of the group's social side), and a whole series of generals, including 'General Silence', responsible for stopping quarrels, and a 'General Police'. There are also dignitaries among the ladies, such as *'Reine La-place'*. Every official, whether elected or chosen by the president, is jealous of his prerogatives and performs his duties with enormous dignity. One gets the impression that this complex hierarchy has very little to do with the actual work that is carried out, but rather fulfills a purpose which we may term 'psychological compensation'. This compensatory function has its roots in the humiliating condition of slavery. The military character of these organisations when in action is suggestive: in particular the council meetings which take place between one job and the next, with their lengthy debates, punctilious protocol, and all the ritual of a deliberative assembly. Such practices betray a desire for posthumous revenge on the white rulers, with their own strictly graded military ranks and free political assemblies, from which the slave was debarred, and which he viewed with an envious eye. In Africa, colonisation brought about the organisation of comparable young men's labour associations, with much the same hierarchical structure. Again, what we find here is parallelism rather than formal continuity. On the other hand, collective labour operates according to the same rules in America as it does in Africa (though we cannot confidently assert that such rules are Dahomean rather than Bantu: many of the associations in Haiti go by the name of 'Sociétés Congo'). The workers stand in a group behind the orchestra, which adapts its rhythms to the various gestures associated with work. Someone, anyone, starts singing. The songs may be Voodoo chants, but more often take the form of satirical ballads, improvised on the basis of day-to-day events in the village community. They both get people laughing and arouse their will to work; though the latter is somewhat relative, being interrupted by meals, meetings and official deliberations (at which society business is discussed, absentees are noted, and penalties are inflicted on late-comers). In the evening the group's solidarity has the seal put on it by a communal feast – which also serves to emphasise the superior status of the society's various employers, through a species of potlatch or distribution of food.

Thus even in an area where parallels (and indeed some sort of historical continuity) with Africa are undeniable, we should take heed of M. G. Smith's well-justified caveat:[7] that a clear and careful distinction must always be drawn between form, function and the evolutionary process. The actual form may be African, yet, in order to survive, be forced to adapt itself functionally to conditions of existence that often differ substantially from those it originally enjoyed. Since such conditions are just as liable to change, over the years, in Africa as in America, we have to be at least as much on the look-out for the phenomenon of convergence as for that of continuity. Similarities may turn out to share a common origin, and be derived, after the event, from conditions analogous to those governing the colonial pattern – on either side of the Atlantic.

If we regard the machinery by which collective labour is operated as highly complex, what are we to say when we turn from the economic sphere to that of the family? Here, before we even attempt to tackle the problem personally, and endeavour to sketch a solution to it, we must first examine the various conflicting theories which it has evoked.

The first theory is that of Herskovits, who regards the family group in a Negro community as a survival of the African family. Marriage in Africa takes the form of an agreement between the parents, with polygyny as the common rule. Now the first of these characteristics appears both in Haiti and in the British colonies of the West Indies, where a formal letter of application for betrothal is *de rigueur*. The second appears in the Haitian *plaçage*, or common-law marriage, contracted without any sanction from the civil or religious authorities, and akin to the so-called 'keeper' relationship practised in the British Antilles. Such irregular unions are equally prevalent in the United States, both in the south and among the lower-class emigrants of the north; they are also found among the Caribs and in South America. Their widespread existence might well be a consequence (or a reinterpretation) of native polygyny. One result of such a practice is that the relationship between a father and his children becomes less close, since the wife passes from one 'husband' to another, and thus the family tends to become 'matrifocal'; but in Herskovits' view this matrifocality is likewise found in Africa. It is true that in polygamous families the bond between a child and its mother is closer than that which links the children of different mothers to their common father. Another point, emphasised by Powder-maker, is that the Negro family in the southern states of the U.S.A. tends to identify itself with the household – a larger unit than the marital partnership, and all the more attractive in that such partnerships always remain a temporary arrangement. She notes, further, that this household is run either by the mother or (if she is out of work) the grandmother or eldest aunt, who takes responsibility for all the children, legitimate, bastard, or adopted.[8] Similar observations have been made concerning the Caribs. At Amory (Monroe County) 639 persons were found divided among 171 families, one of which totalled no less than 141 members. Granted such conditions, one could hardly help being reminded of the extended African family, the patrilineal or matrilineal clan system. While it is true that enslavement or economic poverty may have played some part in the formation of these New World Negro families, its role could not be called creative. Certain characteristics that originated in Africa were simply reinforced by the new conditions of existence that America imposed on them. When we study such 'Africanisms', Herskovits concludes, we should not mistake a cause of survival for a cause of innovation.[9]

This thesis, in so far as it relates to the U.S.A., has been vigorously attacked by Frazier. In his view, the 'maternal' family should be regarded as a consequence of slavery, which destroyed the old tribal institutions and *mores*. The white master would habitually take coloured mistresses, and force the slaves on his estate into general sexual promiscuity. Such a régime, by increasing the servile birth-rate, enabled him to acquire cheap replacements for those of his workers who died young, worn out by toil. Thus control by the group was replaced by white domination, a transition which effectively prevented any possible survival of African cultural patterns in America. Since the father was always out at work (and sometimes unknown), the only affective bonds that could exist were those between the child and its mother and later, when the mother went back to work on the plantation, with the old women who looked after it in her stead. Emancipation, by giving the Negro community increased mobility, and destroying the control which the white boss had exercised over the sexual relationships between his slaves, merely accelerated the process of familial disintegration. Gradually, however, and under the influence of examples taken from his social environment, every emancipated Negro who managed to find work and support his family tended to replace this maternally-oriented family by a more 'paternal' régime. Or, to put it another way, we find the 'natural' family – a heritage of slavery – being replaced by the 'institutional' family: this for a number of reasons, the most important being pressure from the churches. Finally, with the Negro migrations to the big cities, especially those in the north, came a further change. By plunging into the anonymity of city life, the adventurous migrant – a kind of black Ulysses – escaped from all normal social restraints. Sexual life reverted to the purely physical, for men at any rate; while what the woman sought through love was, essentially, economic or social betterment. When a Negro couple cohabited under these conditions, the authority lay with the breadwinner; and since it often happened that the wife had a job, while the husband was out of work, the family tended to take on a quasi-matriarchal pattern. The husband, however, was prone to try and establish his own authority by sheer brute force, and as a result of the clash between these two rival authorities the children often found themselves neglected or abandoned. This in turn led to the formation of adolescent street gangs in the poor districts, and goes a long way towards explaining the high incidence of Negro delinquency.[10] Thus for Herskovits' explanation – what one might term the 'culturalist' theory – Frazier would substitute a more purely sociological interpretation. For him, both the matrifocal or maternal family, and the sexual promiscuity of lower-class North American Negroes, are symptoms not of surviving African customs, but rather of the disorganisation brought about by slavery, emancipation, and the migrant drift of Negroes to industrial cities.

The same explanation has been brought forward by Fernando Henriques and Morris Freilich to account for the matrifocal family among the Black Caribs.[11] Freilich, for instance, instead of basing his argument, in the first instance, on evidence from Africa, establishes some highly generalised categories which, *mutatis mutandis*, can describe a 'culture' in terms of certain invariable points of reference (biological, psychological or socio-situational), such as participation in a group, transference from one group to another, sexual habits, orientation in time, type of authority, beliefs and symbols. Now the Negroes of Trinidad organise themselves by households; these range from the nuclear family, ruled over by the father, to the matrifocal family, which is that most commonly encountered. Transference from one social group to another is effected by the movement of the man from one matrifocal family to another, rather than by the woman's removal from her paternal group to her husband's household. Sexual liberty is very considerable, and associated with an exchange of goods and services, sexual intercourse being granted in return for gifts. This inclination towards freedom of action means that authority is generally in the hands of the old women, while the right to carnal pleasure is exercised with complete egalitarianism. Examples could be multiplied. Now none of these characteristics is to be found in Africa. Whether the family be patrilinear or matrilinear, it almost always constitutes a tight-knit group in which there is no sexual licence, and family or clan interests (e.g. the exchange of wives among the men) are governed by inflexible rules. On the other hand, *all* these phenomena were characteristic of families under slavery:

Point of reference	Slavery	Trinidad Peasantry
1. Group membership		
(*a*) kinship	matrifocal family	matrifocal family
(*b*) household	promiscuity	temporary marriages
2. Transference from one group to another	successive polygyny	successive polygyny
3. Orientation in time	the present	day-to-day living
4. Types of authority	hierarchical	egalitarian
5. Sexual life	sexual freedom	sexual freedom
6. Beliefs and symbols	liking for festivals	liking for freedom
	reputation for sexual athleticism	women-chasers highly regarded
		gaiety of festivals

The only innovation, then, is that of the hierarchical system, which rested on the white boss's authority. With emancipation, however, this soon vanished and was replaced by sexual equality between men and women.

One further theory to be noted is the economic one, which has been maintained mostly vigorously by R. T. Smith. Smith begins with the observation that matrifocal families are by no means restricted to the Negroes of the New World. They occur in certain districts of London, among the Scottish mining communities, in villages of Peru (Moche) and Paraguay (Tobati). Secondly, it is not true that all Negro families in the New World are matrifocal; it would be more accurate to say that matrifocality is a particular point in the domestic cycle rather than an absolute or unchanging characteristic of the system as a whole. During the early part of her married life, the woman is dependant on her husband as a provider, and only when her children are much bigger does she achieve some measure of independence. At the same time, these sons and daughters still remain part of the household, and if the latter have babies before getting themselves 'placed', they leave them in the care of their mothers. Sometimes the husband dies, or leaves home, or contracts another union; in such a case authority passes to the mother, and the family becomes matrifocal. As more often than not wives are longer-lived than their husbands, and the children tend to have pre-marital love-affairs, there comes a point at which the household (though originally patrifocal) consists of nothing but the mother, her own children, and those of her sons. At this stage it may sometimes include, in addition, various other categories of relative, in particular the mother's sisters and *their* children. Nevertheless, such a picture remains the theoretical ideal, and in practice some stages of this *cursus* may be missing. In fact – and this is where the economic factor would appear to predominate – granted the kind of régime prevailing on a large planatation, the Negro worker enjoys considerable mobility. A father may well be persuaded to leave home and try his luck elsewhere, leaving his wife and children behind. When this happens, the mother, to ensure her own and her offspring's livelihood, will take another – temporary – husband, by whom she will have further children.[12] Indirect confirmation of Smith's thesis can be derived from the fact that when the family owns its own land, as in Europe, authority rests with the father, and the domestic group reveals considerable stability. This is what came about in Jamaica. Though church marriages were still rare there at the turn of the century, cohabitation constituted a virtual common-law marriage, recognised by the community at large; and the authority in such a relationship belonged to the father, *qua* owner (or tenant) of the land he worked, and as family breadwinner.[13]

The traditional Haitian family consisted of a group of houses (nuclear families) forming a kind of small village, the *laku*, or 'court', ruled over by the oldest male member of the group. From this it would appear – a fact which lends support to Herskovits' thesis[14] – that after Haiti obtained its independence, the inhabitants proceeded to revive the large patrilinear 'extended family' of their Fon ancestors. Nevertheless, Rémy Bastien, after a close study of the subject, remains sceptical. In his view, once the *lignages* had been broken up as a result of slavery, it would be impossible to reconstitute a wholly lost world by nothing but collective tribal memory. It is true, too, that the rule for landownership is individual holdings, rather than the collective system practised in Africa. However, as such holdings were small, it proved necessary to bring up the children in groups to ensure their survival. The authority of the patriarchs (in point of fact more nominal than real) has its source in the 1801 Constitution of Toussaint-Louverture, a devout Catholic who deliberately borrowed from European models in order to check the moral decline of his fellow-countrymen. Furthermore, as is well known, the *laku* has by now become virtually obsolete. Domestic solidarity has proved no match for the individualism of the 'nuclear' families. The less productive their lands became, the more fiercely did the various heirs fight each other for possession of them. Here, again, it would seem that we must seek economic causes rather than those African survivals so dear to Herskovits' heart.[15]

The present negative trend in scholarly theorising, which seeks to eliminate ancestral influence and the role of the collective memory *in toto*, has left its mark on every culture – even the maroon republics of Dutch and French Guiana, which actually attempted to 'recreate' Africa in the great tropical forests of the New World. These Negro refugees, who organised themselves – just like their Fanti–Ashanti ancestors – into matrilinear and exogamous clans, will form the subject of closer study in my next chapter. Here it is worth noting that within the last few years Jean Hurault has declared (at least as regards the Boni) that 'though one might well assume that a West African system had simply been transported *en bloc*, such a supposition is entirely false'. In his opinion, the Boni familial system evolved against a specific historical background. We have the forma-tion of highly heterogeneous bands of rebel slaves, some Dahomean by origin (and thus patrilineal), while others were Akan (matrilineal, but patrifocal), and others again Bantus. As these bands settled down on the land and began to organise themselves, a new system evolved, under the influence of two factors: first, the independent spirit shown by the women, whose prime concern was to maintain their freedom *vis-à-vis* the men; and second, a system of moral and religious commandments which implied the rejection of violence in any form. 'Under this code there could be no question of removing a woman from her mother's village, if she wished to remain there, far less of exerting any pressure on her to prolong a relationship she had ceased to find desirable.' The proof that these were, in fact, the decisive influences as far as the Boni were concerned is seen in their lack of all matrimonial compensation, which in Africa is the general rule. No claims are made on the husband's *lignage;* and it would follow that – to judge by the Boni's social system – the historical conditions governing their new environment proved stronger than any ancestral tradition.[16]

The mistake, as it seems to me, that *all* these theories make is that of being over-systematic, of attempting to explain what I consider a highly complex and variegated group of cultural features by some one single factor – whether this be collective memory, social disintegration induced by slavery, or the economic conditions prevailing in America. One gets the feeling that in such cases the choice is dictated (more or less consciously) by ideological considerations (e.g. *négritude* or national integration), rather than by any desire to work out an interpretation that fits all the facts. Obviously the investigator's educational background is also relevant. It is no coincidence that Hurault was trained as a geographer, Frazier as a sociologist, and Herskovits as an anthropologist. My own personal feeling is that all these factors have had, or continue to have, some influence – but that some weigh more heavily than others, depending on the social context in which they occur. The most important thing is not to confuse cultural characteristics which bear a superficial resemblance to one another, but in fact are fundamentally opposed.

As regards the Boni, two comments may be made. The Boni constitute the final nucleus of rebellious Bush Negroes, and consequently, when we study them from the chronological viewpoint, they can be seen as the last of the Black refugees. Thus it is possible that their new environment placed more constraint on their previous social organisation than was the case with the Djuka or Saramacca, since these rebelled during the eighteenth century, at the height of the slave-trade, when memories of African customs would still be fresh. In the second place, though it may be true that a new environment consti-

tutes a challenge which demands some response, nevertheless
that response only operates through certain traditional customs.
Ethnologists have observed that the independence of women
tends to be better assured in patrilineal societies which practise
some form of matrimonial compensation than in matrilineal
societies as such; and that in the process of acculturation,
religious beliefs are more tenacious than social attitudes. Consequently, as regards the first point, if the new family had come
about through the woman's urge to achieve independence, it
would have inclined towards the patrilineal rather than the
matrilineal type. On the second point, the importance of the
religious factor, there is this to be said. If Boni society has
re-established itself in the form of matrilineal clans, that is
because each such clan is bound up with a hereditary taboo,
known as *kunu*, to violate which calls down sickness, insanity,
or death upon the offender. It is round this spiritual core that
new forms of marriage and property inheritance have crystal-
lised. Slavery had well and truly disrupted the ancient clans, it
is true; but as soon as successful rebellion enabled the *marrons*
to choose their own way of life, and they found themselves
forced to organise their bands for mere survival, their course
of action was never in doubt. Rather than painfully hammer
out a new system, they inevitably drew on traditional African
models. Thus the clans were reconstituted in accordance with
what was remembered of Fanti–Ashanti practices. There is no
hint of even an initial moment of anarchy, no wavering between
rival systems of kinship or alliance; the construction of this new
society was oriented *ab initio* in a predetermined direction, that
of the ex-slaves' African heritage. Theoretically, indeed, the
two factors most emphasised – rejection of violence, and the
woman's desire for independence – would permit of several
solutions. Why, with such a choice available, was one, and one
only, retained? Surely because the traditions of their native
Africa continued to exert an all-important influence over the
rebels' decisions. It is true that some African cultural traits
disappeared, while other new ones came into being; Hurault
is quite right to emphasise the changes. An old system can only
take on a new lease of life by accommodating itself to changed
conditions; but such accommodation does not imply breaking
faith with the past. It is, in point of fact, the most touching

evidence for fidelity. Survival does not mean a hardening of the mould, a divorce from the ever-changing flow of life. On the contrary: survival presupposes plasticity, it is a kind of cultural cyst. We should, then, refuse to accept the survival-adaptation dichotomy which writers still try to force on us. This depends on certain concepts postulated in regard to *physical* survival and creative adaptation, the survival of the fittest as living reality.

As regards 'matrifocality', common-law marriages, and polygamy, the problem is more complex. The trouble here lies in the fact that scholars have arbitrarily lumped together various phenomena of diverse origin, and then proceeded to make a system out of them. In the first place, we must make a clear distinction between urban and peasant communities (even if the former are composed, to begin with, of rural migrants). I cannot, for instance, accept the thesis propounded by René Ribeiro, who regards the Negro families of Recife (Brazil) as still adhering to an inherited African model. In point of fact, even though – for economic reasons – some of these families rest on a stable basis, that does not enable us to interpret sexual unions there as common-law marriages; what we have is straightforward cohabitation or concubinage. This latter category is as important for the white sector of the lower classes as it is for the black. Matrifocality is a direct result of the temporary nature of these relationships, and of the fact that the child is necessarily more close to its mother. This type of matrifocality has parallels in Europe (e.g. unmarried mothers, children who are brought up by the grandmother). There can be no doubt, I would submit, that the urban Negro family derives its structure, originally, from African models; but at the same time these models have been subjected to a steady process of disintegration for which two main factors are responsible. The first of these goes back to the sexual promiscuity associated with slavery; the second to the social anarchy which followed emancipation, and encouraged Negroes to live in towns, outside the control of any social group. This does not apply to rural communities, or folk societies, as they have sometimes been called. Here, the Negro family can be viewed in our Western Christian perspective, either as showing a lack of real family roots, or as a 'natural' family unit. In fact it is controlled by the community, and conforms to its own proper rules:

marriage in this context *is* a type of common-law relationship, and not mere cohabitation. Here Smith's theory strikes me as more persuasive than Frazier's. The predominant motive forces are economic, and the family is liable to assume different forms according to the type of production method involved. We find matrifocality and successive polygyny in the region of the large plantations, with mobility a constant characteristic of the men. In farming areas largely populated by smallholders, the régime tends to be paternal, whether it takes the form of extended households or independent families. Social organisation is shaped by the material conditions governing life – or perhaps rather survival. However, even in these rural communities we should not assume that the old African systems have totally vanished. Here we must make a further distinction, between simultaneous polygamy and successive polygyny. When Negroes have several wives, they doubtless feel obliged to 'rationalise' their conduct, and to justify it in white eyes; they will therefore refer to their 'wife' and to their '*chérie*', or mistress. As Herskovits has clearly seen, what we have here is simply a reinterpretation, in Western terms, of old-style African polygamy, with its classic distinction between the 'number-one wife' and the rest. The wives are all well acquainted with their husbands' sexual habits, and feel no jealousy of one another; all they ask of a man is economic support. Secondly, the husband keeps his '*chéries*' in different parts of town if he is an urban Negro; his rural counterpart keeps mistresses all over the countryside, and gives them allotments, the produce of which they sell off for their own exclusive benefit.[17] The man spends a night with each of these 'wives' in turn, according to a regular cycle.

This is a precise copy of the African 'compound', where each wife has her own hut, and the man regularly sleeps and eats with all of them, turn and turn about. Clearly we cannot talk of genuine 'matrifocality' in such a context. Though the mother does live alone with her children, the children nevertheless have a father who brings them up and knows them. Finally, polygamy of this sort occurs most frequently when other areas of culture, religion in particular, show a high level of African survivals. It is as though religion constituted a core round which revived ancestral traditions could crystallise. We find such conditions, for instance, among the country Negroes of Maranhão; and, in the towns, not so much among the ordinary workers, who have been subjected to acculturation, as in the priestly caste, the *babalorisha* or *babalão*, those secret religious fraternities peculiar to the Afroamericans.[18] Thus by concentrating on one example, that of domestic society, we begin to isolate a certain bipolarity between types. On the one hand we have something which in its broad outlines is clearly African; on the other a Negro pattern, distinct from both African and western models, the original product of its environment. At the same time, this distinction is by no means always clear-cut. African features persist even in the folk communities: one good example is the contractual attitude to sex. Pure gratuitous eroticism is a Western invention; here we find intercourse offered in exchange for economic benefits. Furthermore, as situations change, such African characteristics as have survived tend to be modified by various innovations.

I have dwelt with some emphasis on this second area of controversy, since its theoretical importance is considerable. I propose to touch more briefly on the final topic to be examined here, that of music, since I am not myself a musicologist. One incontestably established fact is that the chants of the so-called 'fetishist sects', in Cuba and Brazil, are authentically African.[19] But the moment one turns from this 'survivalist' music to the kind of thing produced by Negroes in the southern states of the U.S.A. (Negro spirituals, plantation working songs, and thence to modern blues) controversy begins. Moreover, because of our relatively scanty knowledge concerning the various regional types of music on the African continent, such disagreement looks like going on for ever. Nevertheless, a number of scholars insist that African features exist in this music, having survived not only a change of environment but also the process of Christianisation. Among them we find M. J. Herskovits, DuBois (at least in part, and to the extent that, with such chants, rhythm tends to predominate over melody), J. W. Johnson, who emphasises the stamping and clapping, the monotonously repeated phrases, the dialogue between soloist and chorus, Krehbiel, who compares Afroamerican chants with those of Dahomey, Kolinski, Waterman and Courlander, amongst others. They base their theory on certain specific elements: the prevalence of percussion instruments, rhythmic hand-clapping (whether in religious chants or children's games), dialogue between chorus and soloist, employment of the pentatonic scale, falsetto singing, and so on.[20] Against this, other folklorists emphasise the fact that the Negro has been forced to assimilate Anglo-American culture very rapidly (language, religion, customs) and as a result has been influenced by white music.[21] G. P. Jackson and Guy B. Johnson remark that most, if not all, of those features that are regarded as being characteristic of Negro music – the pentatonic scale, stamping and clapping, etc. – also occur in traditional Anglo-American folksong – not to mention in white revivalist hymns.[22] This strikes me as a somewhat profitless debate. Surely the interpretation put forward earlier in respect of the Negro family in Guiana could, with certain modifications, be applied here also? The Negro has, indeed, been exposed to the influence of a white musical environment; but he has only borrowed what suited him, and his choice has been dictated by his traditional African attitudes.

There we may leave the matter. From this analysis certain conclusions emerge. To begin with, Negro society never reached a state of disintegration. Even when slavery, and the new urban ways of life which succeeded it, destroyed the original African models, the Negro reacted by reconstructing his community. He did not live in a state of nature; he fashioned himself new institutions, worked out new norms of existence, in short built up his own social organisation, quite separate from that of the whites. In particular, the Negro's sexual life always remained subordinate to the laws of his group, controlled by incest taboos and the rules governing exchange of services between the sexes. One cannot help admiring the flexibility and inventiveness of the solutions he arrived at, even if they seem to clash directly with our own Western way of life.

Secondly, our investigations have led us to distinguish two types of community, according to area. There are those in which the old African traditions have won out against pressure from a new environment, though even here modifications are inevitable to facilitate adjustment and acceptance. We can call these the African communities. There are others where the pressure of the environment has proved stronger than such fragments as collective memory managed to preserve through centuries of disruptive servitude. In such cases matters were made worse by racial segregation, which debarred the slave's descendant from adopting the cultural patterns of his former masters. As a result the Negro was forced to invent new forms of social life, in response to his isolation, his type of work, and all his new requirements. These we shall call Negro communities – Negro, because the white population remains outside them, but not African, since such communities have lost all memory of their former homeland.

These two types of community, as delineated here, are no more than ideal projections. In reality we find a variable continuum between them. Thus one sector of society – say religion – may still remain patently African, while others – the family or the economy – are formulated as a response to the group's new environment. Clearly, the closest approach to the first type will be provided by those communities descended from runaway slaves, or *marrons* (Maroons), in particular those founded by *bossales* [first-generation immigrants]. Similarly, it will be those groups formed after the abolition of slave-labour – mainly creoles, leading an isolated existence in the rural areas – that come nearest to the second type. Negro groups in South America, or among the Black Caribs, present an intermediary category, since during the slave-owning period the 'Nations' found it easier to re-establish themselves in such areas without any interference from Europeans, and thus to maintain their own traditions in secret. Elsewhere, however, these Negroes were bound by the laws of the state – matrimonial, political, economic – and thus had to adapt themselves to such models as exile might dictate. I propose to devote the larger part of this book to a study of the African communities, and shall only deal with the 'Negro' communities and their special institutions at the very end.[23]

REFERENCES

1. M. J. Herskovits, 'Les Noirs du Nouveau Monde: sujet de recherches africanistes', *Journ. de la Soc. des Africanistes*, 8 (1938), 65–82.

2. R. Bastide, 'Le principe de coupure et le comportement afro-brésilien', *Anais do XXXI Congresso Int. de Americanistas*, S. Paulo, 1955.

3. 'The African heritage in the Caribbean', *Caribbean Studies: a symposium* (ed. Vera Rubin), Univ. of Washington Press, 2nd ed. 1960.

4. Herskovits, *The Myth of the Negro Past* . . .

5. On the *mutirão* and its origins (whether Indian, European or African), see Clovis Caldeira, *Mutirão, formas de ajuda mútua no meio rural*, São Paulo, 1956.

6. H. Courlander, *The Drum and the Hoe*, Univ. of California Press, 1960; Rémy Bastien, *La familia rural haïtiana*, Mexico, 1951; M. J. Herskovits, *Life in a Haitian Valley*, New York, 1937, chs. I and IV; A. Métraux, 'Les paysans haïtiens', *Présence Africaine* 12, pp. 112–35; Rhoda Métraux, 'Affiliations through work in Marbial, Haïti', *Primitive Man*, XXV, 1–2, 1952; Paul Moral, *Le paysan haïtien*, Paris, 1961, etc.

7. 'The African Heritage . . .', *op. cit.*

8. Hortense Powdermaker, *After Freedom: a cultural study in the Deep South*, New York, 1939.

9. M. J. Herskovits, *op. cit.*

10. Franklin Frazier, *The Negro [Family] in the United States*, Chicago, 1939. A similar view is held by H. Powdermaker (see above, n. 8). Cf. also Frazier, *Negro Youth at the Crossroads*, Washington, 1940, and his essay 'The adolescent in the family', in *The Negro Child* (ed. Burgess). Without wishing to overplay statistics, we may note that an investigation based on Chicago revealed that out of 420 Negro families, 314 were separated; out of 212 mulatto families, 154 were separated. From a sample of 379 young girls in the country, Reid found 47 with two children, ten with three children, and twelve with four or over. In 1920 the proportion of maternal-type families among urban households in the south was between 15 and 25 per cent, while for the rural areas the percentage dropped to between 3 and 15. When we turn to the crime rate, we find that in 1930 the children's courts of Chicago dealt with: 19·5 per cent native whites; 47·5 per cent children of foreign immigrants; 18·3 per cent Negroes. In 1935 the same categories showed the following percentages: 16·1; 52·3; 23. The number of arrests during these two years, expressed in the ratio of x: 1,000 for each racial type, was as follows: (*a*) 1930: native whites, 39; immigrant whites, 29; Negroes 188. (*b*) 1935: native whites, 23; immigrant whites, 24; Negroes, 87.

11. Fernando Henriques, *Family and Colour in Jamaica*, London, 1953; Morris Freilich, 'Serial Polygyny, Negro Peasants, and Model Analysis', *Amer. Anthrop.* 65, 5 (1961).

12. Raymond T. Smith, *The Negro Family in British Guiana*, London, 1956, and 'The family in the Caribbean', *Caribbean Studies* (ed. Vera Rubin), *op. cit.*

13. Martha Warren Beckwith, *Black Roadways: a study of Jamaican Folk Life*, University of North Carolina Press, 1929 (ch. V). Cf. Edith Clarke, *My Mother who Fathered Me*, London, 1917; and Madeleine Kerr, *Personality and Conflict in Jamaica*, Liverpool, 1952, for a study of this Jamaican family in its various aspects.

14. *Life in a Haitian Village*, New York and London, 1937.

15. Rémy Bastien, *op. cit.*

16. Jean Hurault, *Les Noirs réfugiés Boni de la Guyane française*, I.F.A.N., Dakar, 1961.

17. For the rural Negro of Maranhão (Brazil), see Octavio da Costa Eduardo, *The Negro in Northern Brazil*, New York, 1948 (ch. IV).

18. R. Bastide, 'Dans les Amériques Noires', *À travers les Amériques latines*, ed. L. Febvre (Cahier no. 4 des Annales), Paris, 1949.

19. Fernando Ortiz, *La africania de la música folklorica de Cuba*, Habana, 1950, and *Los Instrumentos de la Música Afro–cubana*, 5 vols., Habana, 1952–55; Oneyda Alvarenga, 'A Influéncia negra na música brasileira', *Bol. latino-americano de Música*, VI (1946), 357–408; M. J. Herskovits and R. A. Waterman, 'Música de culto afrobahiana', *Rev. des Estudes Musicales*, Mendoza, I, 2 (1949), 65–127.

20. Herskovits, *Myth*, pp. 267–9; W. E. B. DuBois, *The Souls of Black Folk*, New York, 1961; James Weldon Johnson, Preface to *The Book of American Negro Spirituals*, New York, 1925; Henry Edward Krehbiel, *Afro-American Folk Song*, New York, 1914; Waterman, *Journ. of Amer. Musicological Society*, I, 1, 1948; Harold Courlander, *Negro Folk Music*, New York, 1963.

21. See, e.g., Newman I. White, *American Negro Folk Songs*, Cambridge, 1928.

22. George Pullen Jackson, *White and Negro Spirituals*, New York, 1944; Guy B. Johnson, *Folk Culture on St Helena Island, South Carolina*, North Carolina, 1930.

23. On the other hand, I shall make no attempt to deal with those multi-racial egalitarian societies in which the Negro – with a view to climbing higher up the social ladder – has completely assimilated white values; where, too, we find a mixed population that reveals varying shades of skin-colour, but no distinctions in the way of life. Such societies are the preserve of the sociologist rather than the cultural anthropologist.

CHAPTER III

NEGRO MAROON SOCIETIES

I

One point which emerges from the previous chapter is that African cultural patterns should be best preserved in societies founded by Negro *marrons*, or maroons. This term is derived from the Spanish word *cimarron*, which originally signified animals, such as the pig, that had reverted from domestication to the wild state; thus it came to be used of runaway Negro slaves. In point of fact the stereotype of the 'good slave', an Uncle Remus, or Old John reconciled to his servile lot, devoted to his masters, full of cheerfulness and good humour, is little more than a self-justificatory picture invented by the whites themselves. If it has any truth in it at all, it only applies to house slaves. One point all modern historians emphasise is the stubborn and tenacious resistance which these Africans maintained against a régime to which they had been forcibly subjected. Their opposition took a number of different forms. Some committed suicide: this was the refuge of the weak, but still based on a religious notion, the idea that after death a person's soul returned to the land of his ancestors. For women, there was voluntary abortion, the object here being to spare their children the yoke of slavery. The poisoning of their white masters with the aid of toxic plants (e.g. certain lianas) hints at the existence among the Negroes in the New World of the African *baba-osaim* or medicine-man. There was also deliberate sabotage of work (which gave rise to the stereotyped picture of the 'lazy nigger') and, finally, rebellion, or flight.

Revolts were extremely numerous. They occurred in Haiti in 1522, 1679, and 1691; in San Domingo in 1523, 1537, and 1548; and on various British islands of the West Indies in 1649, 1674, 1692, 1702, 1733 and 1759. Aptheker has collected evidence for the occurrence of six rebellions in the U.S.A.

between 1663 and 1700, fifty during the eighteenth century, and fifty-five between 1800 and 1864. Puerto Rico had uprisings in 1822, 1826, 1843, and 1848; Martinique in 1811, 1822, 1823, 1831 and 1833, the latter coinciding with a revolt in Jamaica (1831–2). This is far from exhausting the list.[1] From our point of view, however, it is the circumstances of such rebellions that are most interesting. Many of them, it is true, were spontaneous risings, a violent and passionate reaction to systematic torture or inhuman working schedules. Others, however, were most carefully organised and planned over a long period; and the leaders of such movements tended to be religious figures. In the United States they took the form of Christian prophets such as Nat Turner – who nevertheless went in for practices uncommonly like African magic (documents written in blood, various cabalistic signs). In South America, this role was taken over either by Muslim imams or else by the leaders of 'fetichist' *candomblés*. The first type of revolt can be explained in economic or political, that is to say ideological, terms; it expressed the Negro's opposition to the whole concept of servile labour. But the second was also a movement of what we may term *cultural* resistance, a symptom of Negro protest against compulsory Christianisation, the imposition of European customs and values. It testified to a desire to 'stay African'. Perhaps the most celebrated revolt in this latter category was that which took place in Haiti, and culminated in the island gaining its independence. It began on the night of August 14, 1791, with a Voodoo ceremony held during a thunderstorm in a clearing of the Caiman Forest. At this point Boukman was the leader; and indeed all those who succeeded him, with the special exception of Toussaint-Louverture, always had close links with Voodoo – the woman prophet Romaine, or Dessalines, self-styled son of the gods of fire and war.[2] There were also the revolts in north-east Brazil by Mali Negroes and the Yoruba from Nigeria. Those of 1807, 1809, and 1813 were all carried out by Hausas, while the later ones, in 1826, 1827, 1828, 1830, and 1835, were all the work of Nagos. But in every case the organisation and cadre leadership was provided by Muslim or 'fetichist' holy men.[3]

None of these rebellions, however, succeeded. They did not – and here they form a striking contrast with Haiti – form the starting-point for a return to African cultural patterns; on the contrary, by intensifying the double movement of persecution and assimilation, they actually helped to destroy the old traditions. The same cannot be said of *marronage*, the influence of which can still be felt throughout almost the whole length and breadth of Black America. This is because, in various isolated spots, there survive a number of virtually self-sufficient communities, whole enclaves, as it were, of African civilisation. Here too, however, a certain number of methodological precautions are necessary. We must, to begin with, distinguish – both regionally and chronologically – between the various different types of *marronage*. The recently published study on this topic by Y. Debbash seems to me extremely pertinent; it is, moreover, based on a most impressive array of documentary evidence.[4]

There can be no doubt that *marronage* was most often practised by recently disembarked immigrants from Africa, who would certainly not have forgotten their own ancestral customs. But there was also *marronage* among the creole Negroes – that is, those who were born *in situ*, and had been from their tenderest years subjected to the influence of 'civilisation' and 'Christianity'. In the latter case we merely have evidence of the Negro's attachment to workshop or labour-gang; he bolted when he suspected he was to be sold, i.e. torn loose from the pattern of solidarity to which he had become accustomed. The nearer we come to the nineteenth century, the more *marronage* becomes a practice of the creoles, who fled the plantations to seek refuge in the anonymous life of the big cities. Here they met large numbers of Negroes who were already 'enfranchised', and disappeared amongst them. Thus we see that it is only the *marronage* of the *bossales*, or newly-imported slaves, which can be regarded as responsible for the preservation of African customs. Yet even here certain distinctions must be made. Firstly, we must separate the individual from the collective or group break-out, the latter including the whole Negro population of one or several working gangs. In the former case, hunger would usually drive the Negro to come back and beg his master's forgiveness. If a group of fugitives were to maintain themselves, they had to be sufficiently numerous to live in the forest, hunting and farming at a primitive subsistence level, or else to set up as a band of marauders, capable – without over-much risk – of attacking nearby plantations. Secondly, it makes a good deal of difference in what actual environment *marronage* took place. A comparatively small and highly populated island would by no means offer the same conditions as the American continent, with its wild mountains and stretches of virgin forest. As Debbash rightly observes, 'not every band becomes a miniature Africa, certainly not to begin with'. In the smaller islands of the West Indies, *marronage* was, for the most part, carried out by bands that were too small, numerically, to re-create a new Africa on the other side of the Atlantic. It is true that such bands were often formed on a basis of ethnic solidarity; but in many cases they depended on the *ad hoc* solidarity bred by the working gang; and as we have seen, these gangs comprised Negroes of the most diverse origins, a policy specifically designed to avoid the development of any sense of communal unity. Thus, because of their heterogeneous ethnic origins, it frequently proved impossible for these bands to preserve their ancestral customs, or even to remodel them in their own way. At the same time their members found them-selves obliged to come to terms with a new environment, to work out hitherto unknown methods of gaining a livelihood and organising their society. The result was a series of new civilisa-tions: Negro certainly, but not in any genuine sense African.

Only faint traces of this lost African heritage still survive – e.g. the ancient forms of marriage. In Mexico a Negro *marron*, Francisco Mozambique, told the Franciscan friar Frei de Bessavides that 'marriage up in the hills isn't the same as marriage in the city'. Discussing the same problem in Brazil, René Ribeiro quotes a similar remark made by a *marron* there, contrasting the African-type marriage of the *sertão* with the Christian ceremony forced on slaves along the coastal strip. Nevertheless, many *marrons* had already been affected by European culture, and the civilisation which they developed was syncretistic rather than African – all the more so since syncretism provided a means of unifying the beliefs of various heterogeneous ethnic groups. At Palmares, in Brazil, the troops sent to hunt down fugitive Negroes found that their abandoned villages had Catholic churches installed, complete with statues of the saints. At Rio dos Mortes, again in Brazil, Europeans exploring the interior were amazed to encounter not only Indian tribes, but also Indian–Negro half-breeds, who had the rudiments of Christianity passed on to them by *marrons* during the eighteenth century.[5] At Lead Mountain in Guiana, the *marrons* pray, in Catholic style, while facing towards Cayenne, as though it were a holy city. The Boni fugitives from French Guiana were influenced, even after their break-away, by Catholic missions, while the Djukas of Dutch Guiana have four villages inhabited by Jewish *marrons*.[6] This phenomenon is so important that it deserves somewhat further consideration.

Many of these 'maroon republics', particularly the oldest ones, have now disappeared. Some were destroyed by colonial armies, and their territories taken over by white settlers, as happened to the republic of Palmares. In other cases their population was eventually absorbed by the Indians or half-breeds around them. But the remainder, those which held out successfully, ended by making treaties of alliance with the governors of the areas in which they had been set up. This process took place in 1739 in Jamaica, in 1750 – for the oldest *marron* community – in Dutch Guiana, in 1761 for the Aucas, and a year later for the Saramacas. Finally, the French colonies absorbed the Boni, who by now had also revolted against the Dutch. We should note, though, that from the time when these republics achieved their independence, and indeed earlier, while they were still fighting for it, they were by no means entirely cut off from society at large. They traded with white planters, they received annual subventions from the parent state, they sent out ambassadors. A number of Europeans, mostly gold diggers or adventurers, settled in their territory. They received visits from missionaries. As a result, certain modifications developed in course of time, which to some extent alienated them from their African heritage. Nevertheless, great efforts were made to preserve this heritage (notably through the practice of group endogamy), and so successful was the attempt that certain archaic beliefs, maintained solely by oral tradition, were subsequently revived. It was, for instance, only when the Boni reached the banks of the Marouini River that they at last discovered the *ouba-oudou*, or 'witch-doctor's tree', hitherto known to them solely by hearsay, on the testimony of tribal elders.

From all this certain conclusions can be drawn.

1. *Marronage* is not solely an economic phenomenon, but also bears witness to cultural resistance. The bands that were formed tended, where possible, to develop along ethnic lines; and when they federated to produce a republic, the various elements did not so much lose their identity as work out a pattern of peaceful coexistence.

2. The need to adapt to a new environment, and find solutions appropriate to a situational crisis, brought about relatively substantial changes in the old native patterns of culture. Nevertheless, it was more often a case of modifying the past to suit the present then of creating wholly new standards and customs.

3. Even though *marronage* was a phenomenon associated, by and large, with Africans rather than creoles, the slave-trade, by its very nature, made some sort of syncretism inevitable; and the republics, though remaining as far as possible in isolation, were nevertheless influenced by the larger society beyond their frontiers. While such isolation undoubtedly helped to preserve certain African traditions, it also facilitated the survival of characteristics inherited from the slave régime, which remained much as they had been during the seventeenth and eighteenth centuries.

It is misleading, however, to compare the 'maroon civilisations' with *contemporary* African societies. Even if Africa has been slow to develop, its various civilisations have undergone some change over the centuries, whereas the Negro refugees in the New World kept to their old archaic customs: time stood still for them. Such Negro civilisations we should rather compare with the features of Africa belonging to the *past*, as reported by travellers during the seventeenth and eighteenth centuries. It would be a grave mistake to assume that all visible change (e.g. between the present Fanti–Ashanti civilisation in Ghana and that of the Negroes in Dutch Guiana) is a result of syncretism or change of environment. The difference may be, so to speak, temporal rather than spatial, with the *marrons* preserving old-time African customs that have since disappeared in their country of origin. But conversely, one must be careful to avoid 'Africanising' other cultural features, simply because they are to be found in refugee villages; this applies to

Indian customs no less than those borrowed from English, French, or Spanish civilisation in bygone times.

II. *The Bush Negroes[7] of Dutch and French Guiana*

The first group of Negroes took to the forest, it would appear, in 1663, when the Portuguese Jews of Surinam sent their slaves there, voluntarily, at the approach of the tax collector, in order to avoid paying head money on them. Naturally, the slaves never came back. In 1712, when French naval forces entered Dutch Guiana, the big landowners fled to the capital. The slaves took advantage of their absence to loot their masters' houses, after which they too went to ground in the forest. In the course of time these primitive bands grew larger, and in 1749, after a ten years' war, their leader Adoc obtained independence for all those under his command. In 1757 a new insurrection broke out, led by a Negro called Arabi – probably a Muslim. Four years later, in 1761, he too succeeded in extracting terms from the Dutch government. By the Treaty of Auca he was granted the right to found a republic, on condition that he gave asylum to no further Negro fugitives. In 1762 another community, that of the Saramacas, also won independence, with the caveat that a Dutch adviser was to act in liaison with the negro ruler, or '*gran man*'. Meanwhile a new tribe that had formed in the forest, under the leadership of one Boni, was aiming at something more than independence: it aimed to drive the white man out of the area altogether. This was the beginning of a long war, during which – as a result of Boni's extortionate demands – the Aucas, followed by other Negro *marrons*, finally went over to the Dutch side. After this, Boni's group was driven back towards the headwaters of the Maroni River, and after the death of Boni himself, his followers placed themselves under French protection. Thus the *marrons* of Guiana – who today, it is estimated, number some 25,000 – have no true geographical or political unity, but rather consist of a group of tribes.

In this group we may note three main subdivisions. There is the Saramaca tribe, located for the most part along the Surinam River; this is the most important tribe of all, with a population of about 14,000. There then is the tribe known as 'Auca', this being the name of the plantation where the treaty was signed that guaranteed its independence. Its members, however, call themselves Djukas, and this title would be more appropriate for the tribe as a whole.[8] The Boni are the smallest tribe of all, numbering no more than 600, and are mostly located along the French bank of the Maroni. Other minor groups are known besides these: for example the Matawaai, the Quintee Matawaai, and the Paramaccas. The latter, about 500 in number, derive their name from the river on which they settled; they are all descendants of a man and two women who escaped together.[9] The Poligudu group began with a nucleus of native troops who deserted during the Dutch wars against the Bush Negroes. Lastly we may note a group of Negro refugees from Brazil, living on the Oyapok River. These various tribes do not fraternise with one another, but still exist as isolated 'republics'. Some of them are known to have been in existence since very early days, and are referred to in accounts published by soldiers such as Stedman and Devonshire, who took part in the campaigns against the *marrons*. But it was the book published by a French explorer, Dr J. Crévaux,[10] which, apparently, first drew the attention of ethnologists to the Bush Negroes. Some of the facts he related – the use of ordeal by poison, certain modes of greeting, the survival of animal taboos handed down inside the clan, the public display of a deceased person's body, the practice of cicatrising the flesh round the navel in a rosette pattern, the names of certain specially revered deities, the tradition of naming children after the day of the week on which they were born – aroused the interest of Delafosse. On the basis of a detailed comparison with the customs of the Agni-Tshi or Agni-Ashanti, whom he had investigated in Africa, he revealed the origin and continued existence, in America, of a near-pure African civilisation.[11] From then on studies came thick and fast; today the Bush Negro culture of the Guianas is a well-mapped terrain.[12]

All the tribes listed above are divided into clans, or *lo* (an Ewe term), and each *lo* into matrilineal families. At the head of the tribe is the supreme Chief (*gran man*), who doubles the roles of civil leader and High Priest. For secular matters, judicial decisions in particular, he has the help of the *gran fiskari*. In charge of each *lo* we find a *gran kapiting*, assisted by a deputy captain and a forest officer. The *lo* is a social rather than a geographic unit; each one includes several villages, these being in the charge of a *basia* (from Bastiaan, a slave-trader), who acts as combined mayor and police chief. What gives the *lo* unity is its connection with some totemic creature (frog, parrot, etc.) which protects it, and which it is *kina* (i.e. taboo on religious grounds) to kill. Despite this hierarchy of officialdom, the political organisation of the tribe is essentially democratic. In every village there is a council of elders (*g'a sembi*), and also the Assembly, open to all grown men (*lanti krutu*); in the last resort decisions rest with the latter. All the *basia* does, in fact, is to implement the rulings of the council of elders. We may note the occasional existence of a female *basia* in addition to the ordinary one; her duties are to watch over the conduct of the women, and deal with any disputes that may arise amongst them. The *gran kapiting* is always the headman of the main village in the *lo*; the *gran man* never intervenes except when quarrels arise between the clans. Each *lo* has its own farming land, its own section of the river to fish in, and its own part of the bush for hunting.

A child belongs to its mother's clan, and is a member of her village. The family is of the 'extended' type, comprising not only mother, father, and children, but also grandparents, uncles, and aunts on the maternal side. Marriage involves free consent on the part of the bride, and obligatory gifts to her parents (substantially higher in value if she is a virgin): but it does not constitute a 'purchase' in the strict sense. All it implies is some sort of compensation to the parents for all the trouble they took in rearing the child – and to the group as a whole for the loss they sustain through being deprived of one of their members' labour. A married woman does not generally live in her husband's house. Either she remains in her own village, with her mother, or else her husband builds her a hut in *his* native village. In any case, he himself stays in his mother's village, and merely pays visits to his wife (or wives, if he has several). He helps her with heavy work, such as burning off scrub and clearing the undergrowth from her 'patch' in the forest. He also brings her presents in return for her sexual favours, while she turns over to him the produce of the allotment. Both husband and wife, in fact, live what amounts to a bachelor existence; married life, in the full sense, does not exist. Thus Hurault maintains that the 'family' of these Negro fugitives is not a reconstituted version of any African model, since the rebels came either from ethnic groups with a patrilineal system, or from matrilineal tribes with patrilocal groupings. By and large this is true enough. Yet even if this family is not a straightforward copy of the African family, it nevertheless preserves many of the latter's characteristic features. This is particularly noticeable among the Saramacas. One striking survival is the famous 'double descent' principle current among the Fanti–Ashanti, who formed the main core of the rebel population. Though a child belongs to its mother, and inherits her totem and her taboos, it also acquires certain *trefu* or taboos relating to its father, and his *obia* or magical objects. Elsewhere, as in the matrilineal areas of Africa, the father is no more than a companion to his son, and authority resides with the mother's brother.[13] When a man dies his property goes, in the first instance, to his mother, brothers, and sisters, and only then to his own children. In the same way, since civic office is hereditary, when the chief dies the council of elders chooses his successor from among his brothers or the sons of his uterine sisters. Among other African features we find clan exogamy, with a ban on having two wives simultaenously from the same related group. Not unless a man puts away his wife can he marry her sister. Matrimonial regulations vary according to the tribe. The Boni (like the Akan in Ghana or the Baoulé of the Ivory Coast) cannot have any relationship with a woman who has been married to 'a brother by the same mother', while the Saramacas compel a sister to marry one of the dead man's brothers.

During his wife's pregnancy, a husband is debarred from having sexual relations with her, so that the child may not be puny or stunted. He is also subject to a series of taboos, including one on digging the soil, since this would bring about the death of his wife. The child is generally delivered by a midwife, known as a *pekein mama*, or 'little mother'; after the birth, mother and child remain separated for seven days if the child is a girl, nine if it is a boy. The baby is named according to the day of the week on which it is born; here – as has already been

stated on the authority of Delafosse[14] – we have yet another
characteristic feature of Fanti–Ashanti culture:

DAY OF THE	BOYS		GIRLS	
WEEK	*Guiana*	*Ghana*	*Guiana*	*Ghana*
Monday	Couachi	Kouassi	Corrachiba	Akouassiba
Tuesday	Codio	Kodio	Adioula	Adioula
Wednesday	Couamina	Kouamina	Amba	Aminaba
Thursday	Couacou	Kouakou	Acouba	Akouba
Friday	Yao	Yao	Yaba	Ayaba
Saturday	Cofi	Kofi	Afiba	Afouba
Sunday	Couami	Kouami	Abeniba	Amoriba

This, however, is not the only name that an individual
possesses. Since a name both determines its owner's character
and to some extent shapes his destiny, the practice is to approach
some honourable acquaintance and purchase his name, which
then becomes that of the child. In addition to this, the child is
a reincarnation of one of its ancestors, and so after its birth the
'sacred scriptures' are consulted to find out which ancestor has
been reincarnated.

On the eighth day after birth, if it is a girl, or the ninth, in
the case of a boy, the child is formally presented to its society
and the gods; on this occasion both mother and child receive
presents from friends and neighbours. When it is two years old,
the child is weaned. Throughout this early period it is normally
looked after by its grandmother, or an aunt, while its education
is in the hands of its maternal uncle. There are no initiation or
puberty rites, except that at fourteen or fifteen an adolescent
receives the *kamisa* (a dhoti-like cotton shirt that tucks between
the legs) and is thus formally enrolled as an adult member of
the group. Tattooing, however, exists, and preserves the
patterns known in Africa. Boys and girls learn their future
tasks according to the rules prescribing a division of labour
between the sexes. For a boy, this involves hunting, both with
a gun and with bow and arrows, constructing a dug-out
canoe, and handling it on the river (Bush Negroes are well
known for their boating skill). The girls learn how to plant and
harvest crops on an allotment, as well as sewing, knitting, and
traditional dances in honour of the gods.

Marriages are not dictated by the parents: prospective
couples have a free choice of partner. As a result courtships

are conducted in a romantic, not to say poetical, fashion. There may be an exchange of little gifts, in which the man's feelings are revealed through the symbolic language of the sculptured figure he offers to the girl of his choice. A boy may ask a girl to braid her hair for him, and the girl's answer will be given, symbolically, by the way in which she braids it. Once a private understanding has been reached, the next step is an official application to the head of the clan. This is made through a representative, most often the maternal uncle or some 'eloquent speaker'. The chief gives this messenger one of the girl's sisters (or a classificatory brother, according to the sex of the applicant); once again approval is expressed in a symbolic form. The fiancé then gathers his friends to help build a house for his wife-to-be, and builds her a canoe. This will enable her to make her way to an area suitable for cultivation, and clear a patch in the forest. Finally, he buys her the basic equipment for running a household. There is no special ceremony involved, except that the girl's maternal uncle gives the newly-weds a lecture on their mutual responsibilities. One point which has struck all ethnographers is that while, more often than not, an unmarried girl leads a very respectable life (I have already referred to the value set on virginity), after her marriage she frequently becomes morally dissolute. (When her husband is away hunting or fishing, for instance, she will receive nocturnal visits from other young men.) Marriages can be dissolved with the same ease as they are contracted, most often on the wife's initiative. She simply notifies the village headman and the *gran kapiting* of her *lo*, and then moves out to the hut of her parents or her lover, as the case may be.

Immediately after death, the body is laid out in a canoe, and washed all over (except for the back) with water containing an admixture of rum and tobacco. All orifices are sealed with tobacco and cotton plugs, and the head is bound up in a white cloth. While the young folk are making the coffin and digging the grave, a wake is held for the deceased person, with songs, stories (in particular those to do with *anansi*, the spider), and a whole series of traditional games, designed to pass the time. When the coffin is finished and the grave dug – the diggers must not let one single drop of sweat fall into the latter, since this would result in their own death – the chanting and dancing begins, culminating in the so-called 'interrogation of the corpse'. Here we have yet another instance of Fanti–Ashanti practice. Since every death is regarded as being supernatural in origin, it is necessary to find out if the deceased has been the victim of divine retribution (for having violated some taboo) or, alternatively, of black magic. The grave-diggers, in a tranced or semi-tranced state, hoist the coffin on to their shoulders, and then move hither and thither as the corpse directs them, while questions are fired at it: 'Who killed you? Was it so-and-so?' The ceremony lasts a long time, and the grave-diggers are kept moving here, there, and everywhere. Only after the corpse has been carried back to the house do the elders assemble to interpret the dead man's message. Burial takes place a week later – or three days in areas where the Dutch government exercises some semblance of control. Then the coffin, whitened with chalk, is carried by river to the site of the open grave, where a final farewell is taken of it. 'The hour has come for us to part. We can do nothing against what earth has decided. We have done all we could. We are giving you fitting burial. Watch over us, deliver us from all evil.' Shots are fired to drive away evil spirits, food is left on the grave, and then all present quickly retire to the river, where they wash themselves in token of purification. Among the Boni, at least, for the duration of the mourning period the surviving partner is placed under the protection of the deceased person's clan, works for it, and can no longer pray to his own ancestors. Eighteen months or two years later a feast is held to terminate the period of mourning. This feast lasts an entire week, for the dead person's influence can only be gradually eliminated, through a series of purificatory rites, dances, and offerings to the ancestral spirits.

Bush Negroes believe in a supreme deity, known by the Aucas as *nana* (originally an Agni word), by the Boni as *masu gadu* (a term of Fon origin), and by the Saramaca as *nyan kompon* or *nyame* (the Fanti–Ashanti name). But beneath this deity we find a wide range of lesser gods or spirits. Some of these are generic, being found among all groups descended from the *marrons*, while others are restricted to one particular clan: for example, the Djuka otter clan (*gwangwella* or *guantata*), of which the totem would seem to have been brought over from Africa by some priest initiated in its mysteries, its functions being to enforce justice among the group's members, and to defend the group as a whole from attacks by sorcerers. Such lesser divinities are termed *winti*, a name most in use among the Saramaca, or *gattu*, the term preferred by the Djukas. The Boni divide them into four categories. First, there are the *kumenti*. These include the *kumenti* proper, who assume the form of jaguars; the *djadja* (ocelots); the *opete* (urubu vultures); and the *bunsunki*, who haunt the rivers and resemble Indian women. Next come the *Ampuku*, the gods of the bush. Third, we have the *vodums*, who achieve incarnation as the serpent *dagowe*. Lastly there are the *kankamasu*, the gods of the termitaries. As regards the other tribes, the only classifications we have are according to the favoured deity's ethnic origin: (1) gods of Fanti–Ashanti origin, such as *asase* (the Earth-Mother), *tando* (name of an African river), *opete* (the urubu vulture), and those forest spirits, particularly violent and dangerous, known as the *kromanti;* (2) gods of Dahomean origin, including *masu gadu*, referred to above, *loko* (the sacred bombax or silk-cotton tree), *dagowe* (the boa-constrictor), *gedeonsu* (god of harvests and female fecundity), and *afrikete* and *legba* (god of the cross-roads and protector of villages); (3) certain divinities of Bantu origin, such as *loango winti*, *zambi* (the Bantus' supreme deity), and *ma' bumba*.

According to Herskovits, individuals can acquire a *winti* in three ways: by family inheritance (man to man or woman to woman); through a personal choice on the part of the divinity; or, lastly, by *kunu*, i.e. as punishment for some transgression. Thus, while in the first two instances the *winti* are a species of guardian angel and receive a normal type of cult, the third category is quite different. Here one is possessed by an evil *winti*, which is liable to inflict poverty, sickness, or even death. Nevertheless, since *kunu* extends to all members of a patrilineal group, it acts – paradoxically enough – as one of the binding elements in the group's unity. It is, similarly, the fear of *kunu* which keeps up traditions in the face of all disruptive influences. Each of these divinities has his or her own special taboos (*trefu* or *kina*), favourite dish, personal colour; each is honoured with a different sacred dance, and provided with individual 'sacred scriptures'.

Cult-worship is in the hands of the priests, such as the *gran moun*, who officiates for the *guantata* clan, and neutralises the maleficent effects produced by any violation of a taboo – besides healing the sick and acting as a rain-maker. The *gedeonsu* have ministrants known collectively as the *pedri-lo*, with a high priestess at their head. The *winti*, or *gado*, are represented by priests known as *lukuman*. Worship takes the form of sacrifices, dances and chants, which culminate in fits of ecstatic possession, to the rhythmic accompaniment of the three ceremonial drums.

Magic is in the hands of the *obiaman*, in contradistinction to the *lukuman*, who are priests. However, it is important to distinguish, equally, between white magic (*obia*), and black magic (*wisi*). The former takes two forms, one defensive, for protection against sorcerers (*tapu*), the other offensive (known as *opo* by the Saramacas and *sabi* among the Djukas), this being employed to win someone's love, succeed in one's activities, and so on. Black magic is that practised by genuine sorcerers (*wisiman*), who call up the spirits of the dead, render them slaves to their malevolent will, and force them to work for evil purposes. These enslaved spirits are known as *bakru*, and recall the famous *zombies* of Haiti.

Every individual possesses an *akra* (known as *kra* among the Fanti–Ashanti), implanted by the supreme being at birth, which vanishes at the moment of death. The *akra* requires worship and sacrifice from its owner, and if it does not get them exacts vengeance for the omission. In certain cases there would appear to be two *akra*, one male, the other female; or perhaps a *nan-akra* (from the father) and an *uman-kra* (from the mother) – both phenomena which, once again, recall the Fanti–Ashanti principle of double affiliation. In addition, every man also possesses a *yorka*, which survives his death. Those of good men arouse no comment, whereas evil-doers give rise to malevolent *yorkas*: the folklore of Negro *marrons* abounds in tales of the disgrace that can be brought on a family by these revenants. It has been argued that the term *yorka* is of Indian origin, and it is true that the Kalina Indians refer to their spirits as *yoroka*. But even if the etymological derivation is sound, the concept implied by such a term has a characteristically African quality about it. In addition to these two component parts of the spiritual personality we must note a third, the *ninseki*, or soul of a reincarnated ancestor. This will normally be from the same clan, but may also belong to an ancestor from some other group, or even one of another race, e.g. a European.

The folklore is essentially Fanti–Ashanti in origin, and characterised by the major role played in it by the spider (*anansi*). On the other hand the language spoken by Bush Negroes has undergone considerable modifications. Since it has to serve as a means of communication between highly diverse ethnic groups, it has gradually become a mixed jumble of words borrowed from various languages – African, English, Portuguese, Dutch, and (among the Boni) French. All these Negro refugees are famous for their decorative skills and their wood-carving. Every tribe has its own original style, and it is easy to tell, at a glance, whether an object has been produced, say, by the Boni or the Saramacas. Herskovits, who has made a special study of Saramaca decorative motifs (on houses, canoes, oars, drums, and combs), insists that they are African by derivation, and has backed up his argument with photographs comparing Fanti–Ashanti and Guiana-produced artifacts. Hurault, on the other hand, comes to quite different conclusions as regards the Boni. Their art, he claims, is of comparatively recent origin: the earliest traveller who mentions it can be dated to 1832. Yet even if Boni art is recent (and in the process of radical change, since today the decoration of house-pillars and house-doors is being done in painting rather than bas-relief) it nevertheless remains African in spirit; its main effect is that of a rebus which has to be puzzled out. Essentially, it consists of a *message*, to be read and understood. Its function, then, is not religious, but purely social, with (more often than not) a specifically sexual reference attached. It provides a means whereby the man who sculpts little gifts for a woman can please her, make her laugh, and insinuate himself into her heart.

To round off our picture of Bush Negro civilisation would involve describing the economic infrastructure. This, however, shows few signs of genuine African influence. What it *does* indicate, with much greater emphasis, is adaptation to a new environment, and the borrowing of agricultural methods from neighbouring Indian tribes. A brief description, then, will suffice. Land is owned collectively by the matrilineal clan, or by that part of it which resides in any given village. The individual merely enjoys the right of using it. The main crops grown on the allotments include rice, maize, manioc, bananas, and yams. Crafts and trade are both unknown (apart from a restricted barter with the Indians, to secure hunting dogs), and because of vampire bats and parasites, stockfarming is quite impracticable. However, they do build and use canoes, and this skill nets them a substantial revenue by putting them in touch with the white community, who pay them.

III. *Other maroon communities*

The case of these Negro refugees in Guiana presents us with a cultural continuum, extending from the economic infrastructure (the least African-looking aspect of their civilisation, since it has always been exposed to the determinist influence exerted by environmental forces) to religion, the most stubbornly African feature of them all. Or, put in other terms, from the Saramaca, who derive the fundamental basis of their culture from the Fanti–Ashanti, to the Boni, who were the last to rebel, and thus more affected by external influences than their predecessors. By and large, however, of all the *marrons* it is the Bush Negroes who have best preserved African patterns for their social organisation and religious beliefs.

Yet we should not infer from this that *marronage* is always synonymous with the survival of tradition; we also have to take the demographic factor into account. In fact a small and isolated community is liable to react in precisely the opposite direction. Faced with a stark struggle for mere survival as a human group, it tends to let its customs degenerate and to lapse into a merely vegetable existence. One fact that has always struck me about Brazil is that the small out-of-the-way hamlets, the fishing villages hidden away by some creek in the mountains, possessed neither folklore nor festivals, and indeed gave signs of having nothing more positive than a vague and rootless religiosity. The *marron*-descended communities that I propose to examine now are all affected by these two opposing trends – the idea of resistance, which makes them cling to their ancestral traditions, and the weakening of these traditions through underpopulation and the overriding demands of mere physical survival.

Beltram has produced an admirable monograph on one of these communities,[18] that of Cujila, in the Mexican state of Oaxaca. It lies beside the Pacific, in a region where the bulk of the population is Indian. Though the village does not consist exclusively of Negroes (there are some Indian–Negro half-breeds and three or four white families, who hold the economic power), nevertheless many African characteristics are preserved. In the field of motor habits we may note the practice of carrying children on the back and packages on the head. When we turn to habitations, we find that the Negroes build round houses, whereas the Indians in the same area have rectangular ones; such round huts as they do possess are direct imitations. The main social unit is the extended patrilocal family, which inhabits a group of houses enclosed within the same outer wall; this is known as the *compuesto*. Polygamy is practised, with the number-one wife living in the *compuesto*, and the others (the *chéries* or *queridas*) in separate quarters of their own. We may note, however, that the status of these secondary wives is actually higher than that of the 'number-one', since the legitimate wife has to live on what her husband allows her, whereas the *queridas* receive agricultural allotments, the produce of which they keep for themselves. Beltram emphasises the aggressive character of this civilisation, due, no doubt, to the tradition of *marronage*. For one thing, the Negro refuses to trade with the Indian – or at least will only do so indirectly, by selling his produce to the white man, who then resells it to the Indians. In this community we also find bands of brigands (*brossa*), who constitute the Negroes' 'offensive arm', as Beltram puts it, against both the whites and the national authorities. This aggressive character is also manifested in the practice of marriage by abduction, the obligatory method here. The fiancé and a group of his friends, all armed with hatchets and pistols, lay in wait for the girl, and when she passes, the young man carries her off on horseback. The abduction, of course, is a symbolic one, or at any rate institutionalised, since the betrothed couple, far from taking to the hills, go no further than the cultivated fields, and return to the village that same evening. If the girl is a virgin, the marriage then takes place; otherwise the girl is returned to her parents. In the first instance, the official demand is made through a messenger (*portador*), and the fiancé's family pays compensation to that of the girl (here we have a survival of the African custom known as *lobola*). Not until the *lobola* has been handed over, and a ritual exchange of chanted insults has taken place between the two camps – the climax of which is the whipping of the two young people – can the marriage be regarded as having been completed.)

In Cujila society, however, we find African survivals side by side with characteristically Indian practices (e.g. nagalism) or such features of Spanish culture as sponsorship by god-parents. The anthropological beliefs of this *marron*-descended group offers a good instance of such syncretism in action. The individual is composed of four elements. First, the body; secondly, the shadow (a feature taken over from African tradition), that is to say the body's double, which can leave it during sleep, and which must never be trapped by sorcerers; thirdly, the soul (a Christian notion, borrowed from European culture); and lastly, the animal-*tono*. This entity is mystically linked with the child from the moment of birth, and its name remains a carefully-kept secret, for if the animal-*tono* is wounded or killed, the man will likewise fall sick and die (here we have an element taken from Indian culture). The *tono* is the first animal seen by the parents between the child's birth and baptism, but the aggressive ethos of the community ensures that it is most often selected from among the more ferocious beasts. Furthermore, syncretism is just as common a feature of Cujila practices as of their beliefs. For instance, the ritual surrounding death and burial follows the Spanish Christian pattern, but it is the deceased person's eldest brother, not his children, who becomes his heir.

The *marrons* of Jamaica are more secretive and retiring, with a tendency to conceal their social customs from the curiosity of ethnographers.[19] They are descended from the Negroes who revolted at the time of the island's occupation by the English in 1739; they marry only among themselves (the ban on out-siders includes the other Negroes on the island), and refuse to receive visitors unless the latter are accompanied by one of their own people. According to M. W. Beckwith, they constitute a species of secret society, isolated from the other Negroes not only politically, but by that tradition of mystery which enshrouds the preservation of their ancient customs. They are said to have the most powerful magicians, to be expert in herbal remedies, and to speak a secret language (Kromanti, which has passed out of use elsewhere). In fact they have preserved a large proportion of their Fanti–Ashanti African heritage. Features we may note include the blood-pact: the war with the English was terminated by such a pact between Trelawney, the English commander, and the *marron* chief Accompong, sealed in their blood, which was mingled and drunk communally, mixed with rum.[20] We also find a similar division of labour between the sexes, with the man hunting while the woman tills the fields, together with marked independence on the part of the latter, who owns, and sells in the market, whatever produce she grows. Other such features include polygamy by the chief, certain musical instruments (the *marrons* will not reveal their African names), and, lastly, the important role played in folklore by stories concerning the spider, *anansi*. As regards their festivals, our knowledge is virtually restricted to public ceremonies such as Christmas. On these occasions they are somewhat more willing to admit strangers, since the festivities consist almost exclusively of English-derived parades and dances – or else historical reminders of their rebellions, which are well known throughout the island (e.g. the cult rendered to their old-time queen, a heroine of the resistance, in the form of a doll called *yumma*). Nevertheless, even here we find some African practices – e.g. the appearance in the crowd during these public celebrations of various masked mummers, such as the 'whooping boy', a horse-spirit which only comes out in August, the 'three-leg horse', which appears just before Christmas, the 'rolling calf', and so on. According to Z. N. Hurston, who has watched the nocturnal dance of the *marrons* as they await the appearance of the horse-spirit, these masked figures are sexual symbols, the fragmentary remnants of some old African initiation ceremony, since the women simultaneously long for their coming and fear their approach. This interpretation is far from certain, but in default of further evidence and any serious investigation of the topic, we may provisionally accept it.

In Venezuela, uprisings took place and *marron* republics were formed, which were known as *cumbes*. These included that of King Miguel in the sixteenth century, that of Andresote in 1732, and above all that established in the Coro region (1795). We know that these *cumbes* contained groups of Negroes 'without any external signs of the Catholic faith'[21] who lived 'like barbarians, in the hills'. We know, too, that one of the leaders at Coro was a fetish priest, Cocofio. However, all these republics were destroyed, one after the other, and – as with Palmares in Brazil – nothing but their names survive today.[22] In Colombia on the other hand, until very recent years – certainly until the spread of sugar-cane cultivation to the area in question – there survived a group which, because of its isolation (no European being allowed to live there except the priest), managed to preserve many features of its original Bantu (Angolan) culture. Its members were descended from some *marrons* led by an African king, Domingo Bioho, who founded the *palenque* (as Negro republics are there termed) of San Brazilia – about which, thanks to the work of Escalante,[23] we now know a good deal. His monograph shows, beyond question, that in its economy, its agricultural methods, its folklore and its religion, this society was profoundly influenced by the far more extensive civilisation of Colombia (though it tended to reinterpret Christianity in terms of protective magic rather than as genuine religion), and that the *palenque* proved incapable of developing an autonomous political organisation strong enough to guarantee the survival of African customs (the only social institution here is the common-law type nuclear family, or else straightforward concubinage). Nevertheless, polygyny continues to be practised, mostly in the shape of bigamy, with the man dividing his attentions between his *mujé de asiento*, or number-one wife, and his *chérie*, or second wife. As at Cujila, marriage takes the form of abduction. The young man carries off the girl (though she is in fact willing, she sometimes puts up a show of resistance) with the aid of his friends. If the girl is a virgin, the news is announced by three drum-beats: if she is not, by six. Three days later the newly-weds return to the bride's parents, who demand a financial compensation of between $200 and $400 – all that survives of the *lobola*. The community retains traces of a certain dualism, visible in the opposition between upper and lower villages. Most striking of all, we have the formation of local groups in each district or quarter: these are known as *cuadros*, and there may be more than one to a quarter. Among them we find adult *cuadros* (though not so many of them as one might expect), with the main function of acting as a mutual aid society in cases of sickness or death; and others reserved for adolescents, these being erotic in purpose, designed both to facilitate social intercourse between the sexes and to institutionalise the ceremony of nuptial abduction. Bantu influence is most apparent in funeral ceremonies. These are conducted by a special fraternity (*cabildo*), known as *umbalú* – the names of the principal drum employed to accompany the chanting in Angolan, with an invocation (according to one participant) of *Calunga*, god of the dead or supreme deity for the various Bantu ethnic groups. For nine days the dead man's soul lingers by his body, and throughout this period the women dance round the corpse, sometimes confessing their sins, while the young men while away the time outside the house by playing various games. On the last day the Catholic altar put up for the occasion is dismantled – an indication of the soul's departure. The subsequent burial ceremony is modelled on the European pattern.

IV

Perhaps we can now draw some reasonably general conclusions from this collection of facts. The most characteristic feature, as I see it, of such *marron* communities, even at this early stage, is the split between the infra- and superstructures. Later, we shall observe it in its fully developed form, but the germ of it is already present here. The split can occur at various levels, between this layer and that of what might be termed, in a sense, the stratified nature of reality. It may exist between social organisation on the one hand and practical and economic know-how on the other; or, perhaps, between social organisation and religious beliefs. These fissures are due to the fact that all such communities find themselves pulled in two ways. On the one hand they have a powerful incentive to adapt themselves to their new environment, to forge new and individual institutions from their struggle for survival.

On the other, there is a strong force driving them to maintain their old ancestral traditions, since these are seen as symbolising their independence (political no less than cultural), and forming the spiritual cement which binds them all together. Obviously tensions will be found in any over-all social group; but whereas in Africa there exists a functional connection between the various levels of what G. Gurvitch has termed 'sociology in depth', and all strata – from the ecological to those embodying social values or the group conscience – form part of the same continuum, in these *marron* communities a quite different state of affairs prevails. Here environmental determinism and the claims of collective memory come into direct conflict.

Undoubtedly an over-subtle dialectic does tend to make a close pattern out of disparate elements, to fit hard technical and physical facts into a context of collective memory – or alternatively, by assuming that collective memory is no less liable to forgetfulness than the memory of the individual, to fill those gaping holes in the web of memory with the aid of new beliefs, themselves thrown up by production methods which a new social and geographical environment has imposed. There are no general rules or constant pattern for 'tie-ups' of this sort, which vary according to time and place. All one can say is that the two basic 'variable factors' involved are the temporal (date of each *marron* republic's constitution) and the demographic variants. The latter depend on the size of the population. Since all memories of the past will be filtered through the sieve of informational exchange between individuals, the number of cultural features known will depend, first, on the number of people in communication with one another, and secondly, on their original position (whether strategic or not) in the African social structure. Thus these communities are at one and the same time resistance groups and pioneers; as *African* civilisations they remain archaic, as *Negro* civilisations they are brand new.

Throughout this chapter my main emphasis has been on the traditional element. But here a further conclusion would seem to suggest itself. Though some communities are relatively homogeneous – e.g. 100 per cent Angolan in origin – the larger ones include the descendants of various different ethnic groups. Even in Jamaica, the Kromanti majority received an admixture of 'Malays', i.e. Malagasy from Madagascar. Every member 'nation', then, contributed its own collective memory to the whole. How did they react upon one another? We always find one culture predominant (the Fanti–Ashanti, for instance, in the case of Guiana); but this still allows the coexistence of whole enclaves based on other civilisations. The very existence of the *vodou* cult, a Dahomean phenomenon, bears sufficient witness to this. As far as the religious superstructure is concerned, in fact, we find ourselves everywhere confronted with 'mosaic' cultures. There is no real difficulty in explaining this. The facts speak for themselves: first, we have a certain homologous affinity between the various African beliefs. Secondly, there is the close bond linking a nation and its cults; the gods form an integral part of human society. As a result, in any *marron* republic a nation can only survive by allying itself with other bands, not by denying its own individuality to serve the common revolutionary cause. Last and most important, we have a factor which explains the actual process of mosaic development. Even in Africa the members of one ethnic group were split up into separate and complementary fraternities, each responsible for the service of a single divinity or a single family of gods. Thus the *marrons* had an *African* model available which would allow them to establish ethnically distinct cults – e.g. the Kromanti *winti* and the Ewe *vodous* – on a basis of coexistence. This they did by setting them up as separate fraternities, with different music, dances and languages for their chants. On the other hand, since in the so-called 'animist' religions the criterion of validity tends to be success, one ethnic group may well accept gods who originated elsewhere, provided that they have made manifest and proved their divine power and efficacy. On the Ivory Coast such religious borrowings are still very much the rule. Thus there is nothing surprising in the fact that Kromanti rebels accepted a Dahomean deity such as *Legba*, since *Legba*'s function was to protect villages against external threats and to halt approaching enemies while they were still on the march. But such cultural mosaics, despite the variety of tone which they possess, nevertheless always reveal one dominant colour – by no means invariably that of the numerically largest ethnic group, and often dependent on the active degree of penetration achieved by any given culture. It was thus, for example, that, in Guiana, the patrilineal Ewes accepted the matrilineal practices of the Fanti–Ashanti.

REFERENCES

1. See, e.g., Herskovits, *Myth*, ch. IV; E. F. Frazier, *The Negro in the United States*, New York, 1949; J. H. Franklin, *From Slavery to Freedom*, New York, 1947; J. Colombian Rosario and Justina Carrion, *Problemes Sociales: El Negro*, S. Juan, Puerto Rico, 1940, etc.

2. Thomas Mandiou, *Histoire d'Haïti*, vol. I, pp. 72–3; J. C. Dorsainville, *Manuel d'Histoire d'Haiti*, Port-au-Prince, 1936; Lorimer Denis and François Duvalier, *Evolution stadiale de Vaudou*, Port-au-Prince, 1944.

3. Nina Rodrigues, *Os africanos no Brasil*, Rio, 1933, pp. 83 ff.; R. Bastide, *Les réligions africaines au Brésil*. Paris, 1961.

4. 'Le Marronage', Pt. I, *Année Sociologique*, 1961; Pt. II, *Année Sociologique*, 1962.

5. R. Bastide, *op. cit.*

6. Debbash, *op. cit.*

7. The classic term by which *marrons* in the Guianas are generally known.

8. '*Djuka*' is the name of an African bird, which they claimed was identical with another similar bird in America.

9. It may be regarded as surprising to find so sizeable a population descended from so tiny a group of fugitives. But the phenomenon is by no means unique: something of the sort can also be seen among the Boni. See Hurault, *op. cit.*

10. *Voyage dans l'Amérique de Sud*, Paris, 1884.

11. M. Delafosse, 'De quelques persistances d'ordre ethnographique chez les descendants des Nègres transplantés aux Antilles et à la Guyane', *Rev. d'Ethnol. et de Sociol.* III (1912), pp. 234–7.

12. See in particular Morton C. Kahn, *Djuka: The Bush Negroes of Dutch Guyana*, New York, 1931; M. J. and F. S. Herskovits, *Rebel Destiny*, New York, 1937; J. Hurault, *Les Noirs Réfugiés Boni de la Guyane française*, I.F.A.N., Dakar, 1961, and *La vie matérielle des Noirs réfugiés Boni et des Indiens Wayana*, Paris, 1965; Van Lier, *Notes sur la vie spirituelle et sociale des Djukas en Surinam* (Fr. trs., roneo, n.d.); also the article by R. de Lamberterie on the Boni, *Journ. Soc. des Amer.* XXXV (1943–6), pp. 123–47, and two studies by M. C. Kahn, 'Notes on the Suramericaner Bush Negroes', *Am. Anthop.* XXI, and 'Saramaccan Bush Negroes', *Am. Anthrop.* XXX.

13. Except among the Boni; here, although the child is placed in the charge of its oldest classificatory uncle, its tutor is selected by a family council (Hurault, *op. cit.*).

14. Delafosse, *op. cit.*

15. Gonzalo Aguirre Beltram, *Cujila, esbozo etnográfico de un pueblo negro*, Mexico, 1958.

16. R. C. Dallas, *The History of the Marrons*, London, 1803; Martha

Warren Beckwith, *Black Roadways: a study of Jamaican Folk Life*, University of North Carolina Press, 1929, ch. XII; Zora Neale Hurston, *Tell My Horse*, Philadelphia, 1938.

17. It seems at least possible that the name Accompong, which survives as the name of a present-day *marron* village, may have been based on the name of the Kromanti god Nyankopon.

18. This was not invariably the case; when the fortified village of Mariscal Castellanos fell, among the prisoners taken was a Negro with mitre and surplice who used to baptise new-born children and celebrate mass. But as far as the negroes of Coro are concerned, historians all agree that 'they were Christians in name only'.

19. C. Restrepo Canal, *Leyes de manumision*, Bogota, 1935; G. Hernandez de Alba, *Libertad de los Esclavos en Colombia*, Bogota, 1956; P. M. Arcaya, *Estudios de sociologia venezolana*, Madrid, n.d.; Enrique de Gandia, 'La insurrection de los negros de Coro en 1795', in *Miscellanea P. Rivet*, vol. II, Mexico, 1958, pp. 695–991.

20 Thomas G. Price, Jr., 'Estado y necessitades actuales de las investigaciones afro-colombianas', *Rev. Col. de Antrop.* II, 2, 1954; Aquiles Escalante, 'Notas sobre el palenque de San Brasilia', *Divulgaciones Etnologicas*, IV, 1, Universidad del Atlantico, 1954.

CHAPTER IV

THE MEETING OF NEGRO
AND INDIAN

I

As a result of *marronage*, the African came into contact with the Indian. The former sometimes tended to keep himself to himself; as we have already seen, the Bush Negroes of Guiana had only the most restricted contacts with the Indians in their area, and then solely for purposes of barter. On the other hand we cannot speak of racial opposition. The very concept of racial opposition is a European invention, like the idea of the happily submissive slave. While the myth of Uncle Remus or Old John was used to justify the continuation of slavery, the myth of Negro–Indian hostility stopped these two exploited peoples from making common cause against the master-race. It was the old familiar precept: divide and rule.

Dollard has shown how close a link there is between aggressive feelings and situations which specifically tend to engender social frustration.[1] Now in theory this aggressiveness of the Africans and their descendants should have been directed against the whites. To avoid such a situation, the latter were obliged to divert Negro aggressiveness on to other targets, to canalise it in a different direction, or else to institutionalise it, in the form of coloured regiments. During the colonial period the Europeans did, in fact, manipulate this aggressiveness for their own benefit, by turning it against their own enemies – i.e other Europeans – for the defence of their colonies. One good example of this process is Brazil, where the Portuguese fought the Dutch. There were also clan struggles between rival families, which led to Negroes fighting each other; each European landowner had his own private slave army. After Independence, this aggression was channelled against the urban ruling class: Anglo-Saxons in the U.S.A., the Spanish in Rio de la Plata or in Cuba, the Portuguese in Brazil. It goes without saying that here again the chief beneficiaries were whites, in this case white creoles, even if the Negroes whose aid they enlisted did sometimes extract personal benefits from the deal, e.g. their enfranchisement papers. Once victory was assured, these creoles made no attempt to integrate the coloured population in the new nation which they had all fought side by side to achieve.

But more often than not – a point of some interest to us – the Negroes' aggressiveness was directed, first and foremost, against the Indians, while the latter, similarly, were whipped up into hostility against the Negroes. The *Quilombo* of Palmares, in Brazil, a refuge and haven for fugitive Negro slaves from Alagôas, only fell after massive intervention by a force of Indians and Mamelukes[2] under Domingos Jorge Velho. After this victory a popular pageant-play was put on (it is still performed in the area) which showed Negroes being taken prisoner by Indians and sold to the whites. The effect has been to maintain, among the population at large, that feeling of mutual hatred which the old-time colonisers controlled and exploited with such skill. The division was even kept up by various laws, such as those forbidding the intermarriage of Negroes and Indians. Since the child inherited its mother's status, and the Indians remained free (the indigenous population being protected by the clergy), marriage between a slave and an Indian woman was liable to deprive the slave's master of offspring which, in other circumstances, would have belonged to him. That these laws did, in fact, stir up racial enmity is made clear by the evidence of certain trials. In Venezuela, for instance, we have testimony which suggests that the Indians were no better disposed towards the Negroes than the whites were. The father of a young Indian girl who had promised to marry a Negro asked the court for an injunction against such a union, on the grounds that 'the Indians, as a class, are set wholly apart by the purity of their blood, inasmuch as each one of them, in his own area, regards himself as on a par with the highest rank of all, that of the nobility'. Thus, he argued, his daughter Libo could not possibly ally herself with 'that class of person which is considered the dregs of our republic'.[3]

Such ideological attitudes, though exploited by the whites (who did their utmost to make them second nature with both Africans and the local natives), did not completely succeed in eradicating the attraction of one race for the other. Saint-Hilaire, who wrote early in the nineteenth century, and was an admirable chronicler of contemporary Brazilian life, observed that Indian women gave themselves to other Indians out of matrimonial duty, to Europeans for money, and to Negroes for pleasure.[4] Mixed blood began to appear from the very first period of contact. Herskovits studied the problem in the U.S.A. by means of genealogical analysis.[5] He took a sample of 1,551 coloured students, and came up with the following statistics: 342 were the offspring of non-mixed families; 798 had some white blood; 97 (or 6·3 per cent) had some Indian blood; while 314, or 20·9 per cent, had the blood of all three races. It is true that we must make allowances for the romantic Indian myth, which may well have led some of these Negroes to claim remote Indian ancestry. But the genealogies which Herskovits compiled are by no means entirely products of the imagination. When we turn to Portuguese America, we find a comparable situation in the sugar-mills of the north-east. Here the three races not only managed to live together, but did so in general harmony. The Europeans owned the land and ran the mills; the Negroes worked on the plantations; while the Indians, armed with bows and arrows, defended the mill against pirates, or attacks by other indigenous tribes that were still 'savages'.[6] Further south, on the colonising expeditions carried out by *bandeirantes* from São Paulo, we find Indian trackers in front of the column, followed by the Europeans and Indian half-breeds, while the Negroes brought up the rear, acting as porters and preparing meals on the march.[7] Thus we see that when the European's interests demanded conflict between the two groups, he would provoke it; but that when, *per contra*, his interests required their reconciliation, he was just as ready to act as peacemaker.

At all events, from these contacts (whether spontaneous or imposed by the master-race) there sprang up a special breed of mestizo, most often known as *curibocas* or *cafusos*, and sometimes as *cabras*. The same phenomenon occurred in Spanish America, and indeed it may be that more cross-breeding between Negroes and Indians took place there than elsewhere. The offspring of such unions constituted a special 'caste'[8] known as *zambos* (or *zobos*, or *chinos*). If a *lobo* carried this cross-breeding process one stage further by pairing off with a mulatto woman, the offspring of such a union was called a *gibaro*. If this *gibaro* then mated with an Indian girl, their child was known as an *albarrazado*. An *albarrazado* who married a Negress would produce a *cambujo* and so on.[9] *A fortiori*, what applied to the Negro slave was equally true of the Negro fugitive, especially when these bands of *marrons* were few in number; being composed almost entirely of men (few women dared to embrace such a hazardous life) they had no option but to seek wives from among the indigenous population.

These mixed marriages made some sort of cultural fusion inevitable; and the two civilisations came into contact – to put it no more strongly – at a time when primitive ways of life had not, as yet, been seriously affected by Western influences. A similar process of fusion took place – as we saw in the last chapter – with certain Bush Negroes, 'those Black Indians now known as Sacatras, the descendants of Auca or Samaraca Negroes and Indian women, whom the Negroes (who were roving bandits) forcibly abducted, after massacring their husbands on the banks of the Maroni River'.[10] Indian tribes have been found in Amazonia which not only adopted Negro fugitives, but made them tribal chieftains or priest-magicans (witch-doctors). But the lack of adequate documentation makes it hard to assess the true impact of Negroes and Indians upon one another. The interpretation of so-called mixed cultural phenomena must always proceed with great caution. For instance, students of folklore have recorded large numbers of animal stories told by these same Amazonian Indians which bear a marked resemblance to other tales collected in various parts of Africa.[11] Yet it is by no means certain whether what we have here is a case of diffusion (the agents being Negro fugitives from Maranhão) or an ordinary process of convergence. In Terra Firma (that part of the north-east coast of South America more commonly known as the Spanish Main), Wassen claimed to have found African features in the magic wands employed by Kuna and Choco witch-doctors, and indeed in most of the Indian medicine-man's equipment.[12]

The *Retzonek* ceremony in Yucatan, designed to ensure normal sexual development in a child, is undoubtedly of Indian origin. An object symbolic of the child's sex is placed in its hands: a needle for a girl, an axe for a boy. However, in certain communities where Negroes are found the ceremony has become more complex: the child no longer plays a leading part in the proceedings, and its birth simply provides an excuse for the alliance of two families, through a series of gifts and counter-gifts consisting of foodstuffs. Herskovits suggests that some African custom might well lie at the back of this change.[13] The matter still awaits confirmation. However, we also possess evidence from another source, documentary records of the Inquisition's missions to Mexico, which reveal some far better attested cases of syncretism. There is, for instance, the 'drawing out' of an illness by native healers, which we also find described in a novel by Adalberto Ortiz, *Juyungo*, set in Ecuador.[14] The medicine-man sucks the afflicted part of the body, and then spits out the illness in the form of little insects, or pebbles, or tiny bones. This type of magic cure undoubtedly exists among certain ethnic groups in Africa, but it is nevertheless a comparatively rare form of therapy there. On the other hand it is typical of Indian shamanism. The Negro has also taken over several magical or religious herbs belonging to the Indians, such as *toboatzin*, for divining the future, *peyotl*, for detecting thieves,[15] and their various local poisons, which were employed to murder white bosses.

However, the best-known – and most thoroughly studied – instance of cultural fusion by contact between African and Indian is undoubtedly that of the Black Caribs.

II. *The Black Caribs*[16]

The West Indies were originally inhabited by the Aruaks, but subsequently occupied by their traditional enemies, the Carib Indians. The latter killed the Aruak men, but kept their wives. This led to an early phase of syncretism, apparent above all in the language, and worth noting here, since the Black Caribs subsequently inherited it; that is, the simultaneous and distinct usage of masculine and feminine forms to describe the same object. When the West Indies were discovered and colonised, the Caribs disappeared from the larger islands, but survived on smaller ones, such as St Vincent or St Lucia. In 1635 two Spanish vessels carrying Negroes sank off St Vincent, and the slaves, after massacring the European crews, made good their escape. A similar fate befell an English slave-ship some years later, in 1672. In both cases the Indians reduced these fugitives to slavery again; but the slaves formed part of the family, and miscegenation between the two races very soon began. This is the origin of the half-breed group known as 'Black Caribs'. Throughout the course of the seventeenth century this first contingent of half-breeds was augmented by all those Negro *marrons* who managed to reach the shores of St Vincent in small boats; and the Anglo-French wars during the same period meant that the population, both indigenous and mestizo, could rely on enjoying a comparative degree of undisturbed independence. Nevertheless, the island finally became an English colony, and as its inhabitants had allied themselves with the French, 5,080 Black Caribs found themselves deported to the beaches of Honduras Bay. Their present-day descendants occupy a long, narrow strip of Central America, stretching from the Yucatan Peninsula to the Mosquitia marshes. According to E. Reclus, in his *Géographie universelle*, they are also to be found in Nicaragua; he regards the Moscos (*moustiques*, mosquitoes) from this area as the descendants of Negro–Indian half-breeds, not of pure-blooded Indians. Nevertheless, the greatest concentration of Black Caribs is in British Honduras, where they have been studied by MacRay Taylor, and in the independant Republic of Honduras, where they have been studied by Ruy Coelho. Physically, they have scarcely any features that could be called Indian; but linguistically it is quite another matter. Though their African pronunciation makes for considerable distortion, what they speak is undoubtedly the Carib language. On the male side, they are descended from the Efik and Ibo tribes of the Niger Delta, who formed that original slave cargo; later, during the seventeenth and eighteenth centuries, these were joined by Yoruba, Fon, Fanti–Ashanti and Congo contingents. On the distaff side, they can trace their ancestry back to the Indian women whom these fugitives married. At the present time, thanks to their natural initiative and ambition, they are steadily rising in the social scale and occupying posts in the police, the civil service, teaching and other such professions; but the large majority of them are still agricultural workers, and it is amongst them that we still find that peculiar mestizo civilisation which first evolved on the island of St Vincent.

Among the Carib Indians the family means the extended family, matrilocal as regards its residence, with the maternal uncle exercising authority over his nephews. Yet though the Black Caribs have retained the Indian nomenclature for relationships, and a bond of solidarity does in fact exist between all related persons, whether close or remote, nevertheless their family unit is the conjugal couple, bilaterally descended, with authority vested in the husband; and marriage, for them, means the common-law variety. Thus the Black Carib family is entirely different from both the Indian and the African pattern: it takes after the European model. Taylor points out that this shift in domestic social *mores* duly influences folklore motifs. Tales current among the Carib Indians tend to hinge round disagreements between husband and wife within a context of polygyny, while those of the Black Caribs concentrate on competition for social status between individuals of the same sex, against a background of the village community. Such communities, which exhibit no liaison with tribal *lignages*, are simply groups formed through propinquity; there is no tribal organisation, since the Negroes are forcibly subjected to the laws and civil constitution of the country which they inhabit. On the other hand, their *social* life is highly developed, with numerous lively festivals. Ruy Coelho, who has made a special study of the latter, shows that they are undoubtedly Western in origin[17] though it is possible to detect certain elements of African totemism in them as well.

The period prior to, and immediately after, the birth of a child is regarded as dangerous. The mother is put on a special diet, while the father, for twenty-eight days, is debarred from fishing, working with sharp-edged tools, and any sexual intercourse (not merely with his own wife, but with all other women). For forty days he is obliged to abstain from certain kinds of food. On the third day after the birth he is even required to take a purgative, the reason being that at this point he is possessed by an evil spirit, known as *Uliburagúdénā*, and must therefore avoid doing anything which might conceivably harm his child. This practice has been recognised as a form of Indian *couvade*: a greatly modified version, however, which has dropped some of the original features, such as taking to one's bed (or hammock) not to mention such bloody rituals as scarification – 'probably because the notion of punishment inflicted on one's own body being a pleasing sacrifice to the gods is wholly alien to the spirit of any African civilisation' (Ruy Coelho). However, the Black Carib civilisation has preserved enough elements of Indian *couvade* for us to be able to say that, amongst them, birth is regarded as the product of harmonious co-operation between the two sexes, and that paternity is recognised as no less important an element in it than maternity. The children are brought up without stern discipline, and play together until they reach the age of puberty; then girls and boys are separated, and begin their apprenticeship for the life ahead of them, under the guidance of the parent who is the same sex as they are (hunting, fishing, agriculture, domestic work). As stated above, the prevalent type of union is a common-law marriage, contracted by free consent of the man and woman, who simply decide to set up house together (often after a previous period of sexual relations). Such a marriage is recognised by their society: the newly-weds can count on getting help to build their house, for instance – there is a day of collective work, followed by a feast and dancing, the expenses of the occasion, moreover, being met by the guests.

Funeral rites are extremely important. In order to understand them properly, we must first examine the anthropological concepts current among the Black Caribs. They believe that every individual possesses three spiritual entities over and above his physical body. There is the *anigi*, or life-force, which resides in the head and blood, and disappears at death. There is the *iuani*, which is the soul, in the Christian sense of that word; when its owner dies it returns to God. Lastly there is the *afurugu*, the individual's double, which reproduces his physical form on the spiritual plane, and remains on this earth until the time is ripe for it to become a *gubida* (ancestor). These rites last for nine days. They begin with a vigil or wake over the corpse, accompanied by feasting, games and story-telling. This is followed by a recitation of the rosary, to free the *iuani* from the sins committed by its owner here on earth. It still remains, on the ninth day, to ensure that the *afurugu* enjoys a good journey into the hereafter, an end achieved by means of a great feast, with dancing. If the soul is driven out of the house at this point, it wanders near the earth for one more year only. The *afurugu* of evil-doers, together with those of murdered persons, protestants, and freemasons, are doomed to such an existence for ever, assuming the form of ghosts, in which guise they persecute the living. But as far as ordinary mortals are concerned, it is held that at the end of a year – on the day when the anniversary of the person's death is celebrated – the *afurugu* enters the world of the ancestors, and becomes a *gubida*.

These *gubidas* must always be honoured by their descendants. If the latter are remiss in their duties, the *gubidas* send them a reminder in the shape of a dream. If they ignore this warning, sickness or misfortune will strike the members of their family. At this point the *buiai*, the priest of the Black Caribs, is called in, and one of two ceremonies will be performed: either the *dogo*, or – if the family's resources cannot run to this, or the law of the land forbids it – the *cugu*. In the *dogo*, a 'house of ancestors' is constructed in which to perform the ritual, and destroyed immediately afterwards, whereas the *cugu* takes place in the two rooms which comprise the ordinary dwelling place. In the *dogo*, the dances are far more dramatic: they are performed by a group of young unmarried girls, who work themselves into a tranced condition prior to receiving the ancestral spirits. By way of preparation for this experience they undergo an apprenticeship which involves learning various sexual taboos and rehearsing the dances themselves, the steps of which are revealed to them in dreams. These dances are interspersed with parody dances performed by clowns dressed up as women, whose jokes are supposed to be inspired by the *gubida* (after the latter have been well wined and dined). None of this takes place in the *cugu*. Otherwise, however, the structure of the two ceremonies is very similar. First of all a number of small piles of earth are made, one for each deceased person (if distant relatives cannot be present at the ritual, they send a messanger with a little earth and water from the river-bank where they dwell). In the centre of these is placed the 'heart of the *cugu*', which draws the spirit of the ancestor; as this operation is considered dangerous, it is carried out by the oldest women in each family. Meanwhile the others weave baskets, one for each dead person. These are hung up from the main beam of the house, with strips of cloth. Early in the morning the fishermen go out to sea and fish, while the women catch crabs along the shore. On the return of the fishing fleet, everyone goes to church and attends mass. The half-burnt candles are removed and taken back home. The 'heart of the *cugu*' is decorated with a crucifix and lithographs of the saints, together with offerings of food and drink, The *buiai* and his acolytes shut themselves in the sanctuary, where they are to communicate with the dead, while the women dance and sing next door. The rite takes place twice, once in the morning for ancestors of the male line, and again in the evening for ancestors of the female line. Children are kept outside, to avoid their coming into contact with the dead. When the ceremony is over, they are thrown the remains of the food, on which they pounce eagerly. This is the ritual known as 'plundering'. Meanwhile the ritual food-offerings are placed in baskets and thrown into the sea, 200 feet from the shore; all objects or utensils used during the *cugu* or *dogo* are purified; and the 'heart', together with the piles of earth, is destroyed and carried off by the same old women who built them. These, too, are cast into the sea.

It is important not to confuse the *buiai* (or *buyé*) with the witch doctor; he is in fact the priest of the Black Caribs. More often than not a son will succeed his father in this office, but the inheritance should be regarded as one of inspiration rather than the transmission of knowledge. Quite separate from the *buiai* are the seers or diviners, who predict the future by studying a candle-flame reflected in a calabash full of water: the healers (*surusié*, a corruption of the French word *chirurgien*) who perform cures with herbs; and, lastly, the sorcerers. These last can transform themselves into animals with the aid of certain prayers, such as that of St Cyprian; but it is also possible to protect oneself against them by means of holy medallions, or little lockets containing special prayers, handed down on either the male or the distaff side of the family. Similarly in the myths, side by side with the *gubida* and Christian angels, we find a variety of other spirits. There are the *hiuruha*, spirits of those who died before the Caribs' conversion to Christianity, whose dwelling-place is a heaven inferior to that of God, Christ, the Virgin, the saints, the angels and the *gubida*; this place is called *sairi*. There are also numbers of nature-spirits, such as the *sucia*, a female spirit who haunts cemeteries, lures men into the forest by assuming the form of the women they are in love with, and there drives them mad. There are the child-spirits of the sea, which let themselves be caught in fishermen's nets in order to spread children's diseases through the village. There are the *mafia* who plague menstruating women, and are led by *Uiani*, whom the missionaries identified with Satan. There are numbers of assorted animal-spirits, both of real creatures (e.g. the cayman) and fantastic ones. This mass of animistic beliefs is superimposed on the Catholic cult of the saints and the Virgin – to whom one can sell oneself as a permanent slave. There are family saints, saints with whom one has made a special pact or alliance, and healing saints, expert in curing the various illnesses that are common among the Black Caribs. However, these saints are reinterpreted in animistic terms, being neither good nor bad by nature; they are just as likely to send thunderbolts as to calm a storm, to collaborate with sorcerers' machinations as to stop them. If you want to ensure that they act for good rather than ill, you must make them 'promises' of recompense.

So the Black Caribs provide us with a good example of syncretism – in which, however, the Indian element remains dominant. This is because education is left in the hands of the women, and when inter-breeding began, in the Antilles, the women were Indian. The practice of *couvade*, the existence of nature-spirits, the methods employed to heal the sick – these are all clear features of Indian culture. On the other hand, the 'Red' Caribs, as those in Honduras are termed, do not appear (from the evidence at present available) to practise the ancestor-cult. All they have are funeral rites, with dances, which last only four days, not nine. It is true that they call up the dead, shaking a *maraca* as they do so, just as the *buiai* does during the *dogo*; but there the resemblance ends. Though we cannot trace the exact genealogical descent of the *cugu* or *dogo* rituals, their essential feature (i.e. ancestor-worship) is undoubtedly of African origin. What we have here is not so much that type of 'mosaic syncretism' outlined in the previous chapter, as a civi-

lisation which is the result of cultural fusion – and one where
the constituent elements have so far coalesced into a single
whole that they are no longer individually recognisable.

III. *Caboclo, Candomblés, and Macumba*

In Brazil, syncretism between popular Indian and African religious cults takes different forms to that which we have noted
among the Caribs. Sometimes African elements survive in a
predominantly Indian structural pattern; sometimes, by contrast, the reverse is true.

In the north-east region we find *catimbo* or *cachimbo* (the
name signifies a pipe used to smoke tobacco), an indigenous
cult which is very widespread – despite being officially banned –
among the half-breed population. *Catimbo* has various features
which clearly distinguish it from African-derived cults. To
begin with, there is a complete absence of dances and percussion instruments; the one musical instrument we find is
the Indian *maraca*. Amongst African sects a state of trance is
solely induced by music and dancing, whereas here it is stimu-
lated by various toxic substances, such as tobacco, *maconha*
(hashish), and above all *jurema*. We may further note the dominant role of the priest, or *catimbozeiro*, who alone receives the
spirits on behalf of the faithful. Though no formal cult organisation exits, public opinion produces a well-defined hierarchy of
prestige, based on the number of spirits which the *catimbozeiro*
can receive. In the areas where this cult is most predominant
we find comparatively few Negroes; but some of these are
devotees, and to the existing list of spirits who speak through the
priest's voice they have added the spirits of various deceased or
mythical Negroes (e.g. Père Joaquim). But this straightforward
addition of Negro spirits to Indian spirits is as far as syncretism
goes. The structure of the cult never changes; it remains, un-
alterably, just as it has been ever since the original colonisation
of the Indians by the whites.[18]

The *caboclo candomblé*, which we will examine in a moment,
offers a contrasting counterpart to *catimbo*, in that the structure
of the cult remains basically African, with *Indian* spirits as the
alien elements absorbed by it. However, mid-way between
these two sects – *catimbo* in the north-east, *caboclo candomblé*

in the Pernambuco–Bahia region – we must note the existence
of another intermediary type of syncretistic cult. This is known
as *pagelance*, and is centred on Amazonia. Among the Tupi-
Guarani the term *pagé* denotes a priest-magician or witch-doctor,
and the word *pagelance* thus embodies an Indian concept. However, a number of Negroes found their way into the area round
the Amazon: first, fugitive slaves, then those who hoped to
make their fortune, or at least to find more remunerative work.
These adventurers brought their own gods with them, Dahomean *vodous* or Yoruba *orisha*: and thus, side by side with the
Indians' *pagelance* (also sometimes referred to, under spiritualist
influence, as the *caboclos'* 'line'),[19] there developed a second
pagelance, the so-called 'African line'. The followers of these
cults realised that they would attract more support by exploit-
ing both 'lines', and would also acquire greater 'powers' if
they reinforced the might of the African gods with that of the
Indian spirits. However, they were also very well aware of
the structural contrast between the two religions. What they
established, therefore, was not so much a process of fusion as a
state of coexistence – though we have already studied evidence
which would suggest that some attempt at fusion had at least
begun. In the temple we find a sharp distinction between the
'territory' allotted to the Indian spirits, and the African sanctuary, or *pégi*, while during ceremonies the *vodous* or *orisha*
are invoked in African, the *caboclos* in Portuguese.[20]

We can trace the origins both of *catimbo* (which goes back to
the earliest syncretistic cults developed by catechised Indians),
and of the two types of *pagelance* (mainly started by the immigration of Negroes from Maranhão), but it is, on the other hand,
quite impossible to determine the origin of the *caboclo candomblés*. They seem to be of recent origin, and yet their success
makes it out of the question that they were simply created,
in an arbitrary fashion, by a group of priests. The most likely
explanation is that *catimbo*-type cults existed through the length
and breadth of Brazil, and that the *caboclo candomblé* was what
resulted when Africans, belonging to Angolan or Congo sects,
adapted them to their own ceremonies. This hypothesis is
based on the discovery, among certain Bantu sects, of pockets of
jurema, which those concerned attempted to conceal from us.
Be that as it may, this cult is restricted to the Bantu groups;

the 'cultural' descendants of the Fon and Yoruba both reject
it.[21] The ritual differs little from the African practices current
among these Bantu sects, except as regards the music and the
type of dance, both being far more violent, with the dances
copied from those of the Indians. The actual form which the
ceremonies take is identical with that of their African counterpart, though they are not held at the same time or on the same
day. In short, we have a juxtaposition of cults, which take
place on different days, but follow an identical pattern. There
is an invocation of the gods to come down and take physical
possession of various members of the group (not just the priest,
as in *catimbo*); this state is induced by music and dancing alone.
Certain toxic substances, tobacco for instance, are utilised *after*
the period of trance, but merely as 'symbols' to indicate possession by an Indian spirit, not to induce it.

These Indian spirits, known as *saints* or *enchantés*, are all borrowed from Tupi-Guarani mythology, or from the folklore of
the so-called 'civilised' Indians. They include *Guarani*, *Tupan*
(god of the thunder), *Jurupari* (an Indian divinity whom Catholic missionaries identified with the Devil), *Caipora* (a Tupi
word meaning 'forest-dweller'), *Curupira*, and others. But some
attempt at syncretism has also been made, with the object of
linking up similar African gods and Indian spirits (much as,
under the influence of Catholicism, the various *orisha* had
already been identified with Catholic saints). Thus *Yemanja*,
the Yoruba water-goddess, and the Angolan deity *Calunga*, were
both assimilated to the mothers of the waters worshipped by
the Indians (Queen of the Sea, Dona Janayna, etc.); while
Ogun, a war-god of the Nago sects, has either taken the indigenous name of Urubatão, or else added various 'Indianising'
titles to his original African name – e.g. *Ogun* of the White
Stone, *Ogun* of the Seven Crossroads, and so on. *Oshossi*, the
Nago hunting-god, is here referred to as the 'forest *caboclo*',
or else takes on the Indian name of *Aimoré*. *Omolú*, whom the
Yoruba made the god of small pox, here becomes the 'saint of
the snake'. One odd fact is that such parallel assimilations are
restricted to the realm of belief, and do not translate themselves
into that of cult-practice. In theory, the members of an African
religious fraternity are bound to one god only (I shall return to
this point later); this applies to the Bantu groups as much as

the others. We might expect, then, that when they pass into a tranced state during ceremonies made on behalf of the *caboclos*, they would receive the same divinity as attends the African votary, but under his alternative title – e.g. the disciples of *Ogun* ought to be possessed by *Urubatão*. In fact this is not the case – doubtless because the number of *caboclo* spirits which manifest themselves exceeds the number of *orisha* available. The result, paradoxical enough, is that members of Bantu fraternities are linked simultaneously to two types of divinity – for example, the African god *Yamsan* and the Indian *caboclo* known as 'Black Stone'. Until recently this odd phenomenon had received little serious attention.

It is difficult to draw a hard-and-fast line of demarcation between the *caboclo candomblé*, the *macumba* of Rio de Janeiro, and the so-called 'spiritualism of Umbanda', at present flourishing throughout almost the whole of Brazil. What in fact distinguishes these various religious manifestations one from the other, we might argue, is the relative extent and development among them of syncretism. Generally speaking, in the first of the three we find a clear division between African and Indian ritual, with each enjoying complete autonomy; whereas in the latter two they tend to coalesce – though by no means always in the same manner, it is true. In the *macumba* of Espirito Santo, for instance, the ritual consists of two parts. The first section is African, and involves the invocation of the *eshú*, since in the Yoruba cosmology it is the *eshú* who 'open the way' and establish a link between the human world and that of the *orisha*. Secondly, we have the invocation of the 'Ancient Negroes' and the *'caboclos'*; this latter part of the ceremony is at once spiritualist and Indian. The *macumba* found in Rio and the state of Guanabara is a wild rout of *eshú*, *orisha*, disembodied souls and *caboclos*, produced at random by casual invocations or spontaneous trances. In the 'spiritualism of Umbanda', which developed from the *macumba*, some sort of dogma begins to appear. The spirits of the dead – in particular deceased Negro ancestors, and the *caboclos*, as spiritualised forces of nature – form great armies known as 'phalanxes'. At the head of each phalanx we find an *orisha*, either under his African name, or the Catholic saint's name corresponding to it. Thus *Oshossi* commands the 'ranks' of *Urubatão*, while *Ararigboia*, one of the 'caboclos of the Seven Crossroads', commands the legions of the Redskins, the Tamoios, and the Jurema *caboclo*. *Shangô* (or St Jerome) leads the forces of Intiaçan, the Sun and Moon, the White Stone, winds and waterfalls and poplars, and Kouenguelê Negroes now deceased: *Omulú*, operating in the blackmagic counterpart to *Umbanda*, known as *Quimbanda*, leads a mixed bag of tribes, some real, some imaginary; souls, skulls, Nagos, Malis, Monurubis (Muslims), and *Quimbanda caboclos*, i.e. souls of local medicine-men. We need not enumerate further examples. The impression one gets is that Negro syncretism, at least in the major urban centres, has moved on from the old spontaneous syncretism of African and Indian practices; the syncretism we now find has been oriented, controlled, turned into a Brazilian religious ideology, parallel to the development of political nationalism in the proletarian class. In this connection we may note what the priests of *Umbanda* assert – namely, that the 'spiritualism' which joins Catholic saints, Indian spirits, and the *orisha* of one-time African slaves in a single act of adoration, also, on the mystical plane, offers a precise translation of the meeting and fusion (on the human plane) of the three major races that constitute the country's population. In contrast to such myths as those of white supremacy or *négritude*, this encounter between Indian and Negro allowed the development of a quite different myth, that of intermarriage and racial fusion.

Such, in broad outline, was the development of a movement which ran flat counter to European propaganda (that of setting Indians and Negroes against each other) and which still leaves its mark on the country, in the rivalry between natives and immigrants as to which group can soonest integrate itself with the national population as a whole. The movement (I repeat) tended towards a process of fusion between these two major civilisations, so that they became subordinated into one single culture. Syncretism, in its most developed phase, undergoes a metamorphosis into a religious ideology, an expression of what we may term Brazil's 'racial democracy'.

REFERENCES

1. Dollard, Doob, Miller, Mowrer and Sears, *Frustration and Aggression*, Yale University Press, 1939.

2. Half-breeds with mixed Indian and European blood.

3. Miguel Acosta Saignes, 'Matrimonios de esclavos', *Suma Universitaria*, Caracas, August 1955.

4. Saint-Hilaire, *Viagem ao Rio Grande do Sul* (1820–21), Portuguese trs., 2nd ed., S. Paulo, 1939.

5. M. J. Herskovits, *The American Negro: a study of racial crossing*, New York, 1930.

6. Gilberto Freyre, *Maitre et Esclaves*, French trs., Gallimard, 1952.

7. Cassiano Ricardo, *Marcha para o Oeste*, Rio de Janeiro, 3rd ed. 1959. See vol. II, chs. IX to XII.

8. Spaniards used the term 'caste' to describe *any* result of mixed breeding between the various races.

9. Some of these classificatory terms (their names varied according to the region) can be found in G. Aguirre Beltram, *La poblacion negra de Mexico* (1519–1810), Mexico, 1946, ch. IX. Cf. Nicolas Leon, *Las castas del Mexico colonial*, Mexico, 1924; Buenaventura Caviglia, *Indio y esclavo 'cabras'*, Montevideo, 1939.

10. F.O.M. Archives, cited by Debbasch, *op. cit.*

11. Camara Cascudo, translation, with notes, of C. Frederic Hartt's book *Amazonian Tortoise Myths*, Recife, 1952.

12. 'An analogy between a South American and Oceanic motif and Negro influence in Darien', *Ethnologiska Studier* 10, 1940.

13. In the discussion on G. A. Beltram's report, 'La etnohistoria y el estudio del negro en Mexico', *XXIXe Congrès des Américanistes*, Chicago, 1952 (volume devoted to acculturation).

14. For Mexico, see G. A. Beltram, *Medicina y Magia*, Mexico, 1955; and for Ecuador, *Juyungo* (French trs. Gallimard, Collection Croix du Sud).

15. Beltram, *op. cit.*

16. E. Conzemius, 'Sur les Garifs ou Caraïbes noir de l'Amérique Centrale', *Anthropos* XXV, 1930, pp. 859–77; 'Ethnographical notes on the Black Carib', *Amer. Anthrop.* XXX, 2, 1928; Douglas MacRay Taylor, *The Black Carib of British Honduras*, New York, 1951; Ruy Coelho, 'Le concept de l'âme chez les Caraibes noirs', *Journ. Soc. des Americ.* XLI, fasc. 1; 'As festas dos Caribes Negros', *Anhembi*, S. Paulo, XXV, 1952; 'The significance of the Couvade among the Black Caribs', *Man*, XLIX, 1949.

17. They include such occasions as Carnival, May Day, Pastorals, and the 'Battle of Moors and Christians'.

18. The best investigation of *catimbo* is that by the great Brazilian folklorist Camara Cascudo. On the part played by Negroes in this cult, see R. Bastide, *Réligions africaines . . . op. cit.*

19. The word *caboclo* carried a large number of different meanings; but in these popular cults it has become more or less synonymous with 'Indian'.

20. An admirable instance of this syncretism (for which I have coined the term 'mosaic') will be found in *Babassuê*, Oneyda Alvarenga (ed.), S. Paulo, 1950.

21. On the *caboclo candomblé*, see A. Ramos, *O Negro Brasileiro*, 2nd ed., S. Paulo, 1940, pp. 159–62; Edison Corneiro, *Negros Bantus*, Rio de Janeiro, 1937, and *O Candomblé da Bahia*, Bahia, 1950.

CHAPTER V

THE GODS IN EXILE

I. *The Institutional Roots of African Survivals*

Despite everything, the descendants of the *marrons* constitute no more than an infinitesimal proportion of America's coloured population. The bulk of this population is accounted for by creoles, whose ancestors were slaves. Now, as we have seen, slavery, together with the passage of time, effectively severed the links attaching these coloured workers to their country of origin. Yet despite everything, Herskovits has been able to compile an impressive list of 'Africanisms' that are still maintained to this day, among *marrons* and creoles alike. These are found not only in religious practices, magic, folklore, language and art (particularly music), but also in everyday life – special ways of carrying babies, or for women to comb their hair; types of co-operative labour in agriculture; marriage laws, diet, birth control, codes of good manners.[1] Our first problem, then, is to find out how and why so many characteristic features of African culture managed to survive the steam-roller tactics adopted by the slave régime. To be sure, we can apply the Bergsonian distinction between memory-as-recollection and memory-as-habit, which may help us to isolate the breaking-point of tradition, the advent of change. In one sense it was possible for the African to preserve memories of his past. Slavery automatically separated a child from his parents, and left him to be brought up by the old women, who were no longer fit to toil in the fields. It was precisely this group which, by reason of old age, would be most likely to dwell on the past. Thus such memories could well have been transmitted from one generation to another, especially since the slave-ships continued to arrive with fresh consignments of human cattle. On the other hand, the new modes of production enforced by the régime accustomed people's bodies to different motor habits; and at the same time the relationship between white masters and black servants introduced a whole new range of social conduct. Thus, while the slaves' minds might remain African, their actions were gradually being Americanised.

Nevertheless, in the long run, and especially after the abolition of the slave-trade, such memories were bound to lose their original clarity. They were out of place in this new environment; slowly but inevitably they became blurred, and at last faded into total oblivion. This, at least, is what happened in the great majority of cases. If these memories were to survive, they had to attach themselves to some existing custom, establish a foothold in the here-and-now, find some sort of niche or hiding-place. Of the conflict between tradition (which is determined to preserve the past at all costs) and society (which remains in constant flux) Halbwachs writes: 'From this it emerges that social thought is, in essence, a matter of memory, and that its entire content consists of accumulated recollections; but of such recollections only a limited number survive, and these not in their entirety. In both cases the criterion for survival is the ability of a society, at any given time, to reconstruct their content within the framework of contemporary custom.'[2] Since Negroes could no longer find, in the New World, anything like the old African context of their joint traditional beliefs, they had to discover – or invent – a brand-new social framework which could contain them.

The survival of African cuisine, both in Brazil and the deep south, can be explained by the fact that the white mistress of the house would employ female slaves to do her cooking. The latter were thus enabled to introduce their own spices, recipes and (on occasion) cooking methods to patriarchal big house society. If Negro folklore has survived, that is because the appalling mortality rate among black slaves forced their masters to let field workers have Sundays and church feast days off. These holidays, during which they were free to amuse themselves as they pleased, formed the institutional context within which chants, dances and various other manifestations of African art (music in particular) could be preserved. If certain agricultural techniques are still in use, that is due to the widespread custom among white employers of giving their workers a small allotment. This not only improved their diet, but also gave them a stake in the plantation, and acted as a deterrent against thoughts of *marronage*. This chapter, however, is mainly concerned with religion (a sphere in which the most striking, if not the most numerous, African survivals are to be found), and I shall restrict myself to exploring the various social contexts within which these African cults operate.

Paradoxically enough, where the whites have not themselves created such contexts, they have invariably accepted them with marked tolerance. In Brazil, Count des Arcos has analysed the policy of colonial government with succinct clarity: 'The *batuques*,[3] as seen through the eyes of government officials, are one thing; to private individuals they are quite another. The difference is profound. The latter regard *batuques* simply as a practice which runs counter to Sunday observance. . . . To the government, however, the *batuque* is an act which, once a week, forces all Negroes – automatically, and without conscious realisation – to renew those feelings of mutual aversion that they have taken for granted since birth, but which tend gradually to vanish in the general atmosphere of degradation which is their common lot. Now such sentiments of mutual hostility may be regarded as the most powerful guarantee which the major cities of Brazil enjoy. Suppose that one day the various African nations forgot their tradition of inbred hatred for one another. Suppose Dahomeans and Nagos, Gêges (Ewe) and Hausas, Tapas and Congos, in fact all the various ethnic groups, became friends and brethren: the result would be a fearful and ineluctable threat to Brazil, that would end by desolating the entire country.' Hence the formation of officially organised 'nations', to maintain tribal or ethnic rivalries. Such 'nations' – they were called various names according to locality, e.g. 'governments', *cabildos*, etc. – were virtually restricted to towns; in the country, they could only exist if they spread over an entire district, which seems to have been rare. The plantation Negroes were of widely mixed origins, even though one ethnic group might predominate over the others. In the rural areas they were not sufficiently numerous to form themselves into 'nations'. Here, moreover, the masters upheld their own rights of ownership in respect of their 'chattels' against the rights laid down by the governor. This is not to say that even here, slaves of the same stock from neighbouring plantations did not slip out at night, dodging the overseers, and celebrate their cults in secret. We have evidence of this for Haitian *Vaudou* (Voodoo) and thc Brazilian *candomblé*. Nevertheless it was in the towns that this institution flourished. The urban slave population was much larger, houses more close-packed in the streets, and the chances of getting out at night correspondingly greater. Slaves with a common origin therefore tended to band together on their own initiative. Gubernatorial policy thus consisted of institutionalising a process that had already begun to develop along independent lines. By so doing a governor could more easily orient it for the benefit of the white population.

Here we see the second role of these ethnic associations for Negroes, viz. to exert indirect control over the general Negro population. In New England – Massachusetts, New Hampshire and Rhode Island – the slaves and free Negroes formed groups, the main object of which was to celebrate feast days, with a 'governor' as their leading figure. Some scholars have argued that what we have here is a perpetuation of African kingship. Others suppose that the Negroes (having no say in political matters) wanted to vote themselves, just as their white masters did; and that they met to 'elect' their own governors, whose jurisdiction sometimes extended – in theory at least – over an entire province. Now we know that the Europeans would send their delinquent slaves before these governors, to be tried, sentenced, and flogged. In this way they diverted the resentment which the slave would otherwise have felt against his master, while the latter could count on keeping good order among his 'flock'.[4] The same phenomenon appears in Brazil, where foreign visitors noticed the existence of kings – often genuine African ones, or their sons – whose task it was to act as intermediaries between the slaves and their masters. The latter allowed them some measure of jurisdiction, so that by settling quarrels between slaves (these were mostly sexual in origin) they could keep the servile labour force working well.[5] In Catholic countries this disciplinary function was a monopoly of the religious fraternities.

But before we deal with the problem of the fraternities, we should take note of another secular institution which also helped to preserve African ethnic traditions, and seems to have existed throughout America. I shall refer to it here by its Brazilian name, *negros de ganho*. City slaves were responsible for certain hard and unpleasant manual jobs, such as unloading ships and carrying large loads (heavy sacks, pianos, etc.). To carry out such tasks they formed into little squads of four to six men, all of the same ethnic group (it was essential that they be able to communicate with one another), and under the command of a 'captain', or foreman. Since they always worked together as a gang, such people were in a better position to preserve their ancestral traditions.[6]

The Negroes were baptised, but their masters paid little heed to their religious education, and thus the clergy were obliged to make themselves responsible for it. However, in these dualist societies, Negro and white Catholicism were two very different things.[7] The Negroes therefore formed special religious fraternities of their own, under the patronage of coloured saints such as St Benedict the Moor, or devoted to Our Lady of the Rosary. But the policy of the church was much akin to that of the governors, and here too the Africans' odd ethnic divisions proved a somewhat pressing problem. As a general rule mulattos and dark-skinned Negroes set up quite separate fraternities; in cities with a large coloured population there were special fraternities for Yoruba tribesmen, and others for those from the Congo. As a result we find the same division into 'nations' cropping up within the ecclesiastical organisation. This facilitated the perpetuation of African languages, and – clandestinely – of African religious beliefs.

Here we come up against what is, for our purposes, the most important and basic fact of all. All those institutions tended to bring people from the same country together, in one single group, thus producing a close degree of solidarity between them. It was this that made possible the survival, on American soil, of African patterns of culture. The institutions and the cultural patterns were closely bound up together: when the former were abolished, the latter faded out.

Aimes, who has produced the best study of this phenomenon in the U.S.A., recognises the fact that such groupings are amenable to the introduction of African cultural elements. He cites, *inter alia*, the despotic powers enjoyed by the 'kings', who are not always elected, but sometimes hereditary, from father to son; the emphasis on military parades (this point would seem somewhat dubious); and the utilisation of magic. In Georgia, we find a Negro from Guinea offering his services as 'governor', and basing his claim on an alleged knowledge of Indian magic, which would enable him to trace and recapture runaway slaves. The revolts mentioned in a previous chapter, such as those of Gabriel in Virginia, or of Nat Turner, were planned under the cover of such associations. The southern whites had no illusions on this score, and were forced to take stern measures, banning the associations *in toto*. As a result they all disappeared, round about the middle of the nineteenth century, thus depriving the North American Negro of the means whereby he could preserve his own cultural traditions.[8] It is very likely that similar ethnic associations existed on Martinique, though in this case they seem to have been no more than tolerated. A letter written by the governor of the island in 1753 refers to military parades and processions, with great ostentation in the matter of costume; at the head went a 'king' and a 'queen', followed by members of the royal family and ministers of the court. However, as such demonstrations frequently ended in disorder, the governor suppressed them. Despite the inadequate nature of the evidence, it is by no means impossible that what we have here is an attempt to re-establish certain features of the African socio-political structure, behind which various elements of native religion had also contrived to insinuate themselves. However, the phenomenon did not last long enough to create a genuine African civilisation. In Cuba, the 'nations' were organised into *cabildos* – Arara, Lucumi, Congo, Mandingo, Nañigos, etc. – with their own special rules; over and above private festivities held in members' houses, twice a year (at Epiphany and Carnival time) they led public masked processions through the streets of Havana. Fernando Ortiz, who has made a study of these celebrations, has shown that the masks were faithfully copied from those in use among African societies; that the musical instruments which accompanied them were just the same as we find employed in Africa; and that the names given to characters in the dance were those of gods or spirits.[9] The government of the island in 1792 promulgated a *Bando de buen gobierno*, Article

8 of which forbade the Negroes of Guinea to erect altars in honour of Catholic saints, when they held their great dances, on ground belonging to the *cabildos;* while Article 9 debarred them from carrying the bodies of deceased members on to the association's premises, and there dancing or otherwise mourning them according to their native customs. Later, the Negroes found themselves also forbidden to parade through the streets in masks during Epiphany and Carnival. But it was already too late: the religious traditions had by now been safely handed on from the native-born African class to that of the Negro creoles. The *cabildo* incontestably forms the starting-point for the African *santaria* of Cuba.

The 'nations' were likewise preserved on Haiti, in the form of religious sects, *Rada* (Dahomean) and *Congo* (Bantu), which divided along ethnic lines: the Mayombés and Monssambés had accepted *Rada* gods and rites (hence their title of *Congo–Guérim*, i.e. Guinea Congolese), while the Wangole had another religion, wilder and more primitive. In Brazil, the various sects still have names indicating their ethnic origin, and enthusiastically keep up their 'national' traditions. One Nago (Yoruba) sect leader, discussing a priest who had founded a new *candomblé*, exclaimed: 'He came out of the *sertão* and wanted to start a *candomblé*. He picked up a little *gêge* (traditional Dahomean lore), a little Nago stuff, a smattering of Congo and local ritual, and so on. What a ghastly mix-up!'[10] Those 'nations' at present represented in Bahia are as follows: Angola and Congo (Bantu), Ketu (the name of a town in Dahomey), Ijesha (the name of a district in Nigeria), Nago (Yoruba), and finally Gêge (i.e. Ewe). At Porto-Alegre there exists yet another Yoruba 'nation', known as Oyo (the name of a town in Nigeria). It is a curiosity worth noting that certain associations – e.g. the Society of Hunters, linked with the cult of Oshossi – have disappeared from the town of Ketu in Africa, while surviving among the Ketu sects of Bahia, such as that of Gantois. In Rio de Janeiro, before progressive urbanisation put an end to them, there existed no less than three independent religions: that of the *Orisha* (the descendants of the Yoruba), that of the *Alufa* (the descendants of the Black Muslims), and that of the *Cabula* (the descendants of the Bantus). In Recife, despite the effects of syncretism, the four traditional sects still preserve the names of the ethnic groups which founded them.[11]

The Negroes of St Lucia also had their societies, each with three (elected) kings and queens; these were strictly hierarchical, the oldest king and oldest queen only appearing on occasions of the greatest solemnity. Most often the societies were for dancing, though at least one of them had a political character.[12] Jamaica, too, possessed its kings and queens; it seems likely that it was these Jamaican groups which kept some Fanti-Ashanti religious traditions alive on the island. I shall return to this point a little later. In Colombia, the Negro *bozales* also formed *cabildos* according to their ethnic origins. We know those of the Mandingos, the Caravali, the Congolese and the Mina, each with its own king and princes. However, since these associations quarrelled with one another, and the quarrels degenerated into physical brawls, the governor banned them. However, they continued to operate in secret, keeping up one of their basic functions, the cult of the dead. As we observed earlier, while discussing the *marron* communities in Bolivia, the funeral club of San Brazilia is still known as a *cabildo*.[13] The free Negroes of Venezuela lived in a special quarter at Coro known as *Los Ranchos*, and seem to have been divided along ethnic lines, since we know that the Loangos had their own chief. We also know that in the mid-eighteenth century there were no less than forty fraternities spread out among the fifteen churches of Caracas – some composed of slaves – which were responsible for the cult of their patron saint and the burial of their members. Some writers, such as Aristides Roja, mention other functions which the Negro fraternities fulfilled. They built houses for their members, provided economic support towards obtaining enfranchisement papers, and gave co-operative assistance in the sphere of agricultural labour. Here we have what looks like a group of genuinely African practices. Other students, such as Miguel Acosta Saignes, are of the opinion that the co-operative character of these fraternities has been exaggerated. Their statutes were obliged to conform to the laws of the West Indies, which only permitted them a religious function. Saignes admits, however, that these fraternities made it possible for Negroes to preserve aspects of their native culture in secret, since – despite the regulations forbidding 'improper and indecent' dances – they maintained the old African festivals under the name of 'drum dances'. What happened was that such celebrations gradually broke away from the church to become purely secular occasions.[14] The *cabildos* or fraternities also existed in Peru. As Ricardo Palma says, 'the Angolas, Caravelis, Mozambiques, Congos, Chalas and Terra-Novans bought houses in the suburbs of Lima and established them as fraternity-centres'. Here they met to celebrate their festivals, under the presidency of a queen or a king, and also clubbed together to purchase members' freedom.[15] On both sides of the Rio de la Plata, in Uruguay and Argentine, the 'nations' likewise existed, in the guise of well-organised institutions, known variously as 'societies' (Uruguay) and *cabildos* or 'kingdoms' (Argentine). The latter referred to their meeting-places as *ranchos*, the former as 'halls'; but in every case there is evidence to show that such associations served as centres for the preservation of African cults. Marcelino Bottero mentions the following 'nations' as existing in Montevideo: Congo, Benguela, Luanda, Mina, Bertoche, Magise and Mozambique. He also observes that the Congo had dances that were 'lascivious' rather than 'religious', and that the Mozambiques – who must have been especially numerous, since they occupied an entire quarter of the city (Cordon) – followed their own laws, and worshipped one god only, whom they represented as a god of war. The Magise or *magices* (?) formed one of the most baffling sects, with mysterious rites. They seem to have had a large number of cult-places, and each one of their divinities (*magés*) had a characteristic dress and special attributes.[16] Ildefonso Pereda Valdes adds that the Congo 'nation' of Montevideo was divided into six provinces: (1) Gunga, (2) Guanda, (3) Angola, (4) Munjolo, (5) Basundi, and (6) Boma; and informs us that on St Balthazar's Day, in addition to the usual Catholic processions, they used to organise funeral wakes in honour of their deceased, presided over by a 'permanent judge of the dead'.[17] In a manuscript by Juarez Pena we read that on this occasion the queen was possessed by the spirit of a deceased person, that invocation was made to all the group's dead *en masse*, and that at the moment of burial those bearing the coffin 'jerked it about in such a manner that it was a wonder it did not fall'.[18] In 1807, however, all Negro dances held in private houses without the supervision of a white (referred to as *tango* or *quilombos* in the documents) were banned. That marked the end of these African cults in Uruguay.[19]

In Buenos Aires, the principal 'nations' of which we have knowledge are those of the Congos, the Mozambiques, the Mandingos and the Benguelas, each with a king, a queen, a president, a treasurer, and a white auditor to certify the accounts. They met every Sunday and feast day at noon; the meetings went on late into the night. On their own special feast day they would march down in procession to the Plaza de la Victoria, with their banners and African musical instruments, and parade round the square, dancing and singing in their own native tongues. The dictator Rosas was a regular attendant at such meetings, which were known as 'drums'; he would turn up every Sunday in his brigadier-general's uniform, together with his family and part of his official household, and take up a position beside either the Congo or the Mina king.[20] The whites, moreover, as a general rule, had no hesitation about patronising these pagan cult ceremonies. Even the Franciscans, in their struggle against the medical order, that of the Bearded Fathers, would send any of their flock who fell sick to Negro healers. Coloured servants, similarly, would take along little white children entrusted to their care. It was thus that José Ingenieros came to leave us his invaluable eye-witness description of the cult celebrated under the name of *bailar el santo*. Members of the sect would dance before an altar (which bore not only lithographs and statuettes of the saints, but also plates of food, bottles, arms, cocks' feet, and other such things), invoking their own deities in African tongues, and finally passing into a trance.[21] A brief hymn of praise preserved by Bernardo Kordon also testifies to the survival in Buenos Aires of the Bantu cult of Calunga:

> A—lé, a—lé
> Calunga, mussange,
> mussange é[22]

However, when Urquiza defeated Rosas in 1852, he assembled all the slaves in their *cabilos* and presented each of them, not only with enfranchisement papers, but also with a passport, so that they could emigrate from the port of Santa-

Fé. A general exodus followed, and the Negroes of the Argentine scattered to the four quarters of the continent. As a result they lost all coherent organisation and forgot their ancestral traditions; by a process of miscegenation they were finally absorbed into the general mass of the population.

Thus we see that African religions only survived thanks to the existence of ethnic associations – which explains why they are mostly found today in the large towns, where their 'nations' were well organised. (The occasional exceptions to this rule, such as Haiti, will be explained in due course.) On the other hand, wherever the *cabildos* have been suppressed, persecuted or victimised (e.g. in Argentine and Uruguay), and wherever the religious fraternities have had their Negro dances banned on grounds of 'indecency' (as in Venezuela or Colombia), African religious traditions very soon withered away. They tended to become assimilated to folklore, and progressively secularised; we shall examine this phenomenon in a later chapter.

II. *The Fanti–Ashanti Religions*

I propose to begin with the Fanti–Ashanti culture, since we have already examined this while studying the Bush Negroes of the Guianas. Thus it will be comparatively easy, when describing the creole Negroes from the same area, to draw comparisons between survivals among the *marron* and creole communities. It is true that the creoles were subjected to various pressures and influences from their social environment which pushed them towards the assimilation of European culture; on the other hand, they were by no means wholly cut off from the *marrons*, whom they admired (or feared) as powerful sorcerers. As a result the creole community could, at any given time, reject the process of assimilation (through opposition to their masters' culture), and 're-Africanise' themselves instead. Because of this we find a large body of religious survivals among those descended from slaves.[23]

The rites connected with birth form a good starting-point. Though the child's main link is with its mother's family, it also inherits a legacy of *trefu* from its father, which corresponds to the Ashanti double-inheritance system, adapted to modern needs. (*Trefu* is a ritual taboo, generally on eating certain foods.) The child receives the name of the week-day on which it was born, but is also baptised in church. Sometimes, in order to avoid the 'evil eye' which might otherwise be put on it, we find the parents taking it also to the rabbi, who gives it a Biblical name. Every individual has two souls. First there is the *akra*, which is born and dies with him, and defends him against the forces of evil. Secondly there is the *djodjo*, which leaves the body at the moment of death and goes wandering abroad, to become a *yorka*. The terms *akra* and *yorka* have their origins in Ghana; *djodjo*, on the other hand, is derived from Dahomey (it is a Fon word meaning 'guardian'). That syncretism between diverse African religions which we observed among the Bush Negroes, combining elements of Fanti–Ashanti, Dahomean and even Bantu cults, also appears here, but in a more extreme form. The term, for instance, which designates what anthropologists usually call a 'taboo' is of Bantu origin – *kina* (or *tschina* in Loango). When fishermen in their boats pass by an area on the bank where *Dagove* (a Fon divinity) has his dwelling, they throw him an offering. Diviners have the English-derived name of *lukuman* (i.e. 'lucky man', someone who brings good fortune), or *bonu*, which comes from the Fon word *gbo*, meaning magic charm. Lastly, we have the names of their gods. These are known variously as *winti* (the Bush Negro name), *borum* or *obosum* in the religious chants (*obosom* is a Twi word from Ghana), and *vodum* or *komfo* (Dahomean appellations).

The creole pantheon, for its part, contains some deities of highly diverse antecedents. The gods of the sky and thunder are known as *Tap-Kromanti*, but one of them, *Sofia* or *Bada*, is the Dahomeans' *Badé*. The earth–mother is known by various names: some, like *Asase*, are Fanti–Ashanti, while others, such as *Aisa*, have a vaguely Dahomean flavour (the earth in Fon is called *ai*). She manifests herself in the form of a serpent, *Dagove* (a Dahomean term) or *Aboma* (from Congo *mboma*), or sometimes an alligator or a crow. River-gods are referred to by an English-derived term, *watra-mama*, while those of the bush – the *Kromanti* gods such as *Opete* (the vulture) – have Fanti–Ashanti names. But a cult also exists, as is the case among the Bush Negroes, to the Dahomean god *Legba*. These *winti* are passed on as an inheritance from man to man or woman to

woman; at the same time a *winti* can, if he wants, take possession of any person he pleases. As among the *marrons*, we find the
notion of *Kunu*, or divine retribution. If a taboo relating to any
god is broken, that god curses the offender's family, and his
curse is passed on from generation to generation. The cult of
these various divinities is in the hands of the *wintiman*, and takes
the form of offerings and ritual dances, which culminate in a
state of trance; the faithful thus possessed are known as 'the
gods' horses' – *asi*, a Dahomean term. Herskovits has described
some of these ceremonies, celebrated in honour of the earth
mother and the ancestral spirits. Rhythmic accompaniment is
provided by *maracas* and three ritual drums. Magic can be
either white (*obia*), or black (*wisi*), against which one protects
oneself by means of *opo*. All these phenomena, we observe, are
analogous to what we have already encountered among the
Bush Negroes of Dutch Guiana.

Certain important features of the *marrons*' culture have completely vanished, in particular the carrying round of the dead:
one can see how this custom was bound to be lost in the big
cities, where funerals and burials were strictly controlled by
law. Other practices, however, including magic and divination,
have assumed even greater importance than before. Here
again, the development is understandable. In a city, the
security of the inhabitants is less assured than in a closed – and
united – community. The problems which arise are far more
numerous, and can seldom be solved by purely rational methods;
thus people have perforce to turn to magic when they are looking for a house, or a new job. Lastly, the atmosphere of a big
city is conducive to erotic freedom. In bush villages, sexual
activities were under social control; the anonymity of urban
life removes all such restraints. As a result of all these factors,
the diviners (*lukuman*) and sorcerers (*wisiman*) have a more
important role to perform among the creoles than they do in
Bush Negro society.

The study in depth which Herskovits produced on the creoles
of Dutch Guiana has no comparable equivalent when we turn
to French Guiana. We do know, however, that dances culminating in ecstatic possession still continue, and attract large
crowds.

The Fanti–Ashanti culture has left its mark on other regions

besides Guiana. It remains a dominant factor in certain enclaves of the U.S.A. and the British dependencies of the
Antilles. From the religious angle, however, all genuine beliefs
have foundered in the American communities, leaving behind
a mere residue of Negro folklore.[24] In Jamaica, on the other
hand, the *Kromanti* cults proved longer enduring. Gardner
mentions the Negroes' adoration of a deity called *Nyame*, also
known as *Accompong;*[25] H. G. de Lisser emphasises that such
ancestral cults are looked after by special priests – except that
of *Sasabonsan*, a kind of devil among the Ashanti, with whom
only a private individual can form any kind of relationship.[26]
This ancient religion is known to us, through the accounts of
historians and travellers, by the name of 'myalism', after the
dance called *myal*, which is performed in honour either of the
minor divinities accompanying *accompong*, or else of the
ancestors. There were various other forms of ceremony in
honour of the river mother, held sometimes in the cotton-fields,
sometimes in the cemetery, or else in private houses. We know
that one ritual involved making a Negro drink some poisonous
concoction until he lost consciousness, after which he was
revived by a herbal tisane; this may have been some sort of
initiation rite, admitting a candidate to full membership of the
sect. We also hear of a ceremony designed to call up the spirits
of the departed, with the aid of two drums, the big one called
panya and the small one *zombi* (Bantu influence), and a
calabash which was beaten with a stick; the ghosts duly came,
but only at the summoning of initiates. During the colonial
period, myalism became an anti-white secret society – which
would explain why, after its disappearance, some features of it
survived in Jamaican magic. As a cure for illnesses it long
outlived the abolition of slavery, surviving until the beginning
of the twentieth century. Every sickness was considered supernatural in origin. People suspected that some sorcerer had taken
the patient's soul and hidden it in a cotton tree; sacrifice was
therefore made to the tree in question, with chanting and
dancing. The latter went on until the soul fell into a basin,
whence it was fished out and restored to the sick person's body.[27]
From 1842, however, we find 'angel-men' operating side by
side with the 'myal-men'; the development, in various forms,
of Protestant religious revivalism meant that myalism was

gradually absorbed by Christianity. We shall meet it again when we come to discuss syncretism, in a later chapter.

Jamaica, then, enables us to observe the decline and break-up of a genuine African religion into two separate fragments. One of these – the ecstatic trance – can be accepted by Christianity, and reinterpreted in Christian terms. The other, being too remote from white religious attitudes, declines into magic. The term signifying magic, *obeah*, is quite certainly derived from the Ashanti word *obayifo*, which bears the same meaning. The '*obeah*-men' are generally male, but there do exist a few '*obeah*-women' too. Their business is to prepare objects that are meant to kill, or cure, or procure someone's love. Such objects are called *obi* (we should not forget that the Ashanti priest in Africa is known as *Obi O Komfo*). The general beliefs concerning the powers of these sorcerers, male or female, are very much in line with the African picture. They can fly through the air, suck the blood of their victims, radiate light from their anus, and turn themselves into animals. They have a special connection with *Sasabonsan*, so much so that *sasa* has come to be used as a synonym for *obeah-man*. In order to recognise them, it is necessary to carry round their corpses after death (hints here of divination from the appearance of the body, such as we have found surviving in Guiana). Miss Beckwith is very emphatic about the dangerous nature of this sorcery, and quotes cases of the ritual murder of children, in 1918 and 1922. *Obeah* is linked with the world of the spirits of the dead (*jumbus*); these too are especially feared, above all the spirits of children who died before baptism (known as 'coolies' or 'Chinese'), and those of criminals.

At the comparatively recent time when Miss Beckwith studied the peasant culture of Jamaica's Negroes, religion still coloured the ordinary person's entire existence. When they were building a house, they sacrificed a cock and buried it in the foundations. Occupations such as farming, stock-raising, hunting and fishing were all subject to a number of taboos. The tree that grew over the hole in which a new-born child's umbilical cord had been buried symbolised his destiny. The child often bore the name of the day on which he was born. Such survivals, however, would seem to have been most numerous in rites connected with death and burial. The coffin was borne in turn by all members of the family, and the children passed under it as their names were called. In it were placed the dead man's pocket-knife, his pipe and tobacco, a few coins, and – so that he could take vengeance on the sorcerer who had killed him by magic – a knife or razor. A cross was planted on the grave to prevent the dead man's soul from coming out and tormenting the living. Nevertheless, the dead man's spirit remained in the house for nine days, and on the last of these every object was moved round, so that the spirit might fail to recognise its surroundings, and so depart. The funeral celebrations concluded with the sacrifice of a cock, dances and songs (in one of these it was claimed that the soul would return to Africa), and games. During the funeral wake stories concerning the spider (*anansi*) were told.[28]

On Barbados we again find Ashanti influence dominant, especially when we examine the funeral customs, which involve eight days of celebration after death, with games, music, dancing, and the inevitable *anansi* stories. On St Lucia we find traces of the *yam* festival, the dedication of first-fruits, which is celebrated throughout West Africa, but in this case derives from the Fanti–Ashanti region.

III. *Black Islam*

If 'myalism' faded out altogether as an organised religion, surviving only as one element in a syncretistic cult, or as magic, it was not the only flourishing nineteenth-century creed of Black America which suffered such a fate.

Black Muslims were by no means unknown in Brazil; during the nineteenth century their religion was known as that of the *alufas* in Rio, and that of the *Musulmis* or *Malis* (inhabitants of Mali) in Bahia. They worshipped *Allah* or *Olorum-ulua* (a syncretism current among the Yoruba Muslims, combining *Allah* with their own chief deity *Olorum*), the Mother of God. They had no mosques but met in the houses of their priests, or *alufas*, to celebrate their cult, under the direction of the *lessano* (corruption of *imam*), assisted by a *ladano*, or sacristan. Cult-practices included two prayers, one in the morning and the other in the evening, saying which the inhabitants of Bahia referred to as *fazer sala* (i.e. perform the *salah*), and a more important ceremony known as 'the mass of the Malis', or *sara* (this last also a corruption of the Arabic term *salah*). In Brazil they continued the practice of circumcising young children (*kola*), and observed the annual fast (*assumy*), which terminated in a great feast, during which a sheep was sacrified and gifts (*saká*) exchanged. But after the Hausa revolts in the first half of the nineteenth century, to which reference has been made in a previous chapter, leading exponents of Black Islam were either condemned to death or deported to Africa; and the faithful, deprived of their priests, were absorbed by that large group of Negroes generally referred to as 'fetichists'. At the beginning of the twentieth century there were still one or two Muslim *candomblés* in Bahia (though no trace of them survives today), and another sect at Alagoâs, that of 'Aunt Marceline', syncretised with the Yoruba cults.[29]

These Muslims were famous for their magical rituals, in which they invoked the *aligenum* (*djinns*), and for their talismans. Consequently all that survives of them today is the term *mandinga*, as a designation for magical objects, and that of *mandingueiros* to denote sorcerers (from the name of the Manding tribes). But the word *mandinga*, meaning 'sorcery', occurs in many other Latin American countries, e.g. Uruguay and the Argentine, thus indicating the former presence there of the Muslim 'nation' formed from the Mandings. The Muslims were also numerous in Cuba, where there used to be the Mandings, Wolofs, and Fulani; the cult of Allah was indubitably established on the island. Yet ultimately, as in Brazil, the adherents of Islam joined the Yoruba group, and *Allah* thereafter became identified with *Olorum*, or even – according to R. Reclus – with *Obatala*, the sky-god, whose name was oddly truncated into *Obbat Allah*.[30] We know that they also existed at Surinam, where they took part in the *marron* revolts, but there are no surviving traces of their religion in Dutch Guiana, either among the Bush Negroes or the creoles.[31]

IV. *Bantu Religions*

The Bantus certainly constituted, at certain periods in particular, the dominant element of the slave population. Yet only a few traces of their religion survive, while their folklore has been preserved from one end of the American continent to the other, from Louisiana to the Rio de la Plata. How are we to explain this odd phenomenon?

The answer is that the Bantus were chiefly valued for their physical strength and endurance, their capacity for work, their known skill as agricultural labourers. While ethnic groups such as the Fon, Yoruba and Mina were chosen as 'house slaves', and thus became relatively numerous in the towns, the vast majority of the Bantus remained 'field-hands', tied to the plantations – where, as we have seen, it was far harder to reorganise 'nations' than in the urban areas. Furthermore (and this was another reason why the whites appreciated them) the Bantus showed themselves more responsive than most to foreign influences. They realised, very clearly, that westernisation and conversion to Christianity would (in a society where European standards provided the criterion for behaviour) offer them a chance for social self-betterment, whereas cultural resistance has precisely the opposite effect. We should note, in this context, that such conversion was rendered easier by the fact that Bantu religions were not so highly systematised as those of the Sudanese or Guineans. Their basis was ancestor-worship, and as I have emphasised throughout, one effect of slavery was to disrupt and disperse family groups, which made this kind of cult impossible. Once it had been destroyed, nothing was left but animism, without the kind of systematised mythology that we find among the Fon or the Yoruba. It should also be borne in mind that their nature-spirits were those of certain specific rivers, forests and mountains *in Africa*. In other words, they were localised, attached to a clearly circumscribed geographical area, and therefore could not be taken into exile. Here, I believe, we have the reasons which militated so strongly against the survival of Bantu cults in America.

To say that they did not exist at all would be an exaggeration. But in their desire for social self-improvement the Bantus generally modified or reinterpreted them. For instance, as I stated earlier, they accepted the *caboclo candomblé*, because of the high esteem in which Indians had been held in America ever since the 'Indian craze' of the Romantic period. Wherever they created Angola or Congo *candomblés*, they grafted their own rituals on to those of the Yoruba or Fon, besides establishing a double series of correspondences, between their own spirits and the Yoruba gods on the one hand, between all these pagan divinities and the Catholic saints on the other. In other words, as part of their drive towards self-betterment, they copied those religions which were considered superior to their own. About 1870–80 spiritualism became all the rage in America, as an organised cult rather than a series of mere psychic experiences. The Bantu were now able to exhume their own old belief in reincarnation, through a fashionable theory – that of Kardecism* – which Europeans accepted. As a result they could also revive their ancestor-cult (for which they retained a secret nostalgia in their heart of hearts), but on a higher level, that of the 'mediumistic' attitude indulged in by their white masters: whereas if they had simply kept up their ancient customs, they would have been written off as unassimilable savages. It is precisely this readiness of the Bantu to take on the colour of his environment that explains why – despite his ubiquity and prevalence – he possessed so few sects that remained genuinely faithful to his ethnic origins. We have already noted, at the beginning of this chapter, that where Bantu 'nations' did exist, their dances were very often secular rather than religious.

Nevertheless, it is important not to exaggerate. What I have sketched in these last few paragraphs is simply the main evolutionary 'trend' of Bantu cultures in Black America. Here and there we do find religious sects or practices which have been faithfully preserved in their original form. In Brazil, for instance, Luciano Gallet has this to say about the ancient *Cambinda* 'nation': 'They worship stones, parallelepipeds, and fragments of stones. They show special reverence to the sunflower, which for them symbolises the moon. The actual ritual of their fetish-worship is known as *macumba*, and during it they invoke their saints: Ganga-Zumba, Canjira-mungongo, Cubango, Sinhu-renga, Lingongo and others. During these meetings, prayers and invocations are also made to the accompaniment of chants, dancing and special musical instruments. . . .'[32] The Bishop of Espirito Santo witnessed a Bantu

* So called after 'Allan Kardec', the pseudonym of Hippolyte Rivail (1804–69), a French spiritualist who wrote two influential books entitled respectively the *Livre des esprits* and the *Livre des Médiums*.

ceremony called *cabula* (held in the same state) and pronounced sentence of anathema against it.[33] It consisted of three main annual ceremonies or 'tables' (the 'table' being the equivalent of the altar), devoted respectively to St Barbara, St Mary Magdalen, and Saints Cosmas and Damian. Meetings were secret and generally held in the forest. They were conducted by a priest, known as *embanda*, with the assistance of a *cambône*; and the meeting of initiates (*camanas*), known as *engira*, had a special function, that of inducing each individual's guardian spirit (*tata*) to enter into him, by means of singing and dancing. This state of trance was known as 'having the saint'. The present-day *macumba* of Rio is directly derived from these cults, but has, as I said earlier, progressively syncretised them with various other elements – Yoruba, Indian, Catholic and spiritualist.

Nevertheless, despite all this it is still the Bantu influence which remains the strongest. This becomes very clear when one studies the list of spirits (or divinities) that are worshipped: *Ganga Zumba* (*Ngana Zumbi*, the Lord God), *Zambiapongo* (the *Zambiampungu* of the Congo), *Lemba* (fertility-god in Angola), *Calunga* (spirit of death and the sea), the *zumbi* (spirits of the dead), *Calandu*, and so on. Bantu influence is similarly observable in the priestly hierarchy. The priest is called *Quimbanda* (*Kimbanda*), whence derives the term *Umbanda;* he is assisted by a deputy called *Cambone* or *Cambonde* (perhaps *Cambambu*, the sorcerer of the Bengalas); the altar is termed *gongá*. We find the same influence at work in the actual cult. The spirits which come and take possession of the living are nearly all spirits of the dead; here we have a survival from the old ancestor cult. However, as there are no more *lignages*, the ancestors who occupy the bodies of the 'mediums' (as, under the influence of spiritualism, the initiates are now known) are no longer family ancestors, but those of the whole enslaved Negro race. Such figures as Old John, Old Joaquim, Aunt Marie and others are now regarded as constituting the new *lignage* for Brazil's black children.[34] In Bahia there exist *candomblés* belonging respectively to the Angolan and Congo 'nations'; but – as I pointed out earlier – these have borrowed their ceremonial ritual and ecclesiastical organisation from Yoruba practice. Nevertheless, a certain number of differences can still be observed. Firstly, the language of the hymns is Portuguese. Secondly, we find the Bantu spirits still preserved – though in direct correspondence with the Yoruba deities, just as though there were some standard dictionary which sanctioned a reciprocal transfer between one religion and the other. Thus the Yoruba thunder-god, *Shangô*, is identified by the Angolans with *Zazé*, *Kibuko*, *Kibuko Kiassubanga*; and by the Congolese with *Kanbaranguanje*. Similarly, *Omolú*, the Yoruba god of medicine and healing, is identified by the Angolans with *Cavungo*, *Cajanja*, and by the Congolese with *Quingongo*. Among the Bantus *Oshunmaré*, the rainbow, becomes *Angoro*, and *Oshala* the sky-god *Cassumbeca*, while *Eshú* reappears as the Angolan *Aluvaia* and the Congolese *Bombonjïra*. Other traces of Bantu influence can be detected in the musical instruments and, indeed, in the music itself, which differs profoundly from that of the other *candomblés*. Finally, we find Bantu elements in the ritual, for example in funeral ceremonies; the souls of the dead do not reside in pots, but among the branches of certain trees, where scraps of white cloth can be seen fluttering. I myself have noted elsewhere the variant forms of funeral *candomblé* practised by the Yoruba, Dahomean and Angolan 'nations'.[35]

When we turn from Portuguese-speaking to Spanish America, we find that the few *marron* communities which survived there kept up Bantu traditions. Amongst the creoles, on the other hand, these traditions are less strictly observed. In the predominantly Negro villages of Venezuela, Acosta Saignes has witnessed funeral wakes during which the women were possessed by the souls of the deceased. Certain districts, such as that of *Ganga* – a name which clearly reveals its Bantu origin – were long famous, and may still be, for their redoubtable sorcerers. In Colombia we find, told in the form of a fairy story, a myth concerning the origin of death which is widespread throughout South Africa, being known as far afield as Madagascar. God, it is said, gave mankind a choice between the stone and the banana. The stone (which they rejected because of its inedibility) would have made them immortal; however, they preferred the banana, because they could eat it. Hence came death – but also the perpetuation of the human race by the begetting of children, symbolised by the bunches of fruit on the banana tree.[36] Funeral practices, like the magic practised by Colombian Negroes on the Pacific coast, also reveal, if carefully analysed, some Bantu survivals, more or less syncretised with their Catholic environment.[37] In the island of St Andrew, on the other hand, which was for long under British influence, and only became part of Colombia at the beginning of the nineteenth century, we may note that both magic and religion (especially the rites for the dead, which last nine days) have been affected by the Fanti–Ashanti traditions characteristic of the British Antilles.[38]

In the Greater Antilles, the so-called 'Congo' religions still flourish, but have been relatively little studied. For one thing, the Congos have a reputation as powerful magicians; for another, as in Brazil, the Bantus have been exposed to the influence of the predominant Negro culture, Fon or Yoruba, according to which island we are considering. The Haitian *bizango*, a kind of African werewolf, which devours children and swallows them through a hole in its back, is analogous to the *Kimbungo* of Brazil. The term *zambis*, employed to designate the 'living dead', i.e those whose soul has been eaten by a sorcerer, is the Congo *zumbi* – a spirit of the dead, a revenant, though here carrying a slightly different connotation. Certain dances practised by the Bantu sects or *petro* of Haiti have Bantu names: *Bumba*, for instance, which is Congolese, or *Salongo*, the name of an Angolan tribe. But in fact the Congo sects were transformed into 'mysteries' and integrated into the general cult of *Vaudou* (Voodoo). We find *Mayombe, Moussondi, Moussai, Bliki* and *Mondingue* 'mysteries', the latter being subdivided into *Mondingue Talmor, Cacapoule, Bratassi,* and *Gé-Rouge*. As was pointed out earlier, this movement towards integration created a tendency to distinguish between two types of Congo: the Guinean, now completely assimilated by ordinary Voodoo, and the French, who remain faithful to ancestral orthodoxy. The main gods of these latter include *Limba Congo*; *Inglessous* or *Linglessous* (who drinks the blood of his victims, and whose worship is held at night, by a fire in the jungle); *Bacoulou-Baca*, a master of black magic (his priest wears a kind of black chasuble, with red facings, a red cap, and a cutlass); and *Mondongue*, who demands dog's meat.[39] Congo religion, it is clear, reacts to the more dominant cult of Voodoo in one of two ways. Either it is assimilated, losing its independence altogether, or else it turns into pure witchcraft.[40]

The development of Cuba's Bantu sects has likewise been oriented in the direction of magic. We may particularly note the *Mayombé* sect (which is subordinated to the Yoruba system, above all in that form known as *Mayombé-croisé*, where we find chants addressed to various divinities in the Yoruba pantheon), and that known as *Gangá*, the main function of which is to arrange funeral rites for its members, and to invoke the spirits of the dead. (As with the Bantus of Brazil, the latter are supposed to inhabit trees.) The principal Mayombé divinities are *Salabanda*, identified with St Peter; *Insancio*, who controls the thunder (identified with St Barbara); *Asambia*, the supreme deity; *Shola* or *Ashola Aguengue*, the mother of the waters (identified with Our Lady of Charity); *Kisimba*, who comes from Nganga Kisi, and is identified with St Francis of Assisi.[41] To this list we must add one of the manifestations of the *Ganga* 'nation', *Kongorioco*, who used to appear at Epiphany. In the Congo, ritual chants are always made in his honour, for he is the master of ceremonies, commonly known as the 'wise fool', combining the functions of counsellor and buffoon. The old *paleros* (*Gangá* priests) told Lydia Cabrera that when *Samba-mpungo*, the supreme god, was distributing divine powers, *Kongorioco* arrived too late to obtain the mastery over any department of nature, and that is why he received, instead, the power of 'seeing' and 'presenting'.

The sorcerers of Cuba are known as *mayomberos*. The very name bears witness to a process we have already observed on Haiti, that of a religion turning into black magic. This magic consists of a pact with the dead. Now, as the dead are located in two separate places, their bodies in the cemetery and their souls among the trees, it follows that the two complementary areas in which these *mayomberos* are liable to operate will be the cemetery and the bush. The first step they take is to ask some spirit if he is willing to serve the sorcerer. There are two ways in which this can be done. Sometimes they explode a number of small heaps of gunpowder; if the reply is in the affirmative, the whole lot should go off at once. The other method is by pouring brandy on the tomb; an affirmative reply is indicated by a crackling sound from the earth. Next, they take the bones –

above all the skull – of the deceased, and make a *nganga*. In addition to the basic ingredients (bones, and earth from the cemetery), certain other substances, both animal and vegetable, must be collected from the bush, together with a few drops of holy water stolen from a church. The spirit thus enclosed within the *nganga*, or receptacle, is known as *Boumba*: henceforward he will obey the magician's orders. *Zarabanda* is a type of magic which first arose in Havana, as a result of syncretism between the Congo and Yoruba cultures. *Zarabanda* is regarded as the Congo equivalent of the Yoruba war-god *Ogun*, whose special prayer is included in the receptacle along with other ingredients – bones (not necessarily human ones) and plants from the bush. Another instance of syncretism with Yoruba culture is the Congos' acceptance of the vegetation-deity *Osain*, at least in connection with their search for medicinal herbs.[42] Thus even in magic, where its influence is strongest, Bantu culture exhibits, as one of its fundamental traits, a capacity for assimilation, a tendency towards syncretism and cultural fusion.

V. *Religions from Calabar*

Also in Cuba, the Efiket and Efor of Calabar have maintained a secret society which is found nowhere else in Black America: the society of the *Nanigos*. As a result of recent studies by Fernando Ortiz, and the remarkable descriptions of Lydia Cabrera,[43] we now begin to have a very fair idea of its nature.

According to adepts, Efor is supposed to have been the 'nation' chosen by the great god *Abasi* as recipient of the secret. A woman of the tribe, Sikàn, went one day to draw water from the river at the foot of a palm tree, and felt something wriggling and moaning in her calabash. Her father, King Mikuere, told her to say nothing of the incident, and made use of the mysterious voice (*ekué*) to aid him in his plans. Nangobié organised a liturgy for the new cult; and since every woman was regarded as incapable, by nature, of holding her tongue, Sikàn was driven out into the forest. Meanwhile the mysterious fish at last died, but its spirit continued to live; and one of the tribal seers, Nasako, made a kind of drum, which fixed *Ekué*'s voice in one place and made it possible to evoke it at will, by striking the drum with a wand (the *ekon*). On its skin Nasako initiated the seven sons of *Ekué*, who then became the first priests of this new secret society. Their first act was to condemn Sikàn to death, on the pretext that she might betray the secret, or perhaps had already done so. Her blood was used to anoint cult-objects, her flesh was made into amulets, and her bones ground down into powder, to help make magic spells against anyone who betrayed the society. Sikàn's spirit, however, remains immortal; she had become the mother who receives the souls of dead initiates. As a result, this religion has developed into something very rare for Africa, a 'religion of salvation', destined to save the society's members from the cycle of reincarnation, and let them enter heaven immediately. A neighbouring tribe, the Efik, who were hostile to the Efor and also jealous of them, wanted to acquire a comparable power: by means of certain plants and animals they too won control over the voice of *Ekué*, and similarly shut it into the *ekón* drum. It was the Efik, likewise, who introduced into the cult the character of *Moruá Yuansá*, who impersonated the woman responsible for fishing the 'voice' out of the river, and was henceforward regarded by the secret society as 'she who goes to seek the spirits and bring about the union with them'. When the Efik were transported to Cuba as slaves, they took their society with them; as the 'society of the *Nañigos*', it has survived to this day.

The temple (*fambá*) in which *Ekué* is hidden stands in an enclosure, and it is here that the society's meetings are held. The leading protagonists in the ritual bear the names of the society's founders, and the ceremony itself recapitulates the story of its foundation. We have *Ekuenon* the slave of *Ekorié*, the leader of the sect, *Moruá Yuansá* the priest, *Empegó* his assistant, *Emkrikamo* the drum-beater, *Nasakó* the seer or magician, *Eribangandó* the purifier, *Aberisum* the executioner, *Isué* the high priest, and so on. Initiate members are known as *okobio*. The initiation ceremony calls, in theory, for the candidate's execution; but in practice a goat is substituted as victim, its blood being drunk by *Ekué*, all the *okobio*, and the postulant himself. Through this communion, this joint partaking of the sacred drink, the novice is formally enrolled in the sect. Though the sacrifice of the goat forms the central feature of this ceremony, it is only one part of it. There are also several official processions; special dances by the *diablitos* (the sect's ritual maskers); the postulant's ritual purification (by the apportionment of a cock, which takes away his sins and is subsequently killed); and various other curious ceremonies, such as the snatching of a piece of the cooked goat's meat by one of the *diablitos*, who then runs off, with *Eribangandó* in hot pursuit. He must not, however, actually catch the thief – who is thus able to offer the purloined meat to the ancestors. The whole drama of initiation is interspersed, at appropriate moments, by groans from *Ekué*.

We now come to a phenomenon the origins of which are still shrouded in mystery. The *Nañigos* reinforce their ceremonial acts with patterned ritual drawings. It is true that the Bantu sometimes employ such patterns in their magic; the Bantu *candomblés* of Rio have something called *pontos riscados*, patterns which they chalk on the ground as a means of summoning spirits. Gunpowder is placed in the middle of them, and exploded. These designs, however, remain rudimentary, and are simply one more device for ensuring success in magic. The case of the *Nañigos* is quite different. Here the patterns reveal a wealth of complex symbolism; we shall find a very similar phenomenon when we come to study Haitian Voodoo. In the first instance they serve as a kind of heraldic blazon; each sect or 'power' and every priest of the cult has an individual one. They also constitute a form of writing. For example, when a member of the society commits some offence, and is provisionally suspended from his duties, he is informed of the fact by a certain written sign. If he divulges the society's secrets (for which the penalty is death, by poisoning), once again a sign – not the same one – is employed to notify him. As we might expect, these signs are not merely conventional, but also have religious force. During the rite of initiation they are drawn, in yellow chalk, on the spot where the ceremony is to take place. They are employed to trace out the mystical map of the Efors' and Efiks' homeland. They herald the entry of the goat for sacrifice, being inscribed on its body; they are also traced on the postulant's head, arms and legs for his participation in the mysteries of *Ekué*. When an initiate dies, his corpse is adorned with the same signs as on the day of his initiation –

but this time in white chalk, and with the addition of certain special devices; that of *Isenekué*, who keeps what is secret hidden, and *Anamangui*, the god of the dead, and various others. But the arrows which, at the time of initiation, were drawn pointing downwards, now have their tips directed towards the sky, thus symbolising the direction in which the initiate's soul – granted delivery and salvation – will take its flight.

Unfortunately we know very little about the religion of the Efik and the Efor peoples, though it was from them that the society of Cuba first developed.[44] We cannot tell whether this concept of 'salvation' really originated in Africa, or was no more than a latter-day rehash of African beliefs, under the influence of Christianity, thrown up by the new Cuban environment. But in any case we have here an (equally beautiful) Negro counterpart to the Eleusinian mysteries.

VI. *Yoruba Religion*

Of all the African religions that have been preserved in America, it is undoubtedly that of the Yoruba which has remained most faithful to its ancestral traditions. It is found above all in Brazil, where it goes under the name of *candomblés nagôs*[45] (Bahia) or *Changô* (states of Pernambuco and Alagoas),[46] or *batuque*, an onomatopoeic term imitating a drum-beat (state of Porto Alegre). On Cuba the term used to describe it is *santeria*; we also find it on Trinidad, in the West Indies, where it is also known as *Changô*. We may further note that the Yoruba of Brazil are called *Nagôs*, whereas those of Cuba go under the name of Lucumis. One last preliminary observation: all these terms are the ones employed to designate the various cults by the inhabitants of the areas concerned, but they are *not* the names by which the members of the sects refer to their religion.[47]

There are two great differences between Yoruba religion in Africa and in America which must be made clear at the outset, since they constitute a point of departure for my analysis. In Nigeria, the cult of the gods (*Orisha*) is linked both with the fraternities and with the *lignages*, or family groups. The *Orisha* is regarded as the ancestor of the *lignage*, and his cult is always kept up by the oldest chief in the group, generation after generation, though without any recourse to a state of trance. On the other hand certain members of the *lignage*, together with other non-related persons who have received the call from the deity (e.g. after an illness or as a result of a dream), form fraternities, the members of which dance for the *orisha* and are possessed by him. The former are known as 'sons' of the *orishas*, whereas the latter are said to be 'born' of them.[48] Now as we have had occasion to note more than once, slavery totally destroyed these *lignages*. Though the notion that one can 'inherit the god' – on the distaff as well as the male side – still survives in America, the only true reality which has been preserved is, of necessity, that embodied in the fraternities. The family-group cult has disappeared.

At this point, however, we come up against another difficulty. In Nigeria, each *orisha* has a separate fraternity. In America, this was no longer possible, especially when the reconstituted 'nation', far from embracing an entire ethnic group, was restricted to the slaves of one particular town, as was the case with *Quetu* or *Oyo*. The priests then found themselves obliged to lump all the devotees of all the various *orisha* in one single organisation; and this in turn brought about a change in the ritual. It was no longer a matter of invoking the same deity on every occasion. *All* of them now had to be mentioned, one after the other, in a special predetermined hierarchical order known as *shiré*. As far as ecstatic phenomena were concerned, this had one interesting consequence. In Africa, generally speaking, once a person has been possessed, that is the end of the matter; but in America there is liable to be a whole series of divine possessions.

This caveat made, we only have to compare the myths, priestly organisation, types of ceremony, and ritual patterns to see with what reverent fidelity the Yoruba religion has been preserved by its American devotees. The main divinities worshipped in Brazil are *Obatala* or *Orishala*, the skygod, who has long maintained his archaic character as an androgynous deity (expressed symbolically by means of the double calabash); *Shangô*, god of the thunder, with his three wives – *Ova*, better known by her alternative title of *Yansan*, who presides over storms; *Oba*, and *Oshun*, goddess of fresh-water streams and sensual love; *Ogun*, *Shangô*'s brother, god of smiths and war; *Oshossi*, god of hunters; *Shapanan*, who is at one and the same time god of smallpox and medicine, but whom we find more usually worshipped under the names of *Omolú* or *Obaluaié*; *Yemanja*, a freshwater divinity in Nigeria who has become the goddess of salt waters and chaste love in Brazil; *Oshunmaré*, the rainbow; and, finally, *Eshú* or *Bara*, who acts as the obligatory intermediary between the *orisha* and mortals, and as a result, is always the first deity to be worshipped. It goes without saying that this is not an exhaustive list of the deities known in Brazil; but the others – such as *Inle*, a double divinity, who spends six months as an earth-god and six as a water-deity, or *Anamburucú*, the oldest of the water-goddesses – have fewer worshippers. *Olorum*, the supreme deity, is known, but, just as in Nigeria, no special cult is paid to him. Lastly, the phytolatric cult of *Iroko* (also known as *Loko*) still survives. The list of *orisha* known in Cuba is more or less the same, though some of them have different names. *Olorum* is more often referred to as *Olafi*, and *Obatala* under the contracted form *Batala*, embracing both a masculine principle (*Batala*) and a feminine principle (*Iyámba*). *Yemanja's* name has been softened into *Yemaja*, while *Omolú* is known as *Baba-byu-aye*, and so on. However, Cuba also preserves certain other deities who have disappeared in Brazil, such as *Olokun*, the god of the sea. The public ritual observances associated with each of these divinities are fundamentally the same in Cuba, Brazil and Nigeria. We may note, *inter alia*, their connection with some special day of the week – though the emigration from Africa to America involved a change from the four-day to the seven-day week, which in turn meant that the gods were more spaced out in time, as it were. Each one, moreover, had his or her special colour and favourite animal; each received a different type of offering, and was hedged about by special taboos. While mythology certainly survives in Brazil (I have recorded certain stories connected with the gods in my book *Candomblé de Bahia*), there can be no doubt that it is much better preserved in Cuba, where it assumes a far richer and more complex form. In any case, mythology in Brazil mainly survives where it is most closely tied to ritual, as though the ideas which it enshrined could only live in so far as they were formalised through a pattern of action; whereas in Cuba – as the accounts collected by Lydia Cabrera make clear – mythology still flourishes as an organised way of looking at the world, in its own right, complete with an account of how the universe began, stories concerning the quarrels and love-affairs of the gods, and so on.

Yoruba priestly organisation is also found in America, though with minor variants. In Nigeria we have, first, a markedly centralised group of priests, the seers or *babalaõ*, with their own clear hierarchy. Next come the leaders of the various fraternities, known as *babalorisha* (men) and *iyalorisha* (women), whose authority extends no further than the group over which they have control. Finally, there are a number of secret societies, often at least as much political as religious in nature – the *Ogboni*, the *Oro*, the Society of the Dead (*Egun*). As I have suggested elsewhere, it would appear feasible to divide the priests of Brazil into four categories. First, we have the diviners, the *babalaõ*. Next, there are the 'leaf-doctors', the *clossain*, linked with the leaf-deity *Osaim*: in Nigeria these remain a subordinate branch of the first category. Thirdly, there are the *babalorisha* or *iyalorisha*, who run the fraternities, or *candomblés*, with the assistance of the *Iya Kêkêre*, or 'little mother'. Finally we have the *ogés*, who form the membership of the *Egun* secret society. All that survives of the *Oro* is its name, now fast being forgotten. Again, it goes without saying that I have mentioned only the most important priests; in fact the comparison with African tradition could be carried still further. The *babalaõ*, for instance, are assisted by female acolytes known as *apetebi*, and every girl dedicated to a god has a waiting-maid (in Africa they speak of 'the *orisha*'s slave') who helps her during her dances and trances, and is termed an *ekedi*. But at the same time we find a new group making its appearance, as a result of the new social situation (the need to protect the *candomblés* against persecution by the police, or to represent them in civil actions). Members of this group are known as *ogans*, a word derived from *ouranga*, the Gabon term for a priest. All animal sacrifices are in the hands of these *ogans*; the *axôgun* and players of musical instruments, in particular those who perform on the sacred drums, also very often come under their jurisdiction. We find precisely the same names in Cuba: *babalaõ*, *apestevi*, *babalocha*, *iyalocha*. On the other hand, the *Egun* secret society does not exist there. In Brazil, *per contra*, it is the *babalaõ* who perform divinations with the aid of the necklace of *Ifa* or *Okuelé* who are gradually vanishing; the type of divination which is more and more tending to replace theirs is that known as *dilogun*, performed with cowrie shells, and associated with *Eshú* (not, like its predecessor, with *Ifa*). This marks a sharp contrast with Cuba, where Bascom goes so far as to speak of between 200 and 300 *babalaõ* operating in Havana alone. Even today the cult of *Ifa* (known in Cuba as *Orumila*) is in a flourishing state there. The processes of divination, whether by means of the *okuelé* or cowrie shells, are very similar; they all belong to the same general type, geomancy, and every such act (*odu*) is associated with various stories, which are traditionally preserved alike in Bahia, Recife and Cuba.

The ritual varies from one ceremony to another, but most often takes the form of dances which mime the major adventures of the gods. Nevertheless we can, broadly speaking – and if we restrict ourselves to the formal structure of the chief annual festivals – isolate a number of fixed points in Brazilian ritual. Early in the morning animal sacrifices take place: two-footed beasts for *Eshú*, four-footed ones for the principal deity whose day it is. Next comes the preparation of the feast, especially the cooking of those dishes that will be offered to the gods who are being invoked. Towards evening comes the *padê de Eshú*, which opens the dancing, and involves an invocation to the god who intermediates between human beings and the *orisha*. This is immediately followed by the 'summons' to all the known *orisha*, beat out on the three drums, its rhythms varying according to the god who is being addressed. Each one is also honoured by the performance of three 'hymns' in the Yoruba language (more or less corrupted, naturally). During the course of the dances which accompany these musical offerings, the *orisha* descend on their children, who pass into a tranced state and are carried inside the sanctuary. After a short break the singing and dancing are resumed, exclusively by those initiates who have undergone possession, and who have now reassumed their liturgical vestments. Finally, the gods are expelled (i.e. the trances are brought to an end) by a series of 'hymns' performed in the reverse order to that which accompanied their summoning. The 'daughters' of the various *orisha* are often united by means of a communal feast. On Cuba, the drums which set the rhythm for the *lucumi* dances – and which 'talk', like their African counterparts – are *batá* drums, identical with those of Nigeria; they are unknown to Brazilian Negroes. Another feature which Cuban ritual shares with Nigerian is a greater emphasis on singing unaccompanied by drums. But, these minor differences apart, we find – if we restrict our investigation to formal structure – exactly the same sequence of events; animal sacrifices, the preparation of the feast, an initial summons to *Eleggua* or *Eshú* followed by the invocation – in canonical order – of all the *orisha*, ecstatic possession, dances miming tales from Yoruba mythology, and so on. One odd point: though we possess admirable descriptions of Afro-Cuban ceremonies, and of every step in the various divinatory rites, we have very scanty material on the successive phases of initiation into the fraternities – perhaps because the secrets of the latter are more jealously guarded. On this topic, then, we must make do with such facts as can be gleaned from Brazil.

The candidate for initiation (in the Yoruba fraternities nearly always a woman, which marks a contrast with the Bantu *candomblés*) is, first of all, taken through a number of rites that detach her, step by step, from the secular world. These include a lustral bath, a change of clothing, and the plucking out of large tufts of her hair. After this she spends several weeks, or even months, in the sanctuary, where she learns the music and dance-steps connected with the cult, the *orisha*'s myths and taboos, and the African language. It is during this transitional period that there takes place the ritual known as 'eating the head' (*bori*). This can also be celebrated outside. Its function is to strengthen the head (*ori*) of the candidate before the great ecstatic crisis of initiation. At the same time certain ritual tests are performed, the object of which is – if I may put it in such terms – to verify or check up on the candidate's *orisha* (for it would be a terrible thing to make a mistake, and implant in the head of some future 'daughter of the gods' a god that was not hers). Finally we come to the most dramatic part of the ceremony. In this the girl is 'put to death', and then resurrected as the child of some predetermined divinity. It lasts no less than seventeen days, and involves, *inter alia*, the shaving of the head and its decoration with chalk (the latter process is repeated several times). Finally there comes the 'blood-bath', during which the candidate, who has previously been put into a deep trance by means of a herbal bath, has an animal sacrificed over her head. While the blood trickles down over her bare shoulders and breast, a tiny incision is made in the top of her head with a razor, so that the *orisha* can take possession of his 'horse'. As a substitute for the ancient tattoo mark (this art is no longer practised) the device of the ethnic group is now scratched on her forearm. The girl, still in a tranced state, feels no pain. All this takes place during the hours of darkness. During these seventeen days the candidate emerges three times; but her final appearance, which takes place immediately after the blood-bath, is the best known, since its object is to present the new initiate, publicly, to the members of the *candomblé*. This ritual is known as the *orunko*, and is a joyous celebration. During it the new 'daughter of the gods' reveals her new name. Afterwards she remains in seclusion for another week, still in a state of trance (or, to be more accurate, of semi-trance, what is known as 'childish trance', *éré*). The following Sunday there takes place the ceremony called *pañan*, during which the initiate relearns the behaviour appropriate to secular life, which she had forgotten in the course of her metamorphosis.[49] She can then return to her own home, but she still remains to some extent under the control of the priest who has initiated her. This subjugation is symbolised by the wearing of a necklace, the *kélé*. Not for another three months does she recover her liberty completely, and dedicate this necklace at the stone of her special god.[50] (In religious matters she remains permanently under the control of her *iyalorusha*.) From now she is the 'bride' (*iao*) of this god. Her career advances in stages. After seven years she can rise to the rank of *ebomin*; from this group are recruited minor priestesses, such as those of *Dagan* and *Sidagan* for the cult of *Eshú*, for instance. After another seven-year period she qualifies as an *abourisha*; she can then become an *iyalorisha* and lead a *candomblé* of her own. Now all this exactly duplicates the picture we find in Africa; the only differences I have noted from Nigerian sources are of the most minor and unimportant kind.[51]

To conclude this discussion of Yoruba-based religions, we must say a word or two about Trinidad's *Shango* cult. On this island, *Olorum* is unknown, but the principal deities of the Yoruba pantheon, as known to us from Cuba or Brazil, are generally in evidence. Some, it is true, have disappeared, while others not previously mentioned enjoy a flourishing cult. In the latter category we find a minor Nigerian spirit called *Aja*, here worshipped under the name of *Ajaja*, and *Mama Loaté*, the 'mother of all nations'. The priestly hierarchy here is a very simple one, being restricted to the fraternity leaders and their acolytes. The *babalaõ* are for the most part ignored (or practise only the most simple type of divination, that involving the two halves of the *Obi*, which can give only a 'yes' or 'no' response). There is little sign of any secret societies such as that of the *Egun*. Those writers who have studied *Shango* ceremonies are primarily interested in the phenomenon of possession, brought on by music and dancing. True possession is preceded or followed by a condition known as *réré* (*were*), the 'childish possession' (*éré*) found in Brazil. Every *orisha* has his own *réré* (who acts as his servant or messenger) and each of these has a name – 'Little Boy', 'Mexican Boy', 'Moon', and so on. They are mischievous, child-like sprites; Herskovits, as is well known, drew a blank in his attempts to trace the notion of *éré* back to Africa, but there can be no doubt that it exists there. Here we have one of the most important contributions which the study of Afroamerican religions can make to African studies generally: the tracking down of phenomena which have eluded ethnologists working in Africa (where they tend to be swamped by the wealth of observable evidence), and the resultant establishment of new lines of research.[52]

VII

As the reader may have observed, there is one aspect of all these sects that I have neglected hitherto, and that is their socio-economic background. This is not to say that it lacks importance, or that it has failed to attract the interest, on occasion, of certain sociologists. Herskovits devoted a whole article to working out the respective budgets of feasts, initiation ceremonies, and the day-to-day running of a *candomblé* in Bahia.[53] Here I shall restrict myself to stating the conclusion at which he arrived, which agrees very well with the view I propose to maintain myself on this topic. The status of any particular cult or priests, among the *candomblés* as a whole, is determined not only by their mystico-magical powers, but also according to European values – i.e. in terms of the amount of cash which any given cult or priest acquires and pays out. Acquires *and pays out*, since money must not be capitalised and kept out of circulation, but rather redistributed for the benefit of the faithful as a whole. While Herskovits may be right in his thesis that what we have here is an adherence to European values, this last fact strongly suggests that such values have been reinterpreted in African terms, according to the law of gifts and counter-gifts – and according to the African criterion of prestige, which can be equated with 'giving'.

Ruth Landes, on the other hand, in her lively report on Bahia, is more preoccupied with the part which the *candomblés* have played in the country's political struggles.[54] If these sects survive – and even expand – it is because they answer some real need, and have a useful function to perform, as René Ribeiro showed when analysing the *Changô* of Recife, and Costa Pinto in his survey of the Rio *Macumba*. The vast majority of the Negro population forms a community apart, the lowest strata of society, and for want of education (and hence of professional qualifications) cannot rise in the class hierarchy. Such people find much that they need in these sects: in the first place, an atmosphere of security, a protection against life's hazards, and also a chance to better themselves, in so far as they can mount from rank to rank in the priestly hierarchy. Finally, they enjoy a prestige status which they could never hope to attain in society at large.[55] On the other hand, throughout Black America – Haiti, Cuba and Brazil all tell the same story – Afroamerican religion has been violently attacked both by capitalists and members of the Communist Party. It is charged with being a non-productive form of economy, an obstacle to the country's progressive development in that it maintains pockets of restricted circulation currency, which thus cannot be capitalised or ploughed back into industry.

As should be clear, all these observations tend to confirm what I have described as the 'principle of dissociation'. On the one hand they undoubtedly reveal the survival of a type of economy which has its distant roots well bedded in the African mentality. At the same time they make it equally clear that this economy only survives in limited cultural enclaves. The fact of the matter is that members of these sects also belong to their society as a whole, and in the latter context they act like other nationals. They belong to political parties and trade unions. Their ideological beliefs are generally nationalist and labour-orientated. They are members of a specific trade or profession: more often than not some kind of merchant or craftsman in the case of the priests (who refuse to take money for their services, or, if they do get a *quid pro quo*, turn it over to the community chest, thus providing the wherewithal for lavish public entertainment). The 'daughters of the gods' generally work as cooks, housemaids, or laundresses. In all these activities they subscribe to the European patterns imposed by the white population. Their activities in the 'other' world, a world apart, merely provide them with some sort of compensation for the setbacks they suffer in this one. Both the *candomblé* of Brazil and the Cuban *santeria*, operating as they do in countries where there is little public assistance, have evolved into genuine mutual-aid societies. Such considerations justify my decision to study the Afroamerican religious cults in isolation, as a quasi-autonomous phenomenon. The situation predicated above in my study of the Bush Negroes – a split between the economic infrastructure, reshaped by adaptation to a new environment, and the superstructure, still functioning in terms of African traditionalism – is present to a still more marked degree here. The American Negro lives in two worlds, each with its own separate rules: while adapting to his social environment, he still – in another sphere of existence – maintains his ancestral religion.

REFERENCES

1. M. J. Herskovits, *The Myth . . . op. cit.*
2. M. Halbwachs, *La mémoire collective*, Alcan, 1925.
3. A generic term denoting Negro dances, secular as well as religious.
4. Hubert H. S. Aimes, 'African Institutions in America', *The Journ. of Amer. Folklore* XVIII, 1905, pp. 15–32.
5. R. Bastide, *Religions africaines . . . op. cit.*
6. Manuel Querino, *Costumes africanos no Brasil*, Rio de Janeiro, 1938, pp. 94–6.
7. R. Bastide, *op. cit.*, chapter on 'The Two Catholicisms'.

8. Aimes, *op. cit.*; Newbell H. Puckett, *Folk Beliefs of the Southern Negro, North Carolina*, 1926, emphasises the endogamous nature of these groups: if a slave wanted to marry a woman outside his own kinship group, he had first to obtain the consent of the girl's kinship group members.

9. Fernando Ortiz, *Los Cabildos Afrocubanos*, Habana, 1923, and *Los Bailes y el Teatro de los Negros en el Folklore de Cuba*, Habana, 1951.

10. Cited by D. Pierson, *Negroes in Brazil*, Chicago, 1942, ch. XI.

11. For Bahia, see R. Bastide, *op. cit.*; for Porto Alegre, see Herskovits, 'The Southernmost Outposts of New World Africanisms', *Amer. Anthrop.* XLV, 1943, pp. 495–510; for Rio de Janeiro, see João do Rio, *As religioẽs no Rio*, rev. ed., 1951; for Recife, see René Ribeiro, *O Xangô do Recife*, 1952.

12. Breen, *St Lucia*, cited by Aimes, *op. cit.*

13. A. Escalante, *op. cit.*, ch. I.

14. Juan Pablo Sojo, 'Cofradias etnoafricanas en Venezuela', *Cultura Universitaria*, Caracas, I, May–June 1947; Miguel Acosta Saignes, 'Les Cofradias coloniales y el folklore', *idem*, no. 47, Jan.–Feb. 1955.

15. Ricardo Palma, *Tradiciones Peruanas*, vol. I, Barcelona, 1893.

16. 'Rituals and Candomblés', in *Negro Anthology* (ed. Nancy Cunard), London, 1934.

17. I. Pereda Valdes, 'El Negro Rio Platense', in *Les Afro-Américains*, I.F.A.N., Dakar, 1953, pp. 257–64.

18. Cited by Paulo de Carvalho Neto, *La Obra afro-uraguaya de Ildefonso Pereda Valdes*, Montevideo, 1955.

19. Petit Munzo, M. Morancios, F. Nelcis, *La condición juridica, social, económica y politica de los Negros durante el coloniaje en la Banda Oriental*, I, Montevideo, 1948, pp. 393 ff.

20. According to Vicente Fidel López, in his *Manuel d'Histoire de l'Argentine*.

21. José Ingenieros, vol. XII of his complete works: *La Loucura en la Argentina*, Buenos Aires, n.d.

22. Bernardo Kordon, *Candomblé en el Rio de la Plata*, Buenos Aires, n.d.

23. M. J. and Frances S. Herskovits, *Surinam Folklore*, New York, 1936.

24. Itself possibly imported from the Bahamas. See, e.g., Guy B. Johnson, *Folk Culture on St Helena Island, South Carolina*, North Carolina, 1930; and cf. C. L. Edwards, 'Bahama Songs and Stories', *Amer. Folk Soc.*, 1895, 3.

25. Gardner, *History of Jamaica*, London, 1873. *Accompong* is the Nyankompong of the Fanti–Ashanti.

26. Herbert G. de Lisser, *Twentieth-Century Jamaica*, Kingston, 1913.

27. On myalism in general, see Joseph J. Williams, *Voodoos and Obeahs, Phases of West Indian Witchcraft*, New York, 1932; and Martha Warren Beckwith, *op. cit.*, ch. IX.

28. M. W. Beckwith, *op. cit.*, chs. II and VI.

29. João de Rio, *op. cit.*; A. Ramos, *op. cit.*, ch. III; Etienne Brazil, 'Os Malês', *Rev. do Inst. Hist. e Geogr. Bras.* LXXII, vol. 2; R. Ricard, 'L'Islam noir à Bahia, d'après les travaux de l'école ethnologique brésilienne', *Hesperis*, 1948, 1st and 2nd quarterly issues; R. Bastide, 'L'Islam Noir au Brésil', *Hesperis*, 1952, 3rd and 4th quarterly issues (pp. 3–10); Abelardo Duarte, *Negros Muçulmanos nas Alagoas*, Maceio, Brazil, 1958.

30. E. Reclus, *Nouvelle Géographie Universelle*, vol. XII, 1877, cited by Fernando Ortiz, *Hampa Afro-cubana, los negros bruyos*, Madrid, 1906.

31. G. H. Bousquet, 'Les Musulmans à Surinam', *Rev. des Etudes Islamiques* IV, 1937. On the place and function of Muslims in South America, cf. Dr Rolf Reichert, 'Muslin-Minoritäten in Südamerika', from R. Italiaander, *Die Herausforderung des Islam* (off-print, 25 pp.).

32. Luciano Gallet, *Estudos de folclore*, Rio de Janeiro, 1934, p. 58.

33. Cited by Nina Rodrigues, *Os Africanos no Brasil*, pp. 377–84.

34. A. Ramos, *op. cit.*, ch. IV.

35. E. Carneiro, *Negros Bantus, op. cit.*; Reginaldo Guimaraes, 'Contribuções bantus para o syncretismo fétichista', in *O Negro no Brasil*, Rio de Janeiro, 1940, pp. 129–40. For the Angolan funeral *candomblé*, see R. Bastide, *Estudos afro-brasileiros*, vol. III, São Paulo, 1953.

36. The Colombian version of the myth is found in R. M. Velasquez, 'Leyendas y cuentos de la raza negra', *Rev. Colomb. de Folclor*, II, 4, 1960.

37. P. Bernardo Merizalde del Carmen, *Estudo de la Costa Colombiana del Pacifico*, Bogota, 1921, ch. XXIII.

38. Thomas J. Price Jr., 'Aspectos de estabilidad y desorganisacion cultural en una comunidad islena del Caribe Colombiano', *Rev. Colomb. de Anthrop.* III, 1954.

39. Carl Edward Peters, S.M.M., *Le service des Loas*, Port-au-Prince, 1956.

40. On the Bantu elements in Haiti see, above all, L. Denis and F. Duvalier, *op. cit.*; cf. Harold Courlander, *The Drum and the Hoe*, California, 1960, ch. VII; and A. Métraux, *Haitian Voodoo*, London, 1949.

41. R. Lachatañere, 'Rasgos Bantu en la Santeria', *Les Afro-Américains*, *op. cit.*, pp. 181–3.

42. Lydia Cabrera, *El Monte*, La Habana, 1954.

43. Fernando Ortiz, *Los bailes y el teatro de los Negros en el Folklore de Cuba*, La Habana, 1951; Lydia Cabrera, *La sociedad secreta Abakuá narrada por viejos adeptos*, La Habana, 1958.

44. Cf. C. I. Jones, in Daryll Forde, *Efik Traders of Old Calabar*, London, 1956; K. O. Dike, *Trade and Politics in the Niger Delta*, Oxford, 1956; Waddell, *Twenty-nine years in the West Indies and Central Africa*, London, 1863; and Miss Kingsley, *Travels in West Africa*, London, 1897.

45. The term *nago* is that used by the Fon to designate the Yoruba. Originally pejorative in significance, it has nevertheless become neutral in America.

46. From Shangô, the name of one of the most popular gods in this religion. In order to avoid confusion between the god and the cult, I have throughout written the first with African orthography, and the second with Brazilian.

47. For Brazil in general, see A. Ramos, *op. cit.*, and P. Verger, *Le culte des Orisha et Vodums*, I.F.A.N., Dakar, 1957. For Bahia, see Nina Rodrigues, *L'animisme fétichiste des nègres de Bahia*, Bahia, 1900; Etienne Ignace Brasil, 'Le fétichisme des nègres du Brésil', *Anthropos*, 1908; Manuel Querino, *op. cit.*; Donald Pierson, *Negroes in Brazil*, Chicago, 1942, ch. XI; Ruth Landes, *The City of Women*, New York, 1947; Edison Carneiro, *Candomblé da Bahia*,

Bahia, 1950; R. Bastide, *Le candomblé de Bahia, rite nago*, The Hague (with a general bibliography on the subject).

For Pernambuco and Alagôas, Gonçalves Fernandes, *Xangôs do Nordeste*, Rio, 1937, and René Ribeiro, *Cultos afrobrasileiros do Recife*, Recife, 1952. For Porto Alegre, M. J. Herskovits, *The Southernmost Outpost* . . . *op. cit.*; R. Bastide, 'Le Batuque de Porto Alegre', *XXIXe Congrès Int. des Américanistes*, Chicago, 1952; Dante de Laytano, *Festa de Nossa Senhora dos Navegantes*, Rio Grande do Sul, 1955.

For Cuba, the fundamental study, despite its date, remains that of F. Ortiz, *Hampa Afro-cubana, los Negros Brujos*, Madrid, 1906; the author subsequently published further most valuable material, in great depth and detail, in *La Africania de la Musica Folklorica de Cuba*, La Habana, 1950, *Los Bailes y el Teatro*, *op. cit.*, and, above all, *Los Instrumentos de la Musica Afro-Cubana*, 5 vols., La Habana, 1952–5. To these should be added Romulu Lachatañere, *Manuel de Santeria*, La Habana, 1942; Lydia Gabrera, *El Monte, op. cit.*; Jose L. Franco, *Olorun*, La Habana, 1960; and Bascom, 'The Focus of Cuban San-Santaria', *Southwestern Journ. of Anthrop.* VI, I, 'Two forms of Afrocuban divination', *XXIXe Congrès Int. des Américanistes*, Chicago, 1952, and 'Yoruba acculturation in Cuba', *Les Afro-Américains, op. cit.*

For the Yoruba cult on Trinidad, see M. J. and Frances Herskovits, *Trinidad Village*, New York, 1947 (appendix); Walter and Frances Mischel, 'Psychological Aspects of Spirit Possession', *Amer. Anthrop.* 60, 2, 1958; G. Eaton Simpson, 'The Shango Cult in Nigeria and in Trinidad', *idem*. 64, 6, 1962, pp. 1204–19; Daniel J. Crowley, 'Plural and differential acculturation in Trinidad', *idem*, 59, 5, 1957.

48. Frobenius, *Die Atlantische Götterlehre*; and W. R. Bascom, *The Sociological Role of the Yoruba Cult Group*, Mem. Amer. Anthrop. Assoc. 63, Menasha, 1944.

49. There is a remarkable description of this ceremony in an article by Herskovits, on the *pañan*; see *Les Afro-Américains, op. cit.*

50. The power of each god resides in a stone, carefully guarded in the *pegi*, or sanctuary.

51. To be discussed more fully in my next book, *Confrontations*.

52. Herskovits, 'The Contribution of Afro-american Studies to Africanist Research', *Amer. Anthrop.* L, 1948, pp. 1–10.

53. Herskovits, 'Some Economic Aspects of the Afrobahian Candomblé', *Miscellanea P. Rivet*, vol. II, Mexico, 1958.

54. Ruth Landes, *op. cit.*

55. René Ribeiro, *op. cit.*, and Costa Pinto, *O Negro no Rio de Janeiro*, S. Paulo, 1953, ch. VII.

CHAPTER VI

PRESERVED RELIGIONS AND LIVING RELIGIONS

I

Some years ago I suggested the designation 'preserved religions' to describe Afro-Brazilian cults, as opposed to that of 'living religions', a category including Haitian Voodoo. The former title, however, is applicable not only to Brazilian cults, but also to many of the others that we examined in the previous chapter – especially the Cuban *santeria*.

What are the precise implications of such a label? My aim is to emphasise the fiercely conservative nature of both African doctrine and African customs in America. Negro culture is subject to constant erosion by its social environment, and reacts against this process by refusing to move or progress in any direction, through the fear that even the slightest change might prove fatal to it. We have here an instance of what might be termed cultural fossilisation, or – if one prefers a comparison with the way an individual reacts when he feels his integrity threatened by the world around him – a kind of defence mechanism.

Naturally, this should not be taken as implying that the adherents of such cults do not 'live' their religion. Very much the contrary: on the individual level – as opposed to what can be observed in the sociological sense – the cults reveal extreme vitality. When a child is born, the *babalaô* is consulted, in order to discover the infant's *orisha*. Before any marriage, a sacrifice is made to *Eshú*, the opener-of-ways, and those concerned go to the cemetery and consult the ancestral shades, to make sure that the union has their approval. No person who has been initiated will have sexual relations on the day of the week that is sacred to his *orisha*, or before going to the *candomblé*. (On that day he will also make a food-offering to the stone of his god.) Immediately after a person's death there is celebrated a rite known as the *axêxê*, which lasts for seven days, and the purpose of which is to drive the soul away from the earth. If, rather than concentrating on the major public festivals, we had examined the more private kind of ceremony, we would have seen how the *candomblé* or the *santeria* reflect, in detail, the day-to-day lives led by their faithful adherents.

Religion, then, is a living experience – yet it is not *alive*, in the sense that it does not evolve, does not change with the passage of time, and remains anchored to the performance of such ritual as has been laid down by the ancestors. Even in Bahia – where, as I mentioned earlier, the Bantus let their cult be contaminated with other popular religions, e.g. Indian *catimbo* or European spiritualism – the genuine *candomblés* have formed a federation (despite the rivalries between the various sects) with the object of enforcing fidelity to traditional standards.

At the same time we must be careful not to exaggerate. Innovations *do* sometimes take place. However, if they are to be acceptable, they must operate within the general framework as previously laid down. Let us consider some examples from Brazil. To begin with we must, despite everything, allow for environmental influence. Response to certain stimuli in this environment has produced cases of adaptation – though these, as we shall see, are very limited. Thus at Porto Alegre, where the coloured population is, broadly speaking, more depressed than in Bahia, the length of the initiation ceremony (which keeps a person away from work and thus deprives him of his wages) is markedly less. Yet despite this ritual condensation, the actual *sequence* of the ceremony remains unchanged. Similarly, a person does not make an annual sacrifice to his *orisha* (though this is the general rule), since such an expense is out of the question: four-footed animals come dear. How to deal with such a situation? By not promising anything to your *orisha*. Your god would punish you for failing to keep a vow; as it is, he is quite happy if he gets the occasional chance to drink a victim's blood. As should be clear by now, in such special circumstances practice tends to diverge from principle; but – just as in primitive marriage systems – there exists an accepted gap between the conjugal ideal (preferential marriage) and conjugal practice. Thus the ideal itself remains intact.

Other innovations have come about for quite different reasons. Brazil has never been wholly cut off from Africa; and today, after a period of comparative decline in communications, the two countries are picking up the threads once more. As a result of this, the Afro-Brazilian sects remain in contact with their parent religions. They have thus been enabled to check on any falsifications or omissions that crept in during their period of near-isolation, and also to introduce a number of new customs and practices. One good example of the latter is provided by Martiano de Bomfin, who travelled to Nigeria for initiation. On his return, he introduced into the priestly hierarchy of the *Opô Afonja candomblé* the twelve 'ministers of *Shangô*' – a direct borrowing from the royal court of Oyo.[1] Clearly, the innovation here does not embody an internal process of evolution, conditioned by structural modifications in the general social environment. It is, rather, what has been termed – in reaction against the potential influences of this environment – a 'return to Africa'.[2] The second example I would cite is that of a sect in Recife. This sect has forgotten the traditional ceremony employed for the investiture of its priests, but still has priests to consecrate. In consequence it needs to fill up the gaps which have appeared in the general framework of its collective memory. As René Ribeiro has demonstrated, these gaps have been filled by borrowings from Brazilian folklore, in particular the traditional election of kings and queens in Espirito Santo.[3] Here, it is clear, the innovation does derive from the external society. At the same time no one could doubt that the features borrowed have been carefully chosen, and worked into an African pattern, simply and solely to facilitate the latter's survival. In short, wherever we find innovations, we are dealing with a process of maintenance rather than one of evolutionary development. Thus my term 'preserved religions' has some justification.

This is not the case as regards certain other Afroamerican religions, in particular Haitian Voodoo. In the first place, the island won its independence at the beginning of the nineteenth century, and this event led to a breaking-off of relations with Africa, whereas Brazil maintained its African connections.

Secondly, independence brought about the elimination of the white population. Consequently the Negroes no longer had to fight against the Europeans' desire to assimilate them. They were not obliged to erect that double barrier of social resistance (such as we find in the other Antilles or on the mainland) against racial prejudice on the one hand and the imposition of Western values on the other. A preserved religion is the result of such prejudices, the expression of a threatened culture's will to resist, to preserve its ethnic identity by crystallising tradition and removing it from the flux of history. The Haitian Negro no longer had anything of the sort to struggle against, and his religion could thus more easily adapt itself to changing conditions – which, inevitably, soon took place in the infrastructures of the peasant community. Here we have the negative reasons for the gradual evolution of Voodoo. But beside these negative reasons there exist other, more postive ones, and these illustrate the way in which such evolution came about. The agricultural system which succeeded the colonial régime of the big plantations was, in all likelihood, a return to the African feudal system, which in many ways it strikingly resembles. It consisted in dividing up the land between the victorious military leaders, the peasants remaining tied to the soil.[4] One result of this was a lack of any centralised religious authority. Once the links with Africa were severed, religion proliferated into numerous individual sects, which took off from a common point of departure, but all evolved in their own fashion. It is true that the accounts which various ethnologists give of Haitian Voodoo are, more often than not, very similar to one another; but this is because they are all operating in the same area, the immediate environments of the capital. In fact there are as many different types of Voodoo as there are districts on the island; even in the same district we find marked variations between one cult-centre and the next.[5] Another point to be considered is that after the establishment of independence in 1804, all the French priests left. The result was a period of religious anarchy that lasted for fifty-six years, until the signing in 1860 of a concordat which restored the church in Haiti to the administration of the clergy of the old capital. During this lengthy interregnum, two things happened. The absence of ecclesiastical authority encouraged the development of

Voodoo in the country districts; to dislodge it afterwards proved quite impossible. There also sprang up a Catholic pseudo-clergy, the so-called *prêtres-savanes*, or hedge-priests, who knew a few fragmentary Catholic prayers, and became absorbed into the complex pattern of Voodoo. Hence the importance of Christian-African syncretism.[6] Finally, since Voodoo (for lack of any competition from European culture) became the medium through which peasant society at large organised itself and expressed its needs and aspirations, it was bound to be directly affected by any changes in the general agrarian pattern. The apogee of this religion is bound up with the predominance of the large extended family known as *laku* ('the court'), which settled on the land by gathering together several nuclear families under the authority of the patriarch, the religious head of the *laku* – just as in Africa religion was based on the linear system of kinship. Today, however, the institution has fallen into decadence. The restricted family now enjoys complete autonomy, acknowledging no authority save that of its own head. One logical consequence of this break-up in the African familial structure is the divorce of Voodoo from *laku* and its constitution as a separate entity, henceforward governed by its own laws.[7] Hence the disappearance of the large cult-centres, which have split up into numerous minor sects, under priests whose training is not adequate to keep the ancestral African traditions alive. It seems likely that such evolutionary processes will continue in the future, particularly with the development of urbanisation and the formation of a marginal proletariat – not to mention the regrettable spread of North American tourism.

This is why we must make a careful distinction between the two concepts of *vécu* (experienced, lived through) and *vivant* (alive, vital) when discussing these cults. Every religion is 'experienced', otherwise it disappears; but here the notion of *vécu* refers to those individuals who identify themselves with it. A religion can be considered 'alive' as well as 'experienced' only if it changes and adapts itself to the changing world as a *totality*, a collective complex of mystical rites and cultural observances, a totality both outside and above those persons who form its membership. In order to give a clearer picture of the contrast between 'preserved religions' and those cults I propose to designate as 'living', I shall, in the following chapter, restrict myself to the study of an African religion only, that of the Fon group from Dahomey (after the previous chapter this is, in any case, the only major culture which still remains to be investigated). This I shall consider under the two aspects which it assumes in America, 'living' and 'preserved'.

II. *'Preserved' Voodoo*

The *gégé* (Ewe) nation exists in Brazil, both at Bahia and at Porto Alegre. In both these towns, however, Yoruba influence predominates, and the Dahomean 'nation' – exactly like those of the Bantus – has been obliged to model its own culture on that of the dominant race. It has preserved relatively few cultural traits of its own: among them we may note the Dahomean language, music, and special method of drumming, as well as certain details to do with dress (e.g. leaving the shoulders bare). The most important distinctions I have observed have to do with funeral rites (which keep the Dahomean name, *sìrrum*, as opposed to the Yoruba term *achéché*), and rites of initiation (which conclude with a sale, conducted by the *yaô*, of the objects they have made during their retreat, this being intended to defray, in whole or part, the cost of their initiation). But the gods worshipped are Yoruba gods, and the *Gégé* people, again like the Bantus, have had to establish a system of correspondence between their own *Vodous* and the *orisha*. We should note that the Fon of Dahomey were already in the habit of assimilating to their own pantheon the divinities worshipped by those peoples they conquered in war, and thus had comparatively little difficulty in accepting the idea of expressing one mythological system in terms of another. Here I shall do no more than tabulate the accepted parallels between *Vodous* and *orisha*:

ORISHA	VODOUS
Olorum	*Mahou (Mawu)*
Oshala	*Olissassa*
Eshú	*Elêgba*
Ogun	*Tobôco* or *Gun*
Oshossi	*Agué*

Omolú	*Sakpatan*
Shangô	*Khebiôssô*, or *Sobo*, or *Badé*
Yemanja	*Obotô*
Oshum	*Aziri*
Oshunmare	*Anyé-ewo*
Irôco (sacred tree)	*Lôco*
Ibeji (the twins)	*Tobossi*

Brazilian Africanists went to much trouble in their efforts to discover a Brazil-based snake-cult – something they regarded as an equally characteristic feature of both Haitian and Dahomean Voodoo. Their researches, unfortunately, were based on a false interpretation. A snake-cult *does* exist in Dahomey, but it is a purely local phenomenon, found only at Ouiddah; it is, moreover, highly specialised, being centred on the totem belonging to Ouiddah's royal family. It could have been carried over from there to Haiti, but only by those slaves imported from Ouiddah; it does *not* characterise Haitian Voodoo as a whole. It is also true that in Dahomey the snake symbolises something called *Dan*, which is the cosmic energy circulating the world of nature; but even so there is no such thing as a special serpent-cult. It follows that these African specialists fell into serious errors of confusion. They tried to interpret the snake dance of *Oshunmare* as a survival from some old snake-cult; in fact *Oshunmare* is the rainbow, and the rainbow is visualised as a mythical serpent – which has no connection whatsoever with either *Dan* or the totem of Ouiddah's royal family. They found bracelets representing a snake biting its own tail, but this is either the snake image of *Oshunmare* or else a symbol of Ogun (Ogun being linked with the serpent in Yoruba mythology). Lastly, while investigating a Bantu sect, they found a chest with a serpent inside it. But what we have here, obviously, is the survival of a typical *Bantu* feature, not a Dahomean one: the serpent figures prominently in Bantu beliefs, especially those to do with death. This is not to say that Voodoo is non-existent in Brazil outside the *gêge* (Ewe) *candomblés*, as a 'preserved' cult; but by and large we must look for it elsewhere, in particular at S. Luiz (Maranhão), in the 'Casa das Minas'.[8] This house is something very like a convent, and all the leading 'daughters of the gods' reside there permanently, under the control and guidance of their 'mother' (*Vodunno*) – in sharp contrast to the general practice in Yoruba houses. Members of the fraternity, who are known as *Vodunsi*, can be married; the husbands work outside and rejoin their wives at night. Under such conditions it is easy to see how African religious practices managed to resist corruption or modification, and to retain their original purity. In a later chapter we shall investigate the syncretism which developed between Catholicism and beliefs imported from Africa; here, in *A Casa das Minas*, we find one of the rare exceptions to this rule. The *Vodous* there are not equated with Catholic saints; it is true that the fraternity's festivals have altered their dates to fit in better with the national calendar, but only as a means of camouflaging an essentially 'fetichist' ceremony, which tends to pass unnoticed amid all the public merrymaking.

The first point to note is the division of the '*vodun*' into families, just as in Dahomey – with one important exception; whereas in Dahomey each family has its own special fraternity, here the same fraternity worships the divinities of various different families. Moreover, the limits set between one family and another are precisely the same as those we find among the Fon.[9] The first family is that of *Davisé* or *Dahomé*, comprising *Dadaho*, his wife *Nae*, *Dosu*, and other deities. The second is that of *Da* or *Danbira*, which corresponds to the Sakpata pantheon in Dahomey: *Sapacta*, *Dan*, and so on. The third is that of *Kevioso*, the thunder-god, and includes such divinities as *Bade*, *Avrekete*, *Solo* and *Abe*. But in the *Dahomé* family, over and above these *vodun* (who represent the various forces of nature) we find the linear ancestors of the kings of Abomey, who have been transformed into *vodun*, and receive precisely the same cult-worship. Among them are *Zomadonu*, *Agongona*, *Zaka* and *Dosu Agaja*. It is a fair inference from this that the founders of the house belonged to the royal family.[10]

At this point we come up against two features of Fon mythology which there is good cause for regarding as fundamental elements of Fon culture, and perhaps of African culture generally, even though specialists have not, as yet, succeeded in finding it on African soil. Here again, as with the concept of the *were* or *éré*, Afroamerican research may shed new light on African studies.

The first of these features (concerning which I have initiated on-the-spot investigations in Dahomey) is self-evidently of Fon origin, though it has not proved possible to reach any firm conclusions as regards the way in which the system was originally constituted. The gods are divided into two groups, elder and younger, and the role of the latter – regarded as mischievous spirits – is to prepare the way for the descent of the former.[11] *Avrekete*, for instance, performs this service for *Badé*. The occupants of the *Casa das Minas* refer to these 'younger' divinities as *tokhueni*, and the name *vodun* is restricted to the elders. As a result, every religious ceremony falls into two halves, one invoking the *tokhueni*, the other the *vodun*. The second phenomenon we must note is this: over and above these two main categories of divinities we find a third category, the *tobosa*, or 'little girls'. We have already come across an analogous term in the *gêge* (Ewe) pantheon – tobosi, the 'sacred twins'. One interesting point is that these *tobosa* do not 'descend' during ordinary ceremonies, but only on special occasions (for example, at Christmas), when they precipitate trances of a child-like character (we find the *Vodunsi* playing with dolls, talking like small children, and so on). As a result, every member of the house possesses (or, more precisely, is possessed by) two separate divinities, a *vodun* and a *tobosa*. Here is a phenomenon very similar to that which we have already observed among the Bantu of Brazil. On the other hand it does not exist among the Yoruba, where an individual can only have one god. At the same time it differs, again, from the conditions prevailing in Haiti (discussed below), in that the Maranhão *vodunsi* have only one *vodun* apiece, whereas in Haiti the same individual can be possssed by several *vodun* in succession. One other consequence of this 'double possession' is that there are *two* critical moments in an initiation ceremony – one, the longer, involving the implantation of the *Vodun* in the initiate's head (a process similar to the rites we have already studied in connection with the *candomblés*), and the other to perform a similar function for the *tobosa*. There is every reason to suppose that such a phenomenon did not develop locally, but originated in Dahomey, where we have already found the term *tobosa* (with another meaning, it is true, but nevertheless linked to the initiation of the *vodunsi*).

This all suggests a new possible line of investigation, which would have to be carried out in Africa. One last observation on the pantheon: the sect claims not to worship *Elegba* (no hymn is sung in his honour at the beginning of a ceremony); the role of 'way-opener' or intermediary is performed by the *tokhueni*.

All ceremonies take place out of doors, under the peristyle of the inner courtyard, as in Haiti. As with other Afroamerican religions, their object is to work up the worshippers into a state of trance, by means of African-language chants and the accompaniment of three drums (known, in order of size, as *ruh*, *gunpli* and *hunpli*). We may also briefly note the existence of a ceremony which is not practised by the Yoruba, the so-called 'drum benefit', which involves rewarding the drummers by giving them presents during a public festival. Funeral rites are known as *sihun* (identical with the *sirrum* rites practised by the *gége* sects of Bahia) when they take place six months or a year after a death, and *zéli* (the name of a funeral drum in Dahomey) when they are held immediately following it. One important feature of these rites is the use of a special herbalised water to purify oneself from any potentially dangerous contact with death (*amasin*); in the Bantu *candomblés* of Bahia, on the other hand, such contact is avoided by means of coloured chalk decorations, and sometimes by apotropaic amulets.

Although, as we have seen, Yoruba customs predominate on the island of Trinidad, two *rada* 'houses' exist there (so named after Allada, the ancient capital of Dahomey). One of these was founded by a *bakonô*, or diviner, from Ouiddah, and is consecrated to *Dangbwe*: the other was founded by a *hubonô* (priest) from Dahomey, and worships *Sakpatan*.[12] The principal *vodun* known to them include the following: *Mahou-Lisa*, but only as points of the compass (east and west), the Creator being *Dada Segbo*; *Ogun* and *Dangbwe* (though the latter now no longer 'descends'); *Elegba*, who was for long represented, as in Africa, with a gigantic phallus, but who now appears in the guise of a dressed stone; *Da Zadji*, who belongs to the family of *Sakpatan*, and *Sobo*, who is connected with the thunder; *Agbe* and *Naete*, two sea-goddesses, and various others. The ceremonies performed, and known as *vodunu* or *saraka*, are of two kinds. There are the regular ones, such as sacrifices to this or that divinity, and the *E'minrã* festival for children: and there are those performed on special occasions, such as rites for the dead or ceremonial processions.[13] Members of the fraternity are known as *vodunsi* and recruited by means of initiation. Such few details as we possess concerning the initiation ritual are all clearly African in origin; they include such things as a house-retreat, the identification of a person's god by means of the particular chant which induces possession, and a secret 'head-eating' ritual. The condition of 'childish trance' known as *éré* is also familiar (the Dahomeans have their own term for this, *Nubiedute*). Taken as a whole, the evidence we have available concerning the *rada* 'houses' agrees with what we know of the *Casa das Minas* in Maranhão: purification by means of water specially medicated with herbs, and known as *amansi*: the existence of a special 'drum-benefit' ceremony held at the end of each festival, and so on. We also find a number of practices which do not exist in Maranhão (or more probably do, but are conducted in secret). Amongst these we may note the preliminary offering to *Elegba*, and the consultation of possessed *vodunsi* by other members of the sect when a festival is over. Granted such conditions, it is easy to see how inductive methods of divination, by means of *Fa* or *Elegba*, have come to be replaced by those which depend on pure intuition. All that survives of the former is the simplest type, which employs kola nuts (*obi*).

III. *Haitian Voodoo*

The two examples I have just given, those of Brazil and Trinidad, offer remarkable proof of adherence to African traditions in a European-dominated environment. But on Haiti, which lost its white population at a comparatively early date, Voodoo has been free to develop in such a way that it is not, strictly speaking, an African religion any longer, but rather the island's 'national' creed. What it expresses is not so much the desire for a 'return to Africa' as – something quite different – the sum of all that is specifically and originally Haitian, at least as regards the island's agricultural population.[14]

It was in 1797 that Moreau de Saint-Mery published his

Description typographique, physique, civile, politique et historique de Saint-Domingue, which contains the earliest known description of a Voodoo ceremony. It was presided over by a king and a queen, and involved the worship of a sacred serpent, which communicated its power and its desires through the mediation of a priest or a possessed woman. The candidate for initiation was then put into a similar tranced state by means of a series of frenetic dances, and so, finally, were all the spectators as they gyrated around the casket containing the serpent. It was on the basis of this account that attempts were made to prove Voodoo a primarily ophidian cult, though in fact what Moreau de Saint-Mery was describing – among many other cult-practices – was a purely local ceremony. In any case the snake has nowadays lost its once privileged position. Other popular clichés which passed into circulation concerning Voodoo (child-sacrifice, cannibal feasts, and so on), proved, similarly, to be rumours without any solid basis in fact.

The gods are known as *loas*, or 'mysteries', in the south, and as 'saints' in the north. Métraux employs the terms genies or spirits, restricting the name of 'God' to the supreme divinity. This is the 'good lord' (*le Bon Dieu bon*) of Catholicism, though no special cult is associated with his worship. The old African notion that these *loas* should be grouped in 'families' (*fanni*) still persists; but they are not the traditional families known to Fon mythology, such as we can find still admirably preserved in the Maranhão area. What we have here, rather, are groups of deities all sharing the same name, and distinguished only by a qualifying epithet. The *Ogou* family, for instance, includes Papa Ogou, the father; Ogou Badagri, who is a general; Ogou Ferraille, who looks after soldiers; Ogou Ashadé, an expert in medicinal herbs (and probably attached to the family because of his ability to heal war wounds); Olisha the magician; Ogou Balindjo (both a healer and a general); Ossange (the Yoruba Ossaim), and others. Here we observe the first modification of the original African pattern.[15] The second one is as follows. The principal Fon *Vodun* are still known and worshipped: they include *Legba* (the mediator between mankind and the *loas*), *Ayizam Véléquéti* (the god of markets), *Loko Atissou* (god of the silk-cotton tree), *Maîtresse Ezili* (goddess of love), *Damballah Oueddo* (the rainbow), *Agoué* (god of the sea), and so on. At the same time there also exist, side by side with these divinities, a number of so-called *loa créoles* (meaning spirits born, as it were, on the island). This is a constantly expanding group. What we have, in short, is a progressive enrichment of the religious pantheon, so that it has ceased to be 'Dahomean' and may now be regarded as 'national'. A third modification we may note is the disappearance, *in toto*, of Fon mythology, and its replacement by something quite new and different. What this new mythology does is to identify the history of the *loa* with the conduct of its devotees. As a result we get biographies of the gods' 'horses', complete with miraculous adventures; these form a substitute for the ancestral myths, which have dropped out of the collective memory altogether.

Apart from the *loa*, there are two other categories of divinity which figure in the *rada* ceremonies: the *zaka* and the *guede*. The order of their invocation during these ceremonies (and consequently of the possessions induced) is clearly defined. First come the *loa*, whether African or creole, then the *zaka*, and last of all the *guede*. The *zaka* were originally Fon Vodun, responsible for agriculture, and it is easy to see how a nation of peasants came to preserve their worship and indeed treat them as 'cousins'. When they possess anyone, their 'horses' put on peasant attire and tell coarse jokes. The *guede* are divinities from Dahomey, but have no connection with the Fon; they belong to a people known as the *guede-vi*, whom the Fon conquered, and made into their grave-digging caste. Later, to escape their reputed magical powers and wizardry, the Fon sold them off as slaves.[16] In Haiti the *guede* thus became spirits associated with cemeteries and death. They sometimes appear as scarecrows, with old frock-coats and top-hats, and sometimes as corpses, with plugs of cotton in mouth and nostrils, and a chin-band swathed round the head (Baron Samedi, Baron La Croix, Baron Cimitière, Guede-Nibo, etc.). They are fond of uttering obscenities. Consequently Voodoo ceremonies (like the theatre of antiquity) consists of two parts, one tragic (with possession by the *loa*), and the other comic (with possession by the *zaka* and the *guede*).

The result is something which much astonished Herskovits: one worshipper can become the 'horse' for several *loa*. Each individual, it is true, has a dominant *loa*, implanted in him at the time of his initiation, and known as his *mait'tête* (literally, 'head master'); but during the course of one ceremony he can receive both a *loa* and a *guede*. So far we are still close enough to the system we have seen operating in Brazil, among the Bantus (an *Orisha* plus a *caboclo*), and also among the *Mina* of *Maranhāo* (a *Vodun* plus a *Tabasa*). But the system finally breaks down on Haiti, in that (for want of any strong traditional control) a person can be possessed by several Vodous, and not merely by two different types of divinity, a *loa* and a *guede*. We should further note that though African mythology has disappeared (see above), the pattern of ecstatic possession nevertheless conforms to standard African practice. Everything that happens makes it look as though the motor memory has proved more lasting and more coherent than memory-as-recollection. Thus we find *Dambellah Oueddo* wriggling across the ground or wrapping himself round trees, *Ogun* puts on a martial expression, and *Ezili* mimes the act of love-making.

The last change from African precedent that remains to be chronicled is the creation, not merely of new *loa*, but of a new organised sect specially devoted to them. This took place in 1768, under the guidance of one Don Pedro, a Negro of Spanish origin. As a result there are two main types of cult on Haiti: *Vaudou rada*, which despite its innovations maintains some connection with Africa, and *Vaudou Petro*, a wholly creole phenomenon. 'Wholly' is perhaps going a little too far, since the *loa Petro* are often the same as the *loa rada;* but the former have a special descriptive epithet – *yé-ruj*, i.e. *yeux rouges* or 'red-eyes' – to indicate how malicious they are, red eyes being one of the physical characteristics by which one can recognise a sorcerer, or *diab* (*diable*, devil). Members of the Petro group such as *Damballah-flangbo* or *Marinette Bois-Chêche* are said to be 'tough', 'bitter', 'sharp', or the like. The same cult exists in the north of the island, where it is known as *Lemba*, this being the name of a Congolese tribe. It is legitimate to infer that the underlying function of *Vaudou Petro* was to reinterpret the dominant Dahomean religion in terms of Bantu magic.

The societies of initiates are led by priests, the *hougan* or *papa-loa*, and priestesses (*mambo* or *maman-loa*); their members, even if they are male, describe themselves as *hounsi*, i.e. brides of the gods. There are a large number of specialised priestly offices: the *reine-chanterelle* or *hounguenikon* who leads (or interrupts) the liturgical chants; the *La Place* (an abbreviation of *commandant général de la Place*) who acts as master of ceremonies, and is responsible for maintaining order; a temple administrator known as *la Confiance;* officials known as *Porte-Drapeaux*, who bear the sect's banners; and the musicians – three drummers, their drums being known as *ountor, ountogui* and *ountogni*, plus the *hogantier*, who bangs an iron bell. The sanctuary itself (*Houmfó*) always contains certain obligatory features. There is the gods' chapel (*caye-mystère*), with a stone-built altar on which sacrificial food offerings are laid out. There is a special chamber (*djévo*) in which the secret part of the initiation ritual takes place. There is an open peristyle or cloister, where public ceremonies are held; in the middle of this stands a central post, the *poteau-mitan*, round which the *hounsi* dance, and at the foot of which the priests (using fine flour for the purpose) trace out the various symbols of the *loa* on the ground. These symbolic patterns are known as *vévés*, and their function (like that of the music) is to make the gods 'descend' on their 'horses'.[17] Lastly we have the garden, with its ornamental pool (for the cult of water-*loa*); the black cross of the *guede*, topped with a bowler-hat and draped in a frock-coat; and special trees for the *loa* to rest in, hung with scraps of cloth and little bags in which visitors place their offerings. Each *loa* is associated with one special tree, e.g. *Legba* with the oil tree (*Jatropha curcas* L.), *Damballah Oueddo* with the cotton tree, *Agoué T'Arroyo* with the gourd tree, *Agassou Guenin* with the mango, and so on.

Entrance to the society is by means of initiation, and this ceremony preserves its African pattern. First comes a rite of separation from one's old life, which includes such features as the *chiré aizan*, in which a cabbage-palm's leaves are torn up (this process, as in Dahomey, symbolises the separation of sacred and profane), the scourging of the candidates, and initial instruction in such matters as ritual salutations and sacred dance-steps. There follows the consecration of the novices. They lie stretched out on the ground round the *poteau-mitan*, while water is sprinkled on them, and they are marked with the sign of the cross. When they leave the peristyle everyone weeps, because they are now 'dead'. At this point they withdraw to the *djevo*, where they remain for seven days, stretched out on mats like so many corpses, and bound by various dietary and sexual taboos. The ceremonies held during this period are secret. Nevertheless, we know that they include the *pot-tête* (equivalent to the Yoruba 'head-eating' ritual, but with certain marked differences), the *laver-tête* (which corresponds to the Yoruba herbal bath), and the verification of the *mait' tête*. In this latter ritual all the *loa* are invoked in turn, beginning with *Legba*, until the novice's *mait' tête* is reached, at which point he passes into a trance. Finally, on the night before his release from the *djevo*, the future *hounsi* has a chicken sacrificed on his head; this corresponds to the *sundidé*, or Yoruba blood-bath, but is less violent. Finally come the rites of emergence and resurrection: the *brulé-zin* (so called because the essential part of the ceremony involves burning objects in jars known as *zin*, and purifying the new initiates with fire), and baptism by the *père-savane* (here we have the Yoruba ritual of giving someone a new name). From this moment on the novices are fully-fledged *hounsi-kanzo*. For the next forty-one days they nevertheless remain in a state of semi-seclusion, since they are in a weakened condition which renders them peculiarly vulnerable to the attacks of sorcerers. During this period – as in Africa – they only make one brief emergence, in order to go and beg in the market. Finally, on the forty-first day, they go over the lessons they have learnt – ritual greetings, dances, chants – for the last time, receive the necklace of their special *Vodun*, and change their old clothes for new ones. Here, as opposed to what has happened in the field of mythology, the African pattern of ritual (depending for the most part on motor memory) has been admirably preserved.

It is impossible to give any adequate picture of the countless ceremonies which take place annually in the *Houmfo*. This (we may safely say) is where Voodoo best displays the liveliness and spontaneity which, as I have shown elsewhere, are its most characteristic features. Undoubtedly it still contains certain elements of Fon culture. Animals, for instance, as in Dahomey, cannot be sacrificed until they have first eaten the branch of leaves or handful of grain that is offered them – this being a sign that they accept the sacrifice. The food offerings set out on the *pé* are similarly typical of Fon practice. So is the invocation of the gods by means of appropriate dances and music, such as the *yanvalou* (which also exists in the *rada* 'houses' in Trinidad) or the *Dahomey z'épaules*. However, new elements are occasionally added to the ritual pattern, stemming partly from the aesthetic preferences of the priests, and partly from those colonial traditions which appealed to the peasantry. Amongst them we may note such things as the movements of the minuets popular at the French court, processions with banners (borrowed from the march-pasts of French regiments), or the use of Catholic prayers. Ecstatic trances, being no longer restricted by the requirements of myth, could expand into wholly new fields of dramatic representation, thus constantly enriching the collective cultural heritage. Though it is hard to give an adequate idea of this vast and ever-changing ceremonial repertoire, an exception must be made for the cult of the dead, which merits a somewhat more detailed examination.[18] Haitian conceptions concerning the soul are far from clear-cut. Broadly speaking, a distinction is drawn between the *gros bon ange* ('big good angel'), which is linked to the body, can be caught by sorcerers during its owner's sleep, and becomes a 'ghost' after his death; and the *petit bon ange* ('little good angel'), which, on its owner's decease, takes refuge in the water for a whole year. At the end of this period it is brought back from the liquid element, by means of a special ceremony known as 'return of the spirit from the water', and shut in a pot (*govi*), which is then placed on the *pé*, where it can henceforth be consulted. Through the mediation of the *hougan* or *mambo* it issues advice, or orders, to the surviving members of the family, speaking in a high, shrill, nasal voice.

One odd phenomenon is the near-total disappearance of Dahomean geomancy (though divination by means of *Legba*'s cowries is still sometimes practised). This may be due to the existence of alternative prophetic media; the 'pots of the dead' can answer questions put to them, and the *Vodunsi* are similarly capable of prophesying when in a tranced state. In this way intuitive divination tends to replace the inductive type. On the other hand both Métraux and Courlander note the existence of an African-derived process of divination known as *gambo*. In this, a shell is threaded on a length of string; if it remains still when a question is asked, that means 'no', whereas if it moves, the answer is 'yes'. However, in the field of inductive divination, perhaps the most popular method (and becoming increasingly widespread as time goes on) is that of the European tarot pack – adapted to African requirements in the sense that the person who draws the cards first goes into a trance. Magic as such is syncretistic, with elements drawn indifferently from Fon, Congo, Petro and European sources. A clear distinction is drawn between the sorcerer (*bokor*) and the priest; the priest, at least in theory, works only for good whereas the *bokor* works only for evil. The main types of black magic are as follows: spells or curses (*expéditions, envoi-morts*), cast in a cemetery, with the object of afflicting the consultant's enemies with sickness or death; the fabrication of *wanga* (African *ouanga*) to work harm on people; and finally, the creation of those notorious beings known as *zombies*, the so-called *morts-vivants*. These are persons already dead and buried, over whom the sorcerer has gained control, and whom he employs as slaves to carry out his diabolical machinations. There also, fortunately, exists a whole body of counter-magic: apotropaic amulets, protective formulae, special drugs and potions. The inhabitants of Haiti claim that these sorcerers have their own secret societies, with an emperor, a queen, a president and ministers. These are the so-called 'red sects', and include such societies as *Les Bessages*, the 'Hairless Pigs' (*Cochons sans poils*), the 'Grey Pigs' (*Cochons gris*), the *Vinbrindingues*, and so on, supposedly an inheritance from the Manding and other 'cannibal' tribes of Africa. Métraux believes that these societies are nothing more than the product of peasant imagination, whereas Hurston claims to have attended one of their ceremonies, and describes it. The question remains open.

IV. *The Migrations and Metamorphoses of Voodoo*

One of the most interesting (and least studied) sociological problems posed by the Afroamerican religions is that of how they tend to be affected by migration – either internal (within the boundaries of a single country) or external (from one state to another). The black population is extremely mobile. A large proportion of the workers on the Panama Canal come from the British Antilles. The creole Negroes of French Guiana are reinforced by those from Guadeloupe and Martinique, who mostly hold administrative posts in the civil service. As we have seen, Negroes from the southern states of the U.S.A. tend to migrate to the big cities in the north, while in Brazil the Negroes of the north come down to the plantations and cities of the south – not to mention the migrations from the British West Indies to England, or from the French Antilles to France, which fall outside the scope of this book. Such population movements cannot but have some influence on religious beliefs and practices. We have already seen, in a previous chapter, how the relocation in Amazonia of workers from Maranhão brought about an amalgamation between *Vodou* and *orisha* cults on the one hand, and Indian *pagelance* practices on the other. In an earier work[19] I traced the migration of the *candomblés* of north-east Brazil to Rio de Janeiro and São Paulo. However, since we are here dealing with 'preserved religions', the 'sub-branches' which these *candomblés* set up in the capitals of the centre and south were in no respect modified as a result of their move; their internal structure, their mythology, and the ritual sequence of their ceremonies all remained unaltered. What we have here, in fact, are genuine provincial sub-branches built up by the Bahia sects, their purpose being to provide adequate conditions of worship for those members who 'went south'. Furthermore, the facilities afforded by air travel make it possible for priests of the 'mother-house' to maintain control over such new provincial centres.

Voodoo has been similarly affected by these migratory trends, and it will be advantageous, at this point, to see how it fared as a result. When Haiti declared its independence, the French planters fled to Cuba, taking some of their slaves (of Fon origin) with them; this was how Haitian Voodoo managed to take root in the neighbouring island.[20] More recently, between 1913 and 1925, Cuba imported large numbers of workers from the other Antilles, including 145,000 Haitians and 107,000 Jamaicans. Many of these workers went back home when their labour contracts expired. In 1941, however, there was a fresh call for labour, and this time 80,000 Haitians came over. The result has been that, in certain areas of Cuba we find the same brand of Voodoo as in Haiti. The districts most affected are those where the earlier immigrants settled; more recent arrivals have tended to regard their stay as purely temporary, and leave their religion in cold storage, as it were, for the duration. However, apart from a few scattered references in the work of Fernando Ortiz, this Cuban Voodoo remains virtually unexplored. Another, much better documented, migration is that which brought Voodoo from Haiti to New Orleans, in the southern part of the U.S.A. At this point I would like to examine this New Orleans Voodoo in some detail, and trace the various metamorphoses which it has undergone.[21]

The cult must have been introduced there by the slaves of white refugees from Haiti, at the time of the Franco-Spanish War of 1809 – and in its archaic form, that described by Moreau de Saint-Mery, i.e. the cult of the python (*danh-gbi*) or the snake in general. In New Orleans it took place under the direction of a king and a queen, also referred to as the 'master' and 'mistress'. The ritual consisted, fundamentally, of the queen's possession by the serpent-spirit, which predicted the future and answered questions put to it by worshippers. Membership was conditional upon initiation, and apparently one requirement was the ability to go into a trance. We also know that new members had to swear a secrecy oath on the blood of a lamb that was specially slaughtered for this purpose. The snake-cult contained not only Dahomean but also Bantu elements, since *Zombi* was one of the divinities worshipped, and the hymns in use are full of Bantu references. In addition to this cult we have, on St John's Day, the festival of St John Ewe, complete with the traditional European bonfire, the sacrifice of a black cat, and dancing. New Orleans Voodoo reached its apogee under the celebrated 'queen' Marie Laveau, an extremely intelligent woman, and the maker of magic philtres that were much in demand among the white population. The cult also existed in Missouri, where tobacco and alcohol were taken during ceremonies, and the initiation of adepts involved segregation from secular life for nine days, and a dream-epiphany of the spirit that was the novice's 'head-master' (*maître de la tête*). Voodooism as an institution disappeared after 1895; but there still survive a number of Voodoo witch-doctors, who perform various ceremonies complete with ecstatic dances, and have not completely forgotten the African pantheon. (They know such divinities as *Leba* (Legba), *Blanc Dani*, *Véréquété*, the great *Zambi*, and Green *Agoussou*.) Nevertheless, one only needs to read the most recent studies on the subject to see that Voodooism is steadily turning, more and more, into pure magic, while its cult-priests have become transformed into ordinary healers.[22] It was this brand of Voodoo, bastardised and corrupted by progressive distancing from its original roots, which travelled north in the U.S.A. at the time of the great internal migrations of the coloured population after the two World Wars. Consequently it is still to be found in such places as Philadelphia, Pittsburgh, and New York. What survives in the minds of these northern Negroes is not the beneficent aspect of Voodoo *qua* religion so much as its black magic side (desecration of tombs to make spells or *wanga*).

'You know, they say that down there in Louisiana they've got Voodoo everywhere (*bis*).

You know, they'd kill anyone; they'd do anything for money.'

To end this chapter, there is one last question we have to ask ourselves. Did the Voodoo cult originally exist only on Haiti – or, remembering that slaves for the French colonies were recruited in the same provinces of Africa, did it flourish throughout the French Antilles? Maurice Satineau[23] asserts that it was to be found in Guadeloupe, linked with the worship of reptiles and other animals, in the form of secret societies that plotted against the whites. According to him, it was about 1720 that the 'Don Pedro' ritual was introduced. Adepts of the latter were made to drink rum mixed with gunpowder, and went into ecstatic trances of a peculiarly violent sort. However, these wild dances were banned, and at some time after 1750 they disappeared from the cities, surviving only in the remote countryside. Only a few traces of this phenomenon survive among the modern peasant population, perhaps more noticeably on Martinique than on Guadeloupe. They include such things as the survival of *Damballah Oueddo* in oral folklore (*Dembe wouge*); the flourishing belief in such things as *zombies* or the *maman de l'eau* (a water-goddess); and the sacrifice, out in the country districts, of chickens or cockerels. We may also note the habit, among the *quimboiseurs* (as sorcerers are known in the French Antilles) of decorating their skin with bits of black, red or white cloth; these may be all that survives of the liturgical vestments once worn by Voodoo priests (each Voodoo god has his own special colour). The silk-cotton tree preserves its importance, being regarded – here as on Haiti – as the home of certain spirits, in particular of the *guiablesses* (i.e. *diablesses*, or female devils, equivalent to the Fon *loko*). Lastly, we find a heavy incidence of so-called hysterical *crises* among the women, especially in the night between Saturday and Sunday, or during Carnival. Such tranced states are normal in Voodoo, being attributable to the descent of the gods on their 'horses'. Here, however, where the cult no longer survives as an institution, such *crises* are ascribed to the malevolent activities of the *quimboiseurs*, and explained by the power they supposedly have to send demons into their victims' bodies. In other words, just as in the United States, we find the fragmented remnants of a vanished culture transmuted into magical beliefs or practices. There is even a popular belief on Martinique that all the *quimboiseurs* are united in a single secret society, under the leadership of a king whose jurisdiction extends – they say – throughout the Lesser Antilles. If the rumour had any truth in it, we might regard this as the final avatar of Voodoo.[24]

REFERENCES

1. See Martiano de Bomfin, 'Os doze Ministros de Xangô', in *O Negro no Brasil*, Rio de Janeiro, 1940, pp. 233–6.

2. Aydano de Couto Ferraz, 'A volta à Africa', *Rev. Arq. Munic. de S. Paulo*, LIV, 1939. The only instance I have discovered of liaison between Haiti and Africa, after the former's Declaration of Independence, is Christophe's recruitment in Dahomey of 4,000 Negroes to form his National Guard and keep order in the countryside.

3. René Ribeiro, 'Novos aspectos do processo de reinterpretação nos cultos afro-brasileiros do Recife', *Anais do XXXI Congres. Int. de Americanistas*, vol. I, S. Paulo, 1955, pp. 473–92.

4. J. L. Comhaire, 'The Community Concept in the Study and Government of African and Afro-American Societies', *Primitive Man*, 25, 3, 1952.

5. George Eaton Simpson, 'The Belief System of Haitian Vodun', *Amer. Anthrop.* XLC–VII, I, 1945, pp. 35–59, and C. E. Peters, *op. cit.*

6. Jean J. Comhaire, 'Religious Trends in African and Afro-American Societies', *Anthrop. Quarterly* (*Primitive Man*), XXVI, 4, 1953.

7. Cf. Remy Bastien, *La familia rural haitiana*, Mexico, 1951.

8. Octavio da Costa Eduardo, *The Negro in Northern Brazil*, New York, 1948; and Nuñes Pereira, *A Casa das Minas*, Rio de Janeiro, 1947.

9. M. J. Herskovits, *Dahomey, an Ancient West African Kingdom*, 2 vols., New York, 1938.

10. P. Verger, in *Les Afro-Américains, op. cit.*, pp. 157–60, where it is suggested that the cult of the Abomey *Vodun* may have been brought to S. Luiz in Maranhão by the mother of King Ghezo.

11. It follows that such cases as that of Elegba among the Fon, or Eshú among the Yoruba, are merely individual instances of a more widespread phenomenon, which has not as yet been properly studied.

12. Andrew T. Carr, 'A Rada Community in Trinidad', *Caribbean Quarterly*, III, I, pp. 35–54.

13. Compare Carr's description of the *Gozen* festival with that of the procession for the royal ancestors performed at Porto Novo in Dahomey, in Geoffrey Parrinder's *West African Religion*, London, 2nd. edn. 1961, p. 122.

14. The literature on Voodoo is immense. An exhaustive bibliography will be found at the end of Alfred Métraux's book *Voodoo in Haiti*, London, 1949. Apart from this basic study my own account is most indebted to the following works: H. Price Mars, *Ainsi parla l'oncle*, Compiègne, 1928; Elsie Clews Parsons, 'Spirit Cult in Hayti', *Journ. Soc. des Amér.* XX, 1928, pp. 157–79; G. Eaton Simpson, 'Four Vodun Ceremonies', *Journ. of Amer. Folklore* 59, 1946, and 'The Belief System of Haitian Vodun', *Amer. Anthrop.* 56, 2, 1954, pp. 35–9; Joseph J. Williams, *Voodoos and Obeahs*, New York, 1932; Zora Neale Hurston, *Tell My Horse*, Philadelphia, 1938; M. J. Herskovits, *Life in a Haitian Valley*, New York, 1937; Maya Deren, *Divine Horsemen*, New York, 1953; Milo Marcelin, *Mythologie Vodou*, 2 vols., Port-au-Prince, 1949; Louis Maximilien, *Le Vodou Haïtien*, Port-au-Prince, 1945; Milo Rigaud, *La tradition vaudoo et le vaudoo haïtien*, Paris, 1953; Harold Courlander, *The Drum and the Hoe*, California, 1960.

15. There is another factor involved in this change, which originates with an undoubtedly Dahomean idea (that of the gods having an 'escort'), but has changed its significance on Haiti as a result of strictly local development; 'Nanili . . . walks alongside Dahomé. In the escort, Dahomé and Pétro walk together. . . . There are twenty-one *loas* all told in the escort. This escort has a commander, and there are soldiers under him – that is, minor *loas* who have to obey his orders.' (Evidence collected by H. Courlander, *op. cit.*).

16. One result of this is that the cult of the guede has almost completely vanished from the Abomey region, and only survives on Haiti. Cf. R. Bastide, *Confrontations* (to be published).

17. Certain scholars (e.g. Maximilen) have sought to postulate an Indian origin for these designs; but it seems clear that, though they have undergone considerable modification (whether under the influence of Freemasonry or of wrought-iron patterns), they are actually African in origin. They also turn up in the Brazilian *macumba* (*pontos riscados*), during the Yoruba initiation ceremonies of Bahia (here, however, they are drawn on the worshipper's body, his head and shoulders in particular), in the *nãnigos* sect on Cuba – and in Bantu magic.

18. Besides the works listed in note 14, see also: Yvonne Oddon, 'Une cérémonie funéraire haïtienne,' in *Les Afro-Américains, op. cit.*; Milo Marcelin, 'Coutumes funéraires', *Optique* 11, 1955; and Lorimer Denis, 'Le cimitière', *Bull. Bureau Ethno.*, Port-au-Prince, 13, 1956.

19. R. Bastide, *Réligions africaines, op. cit.*

20. Cuban Voodoo has been described by H. Piron, *L'île de Cuba*, Paris, 1889.

21. There are several early articles on the subject in the *Journal of American Folklore*, e.g. by A. Fortier in 1888, and W. N. Newell in 1889; see also the following works, which are the most important in the field: N. Niles Puckett, *Folk Beliefs of the Southern Negro*, North Carolina, 1926; Hortense Powdermaker, *After Freedom: A Cultural Study in the Deep South*, New York, 1939; Zora Neale Hurston, *Mules and Men*, London, 1936; John Q. Anderson, 'The New Orleans Voodoo, Ritual Dance and its Twentieth-Century Survivals', *Southern Folklore Quarterly*, XXIV, 2, 1960; Robert Taillant, *Voodoo in New Orleans*, New York, 1946.

22. Individual instances can be found in Warington Dawson, *Le Nègre aux Etats-Unis*, French trs., Paris, 1912; and a list of Voodoo witch-doctors, together with their activities (which extend from the fabrication of charms to the reciting of Catholic prayers over the sick) in H. Powdermaker, *op. cit.*

23. *Histoire de la Guadeloupe sous l'Ancien Régime, 1635–1789*, Paris, 1928.

24. Eugène Revert, *La Magie Antillaise*, Paris, 1951; and Michel Leiris, *Contacts de civilisations en Martinique et en Guadeloupe*, U.N.E.S.C.O., 1955.

CHAPTER VII

SYNCRETISM AND AMALGAMATION BETWEEN RELIGIONS

I

In the previous chapters emphasis has been placed on the phenomena of preservation and survival. Nevertheless, on more than one occasion mention has been made of syncretism – both within the framework of a single African religion (e.g. the introduction of Dahomean elements into the Fanti–Ashanti system, or of Bantu features into that of the Yoruba), and between two separate religious systems, such as those of the Africans and the Indians. At the same time, these amalgamations take place within the context of society at large; and the societies in question (if we except that of the Bush Negroes) are almost all Christian. In Latin America, slaves had to be baptised either before leaving Africa or else on entry to the New World; they were also obliged to undergo a course of religious instruction. (In European eyes this justified a servile régime; they enslaved the body the better to liberate the soul.) In the U.S.A. employers disliked the idea of having Christian slaves; if their slaves underwent conversion, they set them free. But the logic of the economic system was to prove stronger than virtuous sentiments. From the end of the sixteenth century onwards the idea begins to gain ground that a man can be a Christian and still remain a slave, that baptism need not modify the human condition in any social sense. From early in the eighteenth century, missionary societies for the conversion of the Negroes appear in ever-increasing numbers. Thus in the sphere of his beliefs and religious practices, the coloured person was subjected to a fearful pressure from his external environment.

At the same time we must distinguish between two quite

different types of environment, each of which produced its own characteristic 'marriage of religions': the Catholic and the Protestant. In the latter, the Negro was not accepted as a member of the church until he had undergone a very thorough course of instruction. Missionary work, therefore, was carried out in depth, and this led to the eradication of 'Africanisms'. Religious amalgamation never (or at best very rarely) took the form of true syncretism; the most common process was what Herskovits has labelled 'reinterpretation'. A slave would reinterpet Protestantism, or the Bible, in the light of his own mentality, sentiments, and affective needs; what emerged was a Negro (rather than an African) brand of Christianity. In Catholic America, on the other hand – perhaps because Portuguese or Spanish Catholicism was (at least on the new continent) a social rather than mystical phenomenon – the newly-arrived slave needed only to learn a few prayers or ritual gestures to be granted baptism, always supposing he had not already been baptised at the port where the slave-ship took him aboard. This is not to say that the assimilation of Western values was completely unknown. The slave régime took care to leave loopholes in the system as a precaution against revolt by the downtrodden masses; and the Negro knew very well that the only way in which he could get his foot on the social ladder was by acquiring 'a white soul'. Nevertheless, proselytisation was, broadly speaking, less intense. As a result, features of African culture could survive more easily, and in Latin America religious fusion most often took the form of syncretism.

The present chapter, then, will examine these contacts, and trace the consequent amalgamation of both types of Christianity with African pagan cults.

II. *Catholic America*

Here it is easy to isolate certain general tendencies, if not outright laws, which have absolute validity for every country in Latin America, from the Antilles to Argentina (an exception being made, naturally, in the case of the British Antilles, which are Protestant).

1. Ethnically speaking, syncretism becomes more noticeable

when we turn from the Dahomeans (*Casa das Minas*) to the Yoruba, and from them to the Bantus, who are the most susceptible of all to external influences.

2. From the ecological viewpoint, syncretism becomes more pronounced when we leave the rural areas (where cultural cross-pollination is intense) and move into the towns, where the slaves, the 'free Negroes', and their descendants have been able to group themselves in corporations and 'nations'.

3. Institutionally, syncretism is more prominent when we turn from 'preserved' to 'live' religions, since the life of any organism – social no less than biological – involves the assimilation of external influences.

4. Sociologically – and thinking in terms of what G. Gurvitch has labelled 'depth sociology' – the types of syncretism encountered vary in nature as we pass from the morphological plane (mosaic syncretism) to the institutional (with, *inter alia*, the system of correspondences between African gods and Catholic saints), and thence to the plane of events dependent on collective awareness (reinterpretation phenomena).

5. Lastly, we have to bear in mind the specific nature of the facts examined. For religion, the rule is to work by establishing parallels; for magic, by simple accumulation.

To deal with all these problems here would be out of the question. I shall, therefore, ignore the first two variable factors (which, by forcing me to deal with countries and ethnic groups separately, would make my analysis too disconnected) and concentrate on the remainder, which are in any case of far greater interest.

To begin with, let us examine the framework within which Afroamerican religions operate. Every religion exists within certain physical boundaries, and shapes its existence in time according to a certain calendar of events. Slavery forced the African to detach his religion from its natural geographical setting, and transfer it to a new environment, where the rhythm of his life had perforce to be modelled on an alien calendar, that of his white masters. From these constrictions and imposed adjustments there emerged the earliest examples of syncretism. Spatial syncretism has one highly characteristic feature. On account of the solid, unalterable nature of those objects which come within its orbit, it cannot achieve true fusion, but remains on the plane of coexistence between disparate objects. This is what I earlier described as 'mosaic syncretism', and it is just as likely to be found in a broad context as in a restricted one. An example of the former category is provided by the *candomblés*, where African *pegi* and Catholic chapels exist side by side. For the latter, we may cite the Voodoo-type *pé* or the altars of the *macumbas*, with their stones, rum-bottles, crosses, statues of saints' pots containing the souls of the dead, wax candles, specially blessed rosaries, and so on. As regards the calendar, however, the priests found themselves torn between the two different chronological systems – the Christian, and the recurring cycle of mythical deeds performed by their own *orisha* or *Vodun*. They had, at all costs, to shift their existing ceremonies to days on which work was not required of them – which meant, in effect, accepting the Gregorian calendar. Thus in its temporal aspect syncretism involved pouring African material into a Western mould, a process which was bound, on occasion, to produce difficulties and discrepancies. The Yoruba liturgical year, for instance, begins with a ceremony known as the 'water of *Oshala*', in which various objects are washed, and the accumulated impurities of the past year ritually purified. Since it does not quite coincide with the first day of the Christian year, there is a gap between the two festivals. For the most part, however, Negroes have taken over the major Catholic feast days as convenient occasions for the disguised celebration of their own rites. We may particularly note the use made of the whole Christmas cycle, up to Epiphany. All Souls' Eve in November is likewise an occasion for ancestor worship. The use of masks during Carnival provides an excuse for processions: those organised by the secret societies, and also special parades (*afoshé*) held by such remnants of the old royal courts as have survived in America. During Easter Week, the death and passion of Christ replace the mourning for deceased royal ancestors. In Dahomey, all the so-called 'fetichist' religious houses are closed during the annual celebrations in honour of the Kings of Abomey, and no Vodun is allowed to go into a trance at this time. This yearly 'shut-down' of cult-centres was assimilated, in America, to Holy Week, by analogy between Christ and the royal ancestor. Finally, as we shall see, a general correspondence was established between the *orisha* or *Vodun* and the various Catholic saints, so that the former's major feast days and sacrifices now take place on those dates proper to the corresponding saint.

Syncretism by correspondence between gods and saints is the most basic of these processes, and also the best studied.[1] It can be explained in historical terms by the slaves' need, during the colonial period, to conceal their pagan ceremonies from European eyes. They therefore danced before a Catholic altar; and though their masters found this somewhat bizarre, it never occurred to them that these Negro dances, with their prominently displayed lithographs and statuettes of the saints, were in fact addressed to African divinities. Even today, the priests and priestesses of Brazil recognise that syncretism is simply a mask put over the black gods for the white man's benefit. At the same time it can be justified, theologically, in the eyes of the faithful. In essence, the argument runs, there is only one universal religion, which acknowledges the existence of one unique God and Creator. However, this God is too remote from mankind for the latter to enter into direct contact with him; therefore 'intermediaries' are necessary – Catholic saints or the angels of the Old Testament for Europeans, *orisha* and *Vodun* for the Negroes. Though this universal religion takes on local forms, varying according to race and ethnic group, such variations are not fundamental. In any case, one can always 'translate' one religion into another, by assimilating each African divinity to a special saint, or to some local variant of the Virgin (Our Lady of Good Succour, Our Lady of Guadeloupe, and so on). Thus when the faithful go so far as to identify *Shangô* (for instance) with St Jerome, there is no point in talking of superstition or logical absurdity. Granted the overall consistency of the system they *can*, in fact, be identified, since they occupy the same intermediary position in a whole network of relationships, and perform precisely the same functions – controlling the forces of fire, directing lightning or thunderbolt exclusively against the evildoer. But how do these identifications operate? The system itself may be consistent, but its content remains arbitrary, in the sense that it varies from period to period, from region to region, and even in the same area, between one cult and another.[2] On the other hand, it is always possible to detect the motives which have dictated a particular choice. Sometimes (in the case of illiterate populations, we may regard this as a general rule) it is the lithographic pictures of the saints which must be held responsible for certain identifications.[3] *Omolú*, for example, the god of smallpox, is identified with St Sebastian; the latter is portrayed shot through with arrows, and the wounds that dot his body suggest the pustules produced by smallpox. In other cases it is the saint's therapeutic, corporate or social function which provokes the equation. Thus *Shangô* can be identified with St John because of St John's fires, and *Yansan* the storm-goddess with St Barbara, the patron of gunners and artillery-men. Finally, in so far as they were acquainted with it, the Golden Legend set Negroes on the track of possible parallels between certain episodes in the lives of the saints and certain myths concerning their own deities. To a great extent the choice remained free.[4] It is impossible to set down an exhaustive list of such parallels in tabular form: I have simply, by way of illustration, chosen the best-known or most currently popular examples (see Table).

SAINTS	BRAZIL (*Yoruba*)	CUBA (*Yoruba*)	TRINIDAD *Fon, Yoruba*	HAITI *Fon*
Jesus Christ	Obatala	Obatala		Aizan
Our Lady of the Rosary	Yemanjá			
Our Lady of Candlemas	Oshum (Bahia)			
Our Lady of the Immacu-late Conception	Oshum (Porto Alegre)			
Our Lady of the Pleasures	Oshum (Recife)			
The Virgin of the Rule		Yemanjá		
Our Lady of Charity		Oshum		
Mater Dolorosa				Ezili
St Anne	Anamburucú		(Oshum) [Agbe]	
St Barbara	Yansan	Shangô		
St Catherine	Oba		(Oia) [Avlekete]	
St Benedict			(Obatala)	

St Patrick				Damballa [Oueddo]
St Anthony	Ogun		[Da Zodji]	Legba
St George	Oshossi (Bahia) Ogun Rio de Janeiro	Oshossi		
St Jerome	Shangô		(Shakpanan) [Obo Zuin]	
St Hubert (transformed into St Albert)		Oshossi		
St Michael			(Ogun)	
St Sebastian	Omolú			
St Francis	Irôco	Orumila	(Osain) [Abobodji]	
St Roche	Omolú			
St Lazarus	Abaluayê (the oldest of the Omolu)	Babaluayé		
St John the Baptist	Shangô		(Shangô) [Sobo]	
St Peter	Eshú (Porto Alegre)	Ogun		Legba
The Souls in Purgatory		Elegba		
The Devil	Eshú (Bahia, Recife, Rio)			
SS. Cosmas and Damian	The Ibeji	The Jima-guas		The Mar-assa

On this web the collective imagination can weave its wildest fantasies at will. Thus the myths of the gods, such as that of *Omolú*, are liable to get mixed up with Gospel parables, for instance that concerning the Prodigal Son.[5] Popular Christian legends get attached to the *orisha*: for instance, the idea that St John the Baptist sleeps throughout his feast day and must not be woken up (since if he came down on earth that day he would set the whole world on fire) is attributed to Shangô. On Haiti, Biblical stories serve to create some sort of substitute for the lost African mythology (the establishment of the *loa* recalls the struggle of the sons of the morning against God in the book of Genesis). Among the Black Caribs, the concept of white Christianity as superior to black paganism is translated into cosmological terms by the superimposition of various heavens according to a fixed hierarchical order. (This novel idea is also found among the Indians.) The lowest heaven is that of the spirits, those Caribs who died before the coming of the Gospel; the highest, at the very apex, is that of the Christians. Last, and most extraordinary of all, on Haiti Catholic saints can become *loa* – without even changing their European names for that of the appropriate *Vodun*, or relinquishing their Western identity: e.g. St James the Greater, who is the chief of the *Ogou*, or Our Lady of Charity, or – one final instance – St Elizabeth.[6]

When we turn from the sphere of collective representation to that of ritual gesture, we find ourselves confronted with a heterogeneous mass of developments; the principal ones are outlined below. Moments in time, like objects in space, can form solid, clearly delimited points, unchanging in the nature of their syncretism. The Christian moment remains Christian, the African moment African; they come into juxtaposition solely as masses in space.[7]

Thus in Brazil, when the initiation ceremony is over, the 'daughters of the gods' attend mass to thank God for granting them the privilege of becoming *yaô*. On Haiti, Voodoo ceremonies begin with Catholic prayers – not inevitably pronounced by the *prêtres-savanes* – designed to invoke a divine blessing on the meeting about to take place. In other cases we find ourselves dealing with convergence phenomena, which enable us to isolate the original custom. In Nigeria, for example, prospective initiates are guided and helped by a 'godmother'; and in Christianity every baptism requires the presence of a godfather and a godmother. The identical nature of the two institutions has made it possible, in Black America, for African and Catholic concepts of the godfather to fuse into a single reality, so that one has difficulty in telling, *a priori*, where the one ends and the other begins. The two worlds are not only in contact, but sustain a to-and-fro traffic between them; as a result we find African elements being absorbed into Catholic worship, while, *per contra*, Catholic practices are borrowed and reinterpreted in African terms. One example of the former phenomenon is the habit (observable in up-country Brazilian chapels) of sacrificing a hen and leaving it at the feet of some saint's statue in order to obtain a special favour – the healing of an illness, the return of a husband who has gone off with some other woman, and so on. Similarly – though this is characteristic not only of Haiti, but also of Brazil – Church sacraments such as baptism and communion tend to be reworked in African terms. Their accepted function is to boost a person's vital force, to heal the sick, or to strengthen the head (where the *Vodun* resides) – as Métraux[8] has clearly demonstrated. In the Haitian cult even marriage has its place: some worshippers actually contract a written and certificated union with a *loa* – who, one may add, is far stricter in the matter of adultery than the majority of wives or husbands. As this paragraph should make clear, it is on Haiti that we find syncretism in its most extreme form – to the extent, indeed, that if a Protestant wishes to return to the Voodoo fold, he will not be accepted by the *houngan* or the *mambo* unless he has previously been baptised – or rebaptised – into the Catholic church.

One last syncretistic variant is provided by magic, though this differs from our previous examples in being subject to the basic rule of magic as such, i.e. effectiveness. The Europeans who colonised the New World brought their own superstitions with them – not to mention a good deal of medieval witchcraft. Such traffic was positively encouraged by the fact that at this time sorcerers and magicians were no longer burnt at the stake, but deported to the recently discovered territories of the west. A crying need for pioneers won out over the demands of orthodoxy. But these magicians and sorcerers were whites: in other words, they belonged to the ruling class. By a simple process of transference – from the social hierarchy to the world of ideas – European magic came to be regarded by the Negroes as superior to their own, since theirs failed to win them deliverance from slavery, while that of the whites guaranteed an unfailing European hegemony. This is why, though they never rejected any of their own African practices which proved effective, the black population would reinforce the unsuccessful ones with some European formula. In case of doubt, two precautions were better than one. This is how we find Catholic prayers for the healing of the sick – e.g. to St Lucia for eye-diseases, SS. Peter and Paul for coughs, or indeed to St Cyprian for casting a spell on someone, or to St Expeditus – being employed on Cuba and Haiti, or in Brazil. It also explains the coexistence of African and European methods of spellbinding. In the former category we have the practice of transferring some illness to a bird, killing it, and then throwing the corpse down at a crossroads, so that anyone who trips over it will catch the disease (Yoruba *ebó*). In the latter we find such tricks as that of working a person mischief by sticking a doll full of pins (*devotio*, sympathetic magic).[9] This accumulative development exactly matches that of the magic practised during the later Roman Empire, which – in order to boost its operative force – laid all the magical practices of occident and orient alike under contribution. It falls, in fact, into the category of a magical *as opposed* to a religious phenomenon. It remains to be said that, while Negroes may borrow European magic to strengthen their own spells, the reverse is also true. Europeans tend to regard Negro magic as more effective, because of its 'weird' character and the old colonial terrors which it inspired; the uses to which they put it range from murdering their political opponents to winning a football match.

One last important point remains to be discussed. Wherever the triumphant influence of Catholicism has destroyed an ancient African religion (this phenomenon, as we have seen, is most liable to occur among predominantly Bantu populations) there is one final semi-African institution which stands firm amid the general collapse, like some ruined castle keep standing amid mere levelled heaps of stones that once were castle walls. This is the cult of the dead. But the keep is ruined indeed, and almost hidden by the rank vegetation that has sprung up all round it. Herskovits correctly attributes these late survivals to the importance of ancestors in every African ethnic group, the Bantus in particular.[10] Sometimes little enough remains, as we can see from the case of Negroes in North America. Those of the big northern cities go no further than assuring their dead decent burial; in the south, mutual-aid societies exist for much the same purpose. This, however, applies chiefly to the Protestant areas. In formerly Catholic regions, such as Louisiana and the immediately adjacent territory, where French or Spnish influence had time to make itself felt, we find African and European elements coexisting. Burial is in accordance with national custom (apart from anything else the law has to be obeyed), but the belief that the dead person has not actually left the house still persists; hence the retention of the funeral wake, or vigil. However, these occasions do not go on for seven or even nine days, as in Africa, but for three only – probably because Christ rose on the third day. Many ritual taboos (e.g. not looking in a mirror), or omens (e.g. it being bad luck when it rains at the moment of someone's death), or ghost stories, come straight from Europe. On the other hand, the offerings that are placed on tombs, such as bottles of brandy, cups of coffee, cigar butts, or lamps (as in Alabama) are clearly African.[11] Leiris has remarked on the importance attached to death and funeral wakes in Guadeloupe and Martinique, and points out how essentially African this is. Such wakes greatly resemble a full-blown religious festival, except that the liturgy chanted is Catholic, and the spirit of the deceased does not achieve possession. In the *velorio de angelito* (wake for a dead child) of Colombia and Venezuela we find a central idea which is strictly European. Faced with the extremely high rate of infant mortality which social contacts provoked in America, the clergy thought up a new ideology according to which all little children who died became angels in heaven; thus one should not weep for them, but rather rejoice. All that the Negroes added here was what they regarded as the characteristic manifestation of joy: a dance round the coffin (Venezuela), or dances, singing and games (*trapiche, yare, vaca pintada*, etc.) in Colombia.[12] In the case of adults, as soon as the coffin leaves the house the doors are shut, to prevent the spirit getting back inside; and the funeral wake, complete with games, goes on for nine days.[13]

III. *Protestant America*

Syncretism here takes entirely different forms. Though it is true that the Negro can find a certain number of intermediary divinities in the Bible to take the place of the saints (e.g. angels and archangels), it has not been possible to establish a general pattern of correspondences. What assumed fundamental importance here were certain very different Biblical texts, the kind which could affect a slave by reminding him of his own condition: the story of Israel's servitude in Egypt and subsequent liberation by Moses, or that of the captivity in Babylon and the prophets of salvation. Lastly, there were the spirits of the apostles, which demonstrated the existence of certain relevant phenomena in the primitive church – e.g. prophetic utterance, or the ability to 'speak with tongues' through the baptism of the Holy Spirit. Such were the original guiding forces behind African-Protestant syncretism, which led to a quite different orientation, in the general direction of angelism, messianism, and the reinterpretation of African ecstatic possession in terms of revivalist sects or the descent of the Holy Ghost.

In the U.S.A., it is true, the Negro has preserved no trace of his ancestral religion; in his quest for violent emotionalism, for some sort of affective faith, he has borrowed wholesale from North American revivalism – itself a continuation of Scottish revivalism. Johnson, who has made a thorough study of what are reputedly the most traditional communities, those of the Gullah Negroes,[14] found nothing in these Negroes' churches which did not also feature in those of the whites: hand-clapping, rhythmic swaying of the body in time with the music, the practice of 'bearing witness' or making 'public confession'– all these were common in both races. Herskovits, while not denying that the Negroes' religion is a 'received' one, nevertheless maintains that from this beginning there evolved something genuinely original and 'creative'. In white revivalism one always finds a good number of non-participating onlookers, who remain outside the generally infectious mood of excitement, whereas among the Negroes, everyone without exception is a performer. The predominant feeling which emerges from the 'testifying' of whites is fear of eternal damnation, whereas the most common sentiment among Negroes is hope – hope for salvation, deliverance from the bondage of a symbolic Egypt. Among Europeans, the movements of the body are far more violent or convulsive, and ecstatic possession, when it occurs, tends to assume the form of a hysterical *crise*. Among Negroes, on the other hand, such movements tend to be rhythmic and organised: their motor behaviour is socially viable. It should also be made clear that we have no reason to assume an exclusively one-way influence in the contact between the two races, *de haut en bas* from white master to black slave. If we compare Scottish revivalism to that of North America, we find that in Scotland it is the sensory elements which are most important – visions, voices, sensory automatisms, accompanied by a lowering of muscular energy. In the U.S.A., on the other hand, motor automatisms predominate: beating of feet and hands, rhythmic body-movements on the spot, increased muscular energy. So radical a contrast, involving Europeans in both instances, surely hints at possible Negro influence on the religious revivalism of native North Americans.[15] Hortense Powdermaker, who has painstakingly analysed the religion of Negroes in the deep south, points out that even structural differences between white and Negro families (the first being paternalistic, the second matrifocal) have repercussions in the field of religious representation. The Negro God, for instance, exhibits certain maternal characteristics which are not to be found in the Europeans' concept of deity. Thus all the evidence leads us to define Negro Protestantism as something *sui generis*, a mode of expression which nevertheless preserves some element that remains identifiably African. Middle-class Negroes understand this very well. To emphasise their 'acculturation', their absorption of white values, they deliberately turn away from the affective creeds followed by lower-class Negroes (which aim at emotionalism, without concerning themselves about their adherents' moral conduct) and embrace a puritan faith compounded of rigid moral imperatives and reflections on dogma.

In the big northern cities prophetic salvationism holds the field, a response to the frustrations of the Negro community. Here the most famous sect, which we can take as a characteristic example, is that of Father Divine.[16] The origins and function of this sect are well known; it arose in response to the great economic depression that hit black workers after the First World War, bringing widespread misery and unemployment. Yet quite apart from all this, the sect embodies certain undeniably African features; it is as though Protestantism could only take root by infiltrating souls, at some deep level, with fragments of an older cultural heritage. First and foremost, there is the importance attached to earthly matters. As Fernando Ortiz observed of the Negro community in Cuba (a statement, moreover, with general applicability), the Negro does not have a 'credit religion', in which one accumulates good actions in this life to win recompense in heaven; he wants the pay-off here and now. Father Divine's message is the Kingdom of Heaven *here on earth:* 'Every day we have the power of Heaven here among us.' Secondly, there is the concept of the Father, the head of the church, as God Almighty: 'Father Divine is God' – and his life is marked by a whole series of miracles. Judge Smith, who sentenced him in the courts, died three days after pronouncing sentence. Rogers, the man who made an attack on him over the radio, was killed in an air crash. Lastly we have a new link-up with African polytheism through the legions of angels, who become priestly acolytes to God the Father in the sect's ecclesiastical organisation. At the same time, we should note that the more conscious of white exploitation United States Negroes become, the more they tend to abandon Christianity altogether (as being too closely bound up with their masters' world), and to explore new creeds which provide an indirect expression for their political protests (e.g. Jewry or Islam). We shall come back to this point later.

In Trinidad there exists a revivalist sect known as the 'Shouters'. This was officially banned in 1917, but has kept up a clandestine existence ever since; it provides us with what is arguably an even clearer picture of African-Protestant syncretism. The first level at which this applies is in the actual place of worship. The temple contrives to blend Christian features, such as an altar complete with Bible, crucifix, and candles, not to mention a preacher's pulpit, with African elements such as the central post (*poteau-mitan*) which we have already encountered in Haiti, and is similarly to be found in certain Bahia *candomblés*.[17] Secondly, there is the matter of ecclesiastical organisation. According to the powers which they receive during the course of initiation (more of this in a moment) the clergy can be split up into the following categories: preachers, who expound the Bible; 'masters', who interpret the dreams of the faithful; 'leaders', who carry out baptism; doctors who have received the gift of healing; seers and prophets, who foretell the future; and nurses, who correspond to the *ekedy* found in Yoruba sects. Thus we find African and Christian concepts of priesthood overlapping in the same well-organised general context. Entry to the sect is by initiation, and this, as in Africa, takes place 'in the bush'. During the course of it – again, as in the African initiation ceremony – the postulant receives a 'power' (or as Christians would say, a 'grace' or 'gift'). This 'power' is made manifest by the carrying of some liturgical object (which is likewise the rule in Africa, where special colours are associated with the various gods, and every *orisha* has his own liturgical emblem, such as Shangô's *oshe* or Omolú's broom). Lastly, the actual ritual involves dancing round the central post (to the accompaniment of various Protestant hymns) until a state of possession is reached – just like the same island's *Shangô* ceremonies, which we have already studied.[18]

In Jamaica the old Fanti–Ashanti religion, Myalism, has disappeared, surviving only in the guise of witchcraft. The African priest himself is still around, but has been meta- morphosed from a *myalmam* into an *angel-man*. In other words, we find that here, too, religious revivalism has been rethought in African terms. The prime objective is still the ecstatic trance, but the devices used to further this end are partially new – e.g. the so-called *tooping*, nocturnal meetings, and military-type processions led by a 'captain' to the accompaniment of muffled drum-beats. The trance itself contains some mixed features – on the one hand communication with the spirits of the dead, on the other a vision of angels. To these we should add the ceremony of healing the sick by immersion in the water of certain *sacred rivers*, a practice which simultaneously recalls Christian baptism and the African 'cult of the waters'. Now these 'angelic' sects have tended, as a result of the Negro's racial and social position within the community, to assume a prophetic role. In 1894 Bedward founded the Jamaican Baptist Free Church, in which we find repeated certain features of the Father Divine sect. Its founder announced himself as a reincarnation, first of Jonah, then of Moses, then of St John the Baptist, and finally of Christ. He too promised salvation here and now, but in a more violent form, that of the destruction of the whites in 1920, an event to be followed by the triumph of his new religion. Nevertheless, despite such survivals, the general trend of development was towards 'de-Africanisation'. But events took a fresh turn which rescued Africa from the near-oblivion into which it had fallen.

The Pukhumerians created a new religion by synthetising magic and revivalist Protestantism – offshoots respectively of the Myalist cult and of angelism. Its leaders, known as governors or 'shepherds', are each attached to a young woman (not a legitimate wife) known as a 'governess' or 'shepherdess'.[19] Both have the key to a secret language which the spirits employ to address them when they are in a state of trance, and which they subsequently translate for the benefit of the faithful. This language includes words taken from Spanish slang and from Kromanti, together with instances of glossolalia. The ceremonies are of two types, known respectively as 'grudge meetings' and 'blood meetings', at each of which the priests wear different turbans. Their central feature is dancing designed to bring down the spirits, which may be either bad or good according to the end in view.[20] It is this latter cult which still flourishes today, being known under the African name of *Bongo*, or in English as the 'Convince Cult'. It acknowledges the existence of God and Christ, but these figures are too remote, and, above all, too closely connected with the whites, for anyone to accept their sovereignty and moral code. Where Negro worshippers establish real contact, on the other hand, is with the spirits of the dead. These are hierarchically divided, according to their special powers, into (1) spirits of Africans, (2) spirits of former slaves or *marrons*, and (3) spirits of Negroes more recently deceased. The object is to obtain immediate material benefits, such as the healing of illnesses, the obtaining of good fortune, or the practice of *obeah* (manufacturing magical objects). The syncretistic rituals, in which Protestant prayers and hymns are found side by side with animal sacrifices and original incantations dictated by the spirits during possession, may be held either in public or in private, according to circumstances. Rites to honour a dead person or placate his angry ghost will be public, whereas the practice of magic (for example) is liable to take place secretly. On the other hand, there is no central organisation and no well-defined priesthood. Rather what we find is a mass of local fraternities (*bongo*) all in competition with one another, each with a cult-leader and a few acolytes. At one time this movement was the mouthpiece for Negro protests against white domination; nowadays, however, it seems gradually to be losing ground. This may

well be the result of the current swing towards political involve-
ment, and the revival of messianism (though with more political
than religious emphasis) in the Ras Tafari movement, to which
I shall return later.[21] In this respect, then, Jamaica confirms
that evolution of escapism into social opposition which we have
already noted as characterising mystery cults in the U.S.A.

IV. *African Spiritualism*

There exists a third type of syncretism, that developed by Negro
converts to spiritualism. We have already come across an
elementary instance of this in Jamaica, where 'Convince Cult'
adherents who undergo possession are known as 'mediums'.
Little is known about the Negro spiritualist movement in Cuba
(*les cordoneros de Orilé*); all we have are a few facts collected by
Fernando Ortiz.[22] The spirits form chains along which passes
the 'mediumistic fluid', and this fluid can send some people
into a special tranced state (temporary possession by the spirit
of a dead man). The 'chain' takes the form of a revolving circle,
as in the African cults, but the movements of those who compose it are regulated by deep breaths, in and out, linked with
contrapuntal movements of arms and feet. These two sound
patterns (breathing and stamping) set up their own resonance,
like a dull two-toned drum; they produce 'a sonorous thrum-
ming, with suggestive and hypnotic side effects, akin to those
produced by the chanting' of the Yoruba sects. It is clear that
what we have here is a reinterpretation of the African ancestor-
cult and cult of the dead through Allan Kardec's spiritualism.
The *macumba* of Rio de Janeiro has been admirably defined by
Arthur Ramos as a syncretistic mixture of *gêge* (Fon), Nago
(Yoruba), Muslim (Black Islam), Bantu, Caboclo (Indian),
spiritualist and Catholic elements. The 'daughters of the gods'
become 'mediums'. The ecstatic trances produced by the dancing
and singing (in Portuguese) involve possession by the spirits of
the dead rather than the *orisha*. We have already seen how this
cult achieved a degree of syncretism with Indian beliefs. What
tends to monopolise the picture increasingly as time goes on is
the syncretistic link-up with spiritualism. Spiritualist concepts
gradually triumph over the original African features. We find
the spirits now divided into various categories: suffering spirits,

malevolent furies, benevolent ghosts. We find the African notion of reincarnation rehashed in spiritualist terms as a return to earth by the souls of the dead to atone for sins committed in their previous existence. There is also the idea of spiritual evolution among the Spirits, achieved by means of successive reincarnations, first on earth, then on other planets, until a point is reached at which the dead become 'Spirits of Light'.[23] But the *macumba*, by thus transforming itself into a form of Negro spiritualism, 'Umbanda spiritualism' as it has been termed, became a 'live religion' (in the special sense I attach to this term) which could give expression to modifications in the country's social structuring – under the impact of urbanisation and industrialisation – as and when they took place.[24]

REFERENCES

1. By Herskovits in particular; see his article 'African Gods and Catholic Saints in New World Negro Belief', *Amer. Anthrop.*, 39, 4, 1937, pp. 635–43.

2. R. Bastide, *Religions africaines*, *op. cit.*, chapter on syncretism.

3. M. Leiris, 'Note sur l'usage de chromolithographies catholiques par les Vodouisants d'Haïti', *Les Afro-Américains*, *op. cit.*, pp. 201–7.

4. To take one example only: *Shangô* is sometimes St Barbara (despite being the wrong sex) because of the association with thunder (Cuba); sometimes St Jerome (Brazil) because St Jerome is represented with a ram beside him, and Shangô's sacrificial animal is the ram; and sometimes as St John the Baptist, because of St John's fires. Even in the same country, therefore, we tend to find a multiplicity of identifications: Ogun, for instance, is equated with St Anthony in Bahia, St George in Recife, and St Onophre in Porto Alegre. Cf. R. Bastide, *op. cit.*

5. D. Pierson, *op. cit.*

6. Milo Marcelin, *op. cit.*

7. In Catholic countries, the moment of tranced possession always remains an exclusively African phenomenon. Catholicism does indeed recognise the ecstatic condition, but is wary of its dangers, and only accepts it in very exceptional circumstances. In Protestant sects, on the other hand (as we shall see), the search for affective religious elements and the importance attached to the baptism of the Holy Spirit eventually led, in Anglo-Saxon America, to the Christianisation of the African trance.

8. Métraux, *op. cit.* Cf. Fr. Thomas Kockmeyer, 'Candomblé', *Sto-Antonio*, 14, 1, 1936, pp. 25–36, and 14, 2, 1936, pp. 123–39.

9. Cf. A. Ramos, *op. cit.*, for Brazil; A. Métraux, *op. cit.*, for Haiti; F. Ortiz, *Os Negros Brujos*, *op. cit.*, for Cuba. There is a large literature on the subject.

10. *The Myth . . . op. cit.*

11. Newbel Niles Puckett, *op. cit.*

12. P. Bernardo Merizalde del Carmen, *op. cit.*

13. Except in those areas where Protestant influence is uppermost, and such games are forbidden – to be replaced by Christian hymns and readings from the Bible; see Th. J. Price Jr., 'Algunos aspectos . . .' *op. cit.*

14. Guy Johnson, *op. cit.*

15. Herskovits, *The Myths . . . op. cit.*; Hortense Powdermaker, *op. cit.*

16. John Hooher, *God in a Rolls-Royce*, New York, 1936; R. A. Parker, *The Incredible Messiah*, Boston, 1937; more recently Hadley Cantril, *The Psychology of Social Movements*, New York, 1941, and Arthur Huff Fauset, *Black Gods of the Metropolis*, Philadelphia, 1944.

17. R. Bastide, *Le candomblé de Bahia, op. cit.*

18. M. J. and F. Herskovits, *Trinidad Village*, New York, 1947.

19. One is reminded of the connection between the *babalão* and the *apetevi*, which was discussed above in ch. V.

20. M. N. Beckwith, *op. cit.*

21. Donald Hogg, 'The Convince Cult in Jamaica', *Papers in Caribbean Anthropology* (ed. S. W. Mintz), Yale University Press, 1960. Similar prophetic or messianic movements are to be found in Puerto Rico; these also feature induced possession, speaking with tongues, messages that carry an eschatological content, healing of sick people by the Holy Ghost, and so on. See also Scott Cook, 'The Prophets: a revivalistic Folk-religious movement in Puerto Rico', *Caribbean Studies* IV, 4, 1965, pp. 20–35.

22. F. Ortiz, *La Africanía de la Música . . . op. cit.* pp. 450–6.

23. R. Bastide, 'La théorie de la réincarnation chez les Afro-Américains', in *Réincarnation et Vie Mystique en Afrique Noire* (ed. Zahn), Paris, 1965, pp. 9–29.

24. I have omitted (as being too exceptional a case) the syncretism which took place between African religions and those of the Indians who were hired *in India* to replace Negro workers in the West Indies after the abolition of slave-labour. At present I am only aware of two instances: the identification of the Yoruba god *Osain* with the Muslim saint *Hossein*, and the use by Negroes in the offerings they make to their divinities of Hindu dishes such as *dhalpuri* or curry. Cf. D. J. Crowley, 'Plural and Differential Acculturation in Trinidad', *Amer. Anthrop.* 59, 5, Oct. 1957.

CHAPTER VIII

THREE KINDS OF FOLKLORE

The folklore of Black America comprises three superimposed layers, or strata, which it would be dangerous to confuse. We must, therefore, make every effort to distinguish between them. First we have an African folklore, a pure traditional core, faithfully preserved. Secondly, there is Negro (or, as we might term it, creole) folklore: this, as its name implies, evolved in America. The process may have been spontaneous, as an expression of Negro sentiments in the face of white domination; or artificial, worked as a method of proselytising the coloured masses. Lastly, there is white folklore, absorbed by the Negroes in their drive to achieve assimilation and social self-betterment. (In the same way the whites borrowed certain dances and types of music from the Negroes, their object being, by hook or crook, to get themselves over the 'threshold of civilisation'.)

I. *African Folklore*

Though religious survivals may be the most spectacular for a foreign observer, they remain a phenomenon restricted to certain privileged areas. African folklore, on the other hand, is to be found everywhere, from the United States to the Rio de la Plata. If we compare their frequency of manifestation, two facts emerge. We have far more evidence for folklore than for religion; and the folklore material is very largely of Bantu origin. So here we have a state of affairs which at first sight might appear somewhat paradoxical: Bantu influence predominates in folklore, whereas – as we have seen – it appears only sporadically in the field of religion.

How are we to explain this? To begin with, we should bear in mind what was said earlier concerning the institutional roots of African survivals. The masters very soon saw that unless they

gave their slaves a chance to dance and celebrate 'their customs', they very soon died, or at any rate worked far less
efficiently. Even aboard the slave-ships the wretched captives
were forced to dance to prevent them dying. Thus both the
dances themselves, and the secular music which accompanied
them, were able to take root wherever slavery existed; and
since the Bantus were firm favourites as field workers, it is not
surprising that 'plantation folklore' everywhere bears traces of
their influence.

There were other elements which encouraged its preservation down the years. To begin with, such dances did not appear
in any way dangerous. They were not a manifestation of
paganism, but simply a form of amusement. The Negroes
were therefore left to enjoy themselves in their own fashion,
without interference (whereas the *candomblés, changô*, and such
things as Myelism or Voodoo were persecuted). Indeed, far
from being dangerous, these dances actually served a useful
purpose during the slave era. Their erotic nature, the whites
hoped, would rouse those who performed them to a high pitch
of sexual excitement; and this, in turn, would lead to the birth
of numerous piccaninnies, a future source of slaves that would
have cost their masters nothing (the labour force was always a
worrying problem). Secondly, the stories managed to survive
because they filled a useful function. They constituted, in one
sense, the compensatory dreams of a subject race, with the
clever animal triumphant over brute force, and little ones
getting their own back on the larger.[1] Furthermore, these tales
gained currency among the whites through Negro nursemaids
and mammies (*mammy, mae preta*); since white mothers often
died young, worn out by too frequent child-bearing, these
mammies were left to look after the orphans single-handed, a
task they carried out with love and devotion – a feeling recip-
rocated by their charges. The Europeans, being literate,
proceeded to publish these stories, thus saving them from the
oblivion which might otherwise have swallowed them up.
Here too, moreover, even after the transference from one race
to another, we find the survival of such tales facilitated by the
fact that they served an equally useful purpose in their new
context. Bantu monsters such as the *quinbungo* underwent a
metamorphosis after crossing the Atlantic, becoming bogeys

used to scare small children. So frightened were the latter of these creatures that they could be enlisted to stop them wetting their beds, going outside the house at night, wandering off into the forest during the day, or refusing to go to sleep when told to by their parents. In other words, they formed the main (African-derived) instrument for teaching small European children good manners.[2] When we turn to the dances, we find it is no longer the black mammy but the coloured lover who exercises a decisive influence, by giving the white male a taste for certain shimmying movements of the hips and other such erotic gestures. Consequently the Negro girl had a valid reason to keep up her choreographic skills, as an instrument of social self-betterment. In this way she could get herself picked as a concubine by her master (or his young son), sometimes ending up loaded with jewels and treated like a queen.

Such, as I see it, are the principal reasons for the importance assumed by African survivals in folklore. There are undoubtedly others, one being the cult of the dead, wherever it has survived. A funeral wake is a special occasion for telling stories, asking riddles and performing dramatic ancestral mimes. On the other hand, the reasons advanced above have universal application, whereas the cult of the dead only survives sporadically. Moreover these reasons also explain the selections and omissions that we find within the body of African folklore as such – why, for example, erotic dances have survived better than the old wrestling matches (the latter are found primarily in towns where robber bands used to be formed, with the object of waylaying and fleecing passers-by).

At this point I will attempt to give a brief descriptive analysis of African folklore in America. At New Orleans, side by side with Dahomean Voodoo, we find the equally popular Bantu *bamboula*, which was danced every Saturday and Sunday evening on the Place des Congo, to the accompaniment of a typically African orchestra: drums made from a hollowed-out tree-trunk, castanets (the two jawbones of an ass), and *marimba*. The women wore bell-bracelets on their ankles. It is, in all likelihood, this same *bamboula* which we find flourishing after the suppression of slavery under the name of *cabinda*. However, in 1843 the authorities banned it because its of obscene nature. The Negroes thereupon transferred their performances from the public square to the taverns; but this change of locale led to corresponding changes in the musical instruments, just as the appearance of Europeans in these 'low-life' taverns resulted in the dances themselves being modified. African folklore gradually vanished, and was replaced by a 'Negro version'. As such, I shall return to it later. On the other hand, the animal tales told by the old-time slaves have survived until our own day, though naturally becoming mixed up in the process with others of European derivation, such as *Renard the Fox*. However, the African Rabbit still remains the principal hero of these mischievous stories. For obvious reasons it is hard to discover a genealogy for the proverbs and riddles so dear to the Negro's heart. On the other hand certain children's games in the deep south (one example – despite its name – being 'King George's Army'), in which two opposing teams are formed according to their choice of some plant or animal, have African parallels.[3] In Mexico, the records of the Inquisition for 1766 refer to a dance performed by four men and four women, the most characteristic feature of which was the *ombligada* (navel-to-navel contact). This is a trait common to all erotic dances in Angola. We also know that in addition to these dances, brought over by the slaves, the Spaniards themselves popularised in Mexico two dances, *El Maracumbi* and *El Paracumbé*, that they had learnt in Africa and subsequently brought back to Spain. The European craze for Negro customs, we see, is by no means a recent innovation.[4] In Ecuador the coastal population is predominantly Negro; yet the only instance known to us of an African dance there, the *bomba*,[5] chiefly danced at Christmas time (though to the accompaniment of songs in Spanish) comes from a northern valley, that of the Rio Chota, now inhabited by the descendants of the Jesuits' slaves.[6] In Colombia, a number of Negro folk-tales have been collected from the Chaco region by Rogerio Velasquez. Some, such as those to do with the spider, are clearly African, as are those concerning the crow and the tiger; others are syncretistic.[7] The musical instruments – drums, *bombo*, *marimba*, *maraca* – are African, like many of the dances which they accompany. These include the *bullarengue*, the *currulao* (which mimes the first amorous approaches between a man and a woman),[8] the *caderina*, *agualarga*, *agua chica* or *madrugada* (which last for several days, and take place on the Pacific coast),[9] and – last but not least – the *bambuco*. This last supposedly derives its name from an African tribe known as Bambouk, and in its sung version has passed into the national musical repertoire.[10]

Venezuela too has dances of Bantu origin, which have survived by attaching themselves to the cults of two saints: one a Negro, St Benedict the Moor, and the other St John the Baptist. To honour the former, worshippers perform the *chimbangueleros* (so named from the drum *chimbanqueli*), for which participants still wear straw skirts. The latter has the *malembe* and the *sangueo* (from the Bantu word *sanga*, to dance), which both form part of the 'Drum Festival'.[11] In Peru, the various dances of the African nations, such as the *panalivio* and the *sereno*, were banned as dangerous 'not merely on account of their movements but also because of the verses which accompanied them'. They did not, however, disappear. The Abbé de la Blanchardière notes the existence of 'African dances' in 1747, and the *Peru Mercury* for 1791 provides us with evidence for these choreographic performances which confirms their Bantu origin. The climax, indeed, took the form of the *golpe de frente*, i.e. navel-to-navel contact. During the eighteenth century mulatto influence tended to oust that of the Negroes; yet even so the Bantu fiddle (*quijada*) and the *cuica* were still used to provide an accompaniment a hundred years later. Meanwhile traditional choreography had blended with Spanish flamenco to produce the great national dance (known variously as *zamba*, *cueca*, or *zamacueca*), which represents the amorous pursuit of a woman by a man, and ends with the couple embracing voluptuously. This rapidly spread to Argentina on one side and Bolivia on the other. Since it was danced both by blacks and whites, it not unexpectedly developed various modifications according to the race or social status of those performing it. In 1841 Max Radiguet remarked of it 'The Negroes are degrading Peru's elegant, passionate dances by introducing into them various grotesque posturings and jerky, disorganised movements borrowed from their own African *bamboulas*.'[12] In Uruguay, African folklore is represented by a few rare animal stories in which the main character is the tiger, and a number of dances, also once found in Argentina, but today virtually non-existent in either country. These include the *calenda* (the same name as that we find in Louisiana, and characterised by navel-to-navel contact); the *bamboula*, here a warrior-dance, with much beating of sticks on shields; the *chica*, an erotic dance; and lastly the famous *candomblé* (this term denotes a secular dance in Rio de la Plata, a religious dance in Brazil) with its dancing processions and *rondes*. Though the *candomblé* has not become entirely obsolete, it underwent considerable modifications about the end of the nineteenth century. In Montevideo it became a dancing procession, that of the *lubolos*, held during Carnival, while in Argentina it survived in the form of the tango.[13]

In Brazil, again, we find Negro folklore coloured by the same Bantu influences. Though its name varies according to the region, the dance remains fundamentally the same: either in two rows, men opposite women, or else in a circle, with a couple performing in the middle, miming the choice of sexual partners. Names for this dance include *bambelô* (a word from the Quimbundo vocabulary), *jongo*, *batuque* or *samba* (*semba* in Angola refers to navel-rubbing; the Brazilian term is *umbigada*). But these dances, especially in the central and southern regions, are accompanied by chanting; and though the language employed is Portuguese, this practice embodies two characteristically African features. First, there is the improvisation of verses by the soloist, to see if they will 'take' – which they do when the dancers pick them up and repeat them. Secondly, we have the tradition of a contest between two singers. The form it takes is as follows. One of the two asks the other a riddle to which he must find the answer. The conundrums posed are not the Western sort, but rather the kind of African riddle which employs a special symbolic language. Using images that occasionally recall those of Mallarmé, they simultaneously conceal and hint at their underlying significance. The *afoshe* of the Bahia Carnival seems to be a reminiscence of royal processions in the Congo. Among the games, we may note the *capoeira de Angola*, a remarkable type of wrestling, once popular with young toughs in Rio and other towns. In Bahia, as a result of intervention by the police, it has been transformed into a kind of ballet, full of vaulting and somersaults and other acrobatic feats. In Rio, similarly, it has become the *cambapé;*

at Recife it survives, in somewhat fragmentary form, as a Carnival dance, the *frevo* (intermingled with movements from military marches). The stories can be divided into two categories. First we have animal fables: these are of multiple origin, since variants turn up in numerous African ethnic groups. The second category covers fairy tales, for which, again, African parallels can be found. The form which such stories assume during performance is identical on either side of the Atlantic. They are part spoken, part sung, with the narrator adopting a different voice and gestures for each character he brings on. For this reason some Brazilian folklorists have labelled such recitals 'theatrical monologues'. Numerous musical instruments have successfully crossed the Atlantic; in consequence the singing is still marked by genuine African rhythms. These accompanying instruments include the *adja* (an iron bell struck with an iron bar), the Yoruba *agogô*, the musical bow (of Bantu origin), the *candongueiro* (a drum made from a hollowed-out tree-trunk), the *marimba* or African piano, the *puita* or *roncador*, and others.[14]

In the Antilles, Haiti yields an especially rich crop, with its tales of Bouki, Malice and Jean Sauté; Malice inheriting the spider's guile, and Bouki her awkwardness.[15] There are also dances of Bantu origin such as the *kalenda*, described by Moreau de Saint-Mery; and Ewe-derived dances like the *bottonie* or stick-dance; and dances that were originally Bantu, but have now evolved into something quite different – e.g. the cumbite *bamboula*.[16] We may note the importance attached to proverbs and riddles, with syncretism between the African and French traditions. There exist various songs of complaint, recrimination and ridicule, their purpose being to make one's enemy look, a fool, or to resolve a quarrel by turning it into songs – as we find being done by the wives of the same polygamous husband in the markets of Dahomey. There are songs of boasting and defiance, political songs, work chants, and so on – but in all of them the African element is being 'creolised'.[17] There are children's games, such as the *alo*, also of Fon origin, not to mention various musical instruments.[18] The *méringue*, found not only in Haiti, but also in Guadeloupe and Martinique, far from being African, is an old French dance, formerly popular at court; it is only the fact of its being danced by 'creoles' which gives it, nowadays, a vaguely African air. The French Antilles also have a 'combat dance', the *laggia*, and various animal stories. To the best of my knowledge, Cuba is the only country where proverbs have been preserved in an African tongue. (Such proverbs, as in Africa, are very often simply the conclusion, or 'moral', of a story – which must be equally familiar to the Cuban peasant.)[19] The Negro population of the island enjoy telling stories at wakes – either animal fables or fairy tales – in which the *orisha* come down and mingle with mankind. Some of these stories have been exquisitely transcribed for our benefit by Lydia Cabrera, in two books available in French.[20] Fernando Ortiz has devoted a very considerable work to the study of Afro-Cuban music, and the various musical instruments of African origin in use in Cuba.[21] In particular, he has shed much light on a number of special phenomena. He notes the existence in Cuba, as in Brazil, of collective improvisation by Negro singers. He recognises the importance of literary contests such as the *puya*, *managua* or *makagua*, which throw some of these remarkable improvisers into competition with one another, using the same set theme. Nor does he neglect the so-called 'songs of sanction', directed against any one who, in terms of the Negro ethical code, has committed some reprehensible act, an. thus form a marvellous instrument of social coercion. He acknowledges the variety of African dances surviving on the island, some of which (such as the *rumba brava*) include navel-to-navel contact (*vacunao*), while the chief ones in evey case (religion aside) are of obvious Bantu origin. They include the *yuka* and *caringa* (calenda), in all likelihood the *danse de mani* (a kind of pugilists' dance which recalls the Brazilian *capoeira*), and, first and foremost, the famous *rumba* itself, which mimes the preliminaries of love-making between two people. If the reader wishes to form some idea of the richness and variety of African-derived musical elements still surviving in Cuba, he cannot do better than consult Ortiz's *magnum opus* on musical instruments of African origin, from knocking-sticks to drums, *ashanti*, *arara*, *congos*, *lucumi* and *abakua*. All of which, taken broadly, goes to show that though Haitian and Cuban folklore have been shaped, to a large extent, by Bantu influence; nevertheless the Ewe and Yoruba have also added their contribution. Fanti–

Ashanti influence, on the other hand, predominates in two areas: first, in Suriname folklore, where we find various features which recall it – *anansi* stories,[22] riddles, proverbs (*taki-taki*), certain special types of dances, songs designed to ridicule a rival in love, or a lover who has deserted you (*lobi singi*, or love songs), perhaps also those curious homosexual love songs designed to celebrate a lover's birthday; secondly, in Jamaica, the Bahamas, indeed generally speaking throughout the British Antilles, where *anansi* the spider, animal stories and Ghana love songs are universally known.[23]

We cannot cite every characteristically African feature of oral and motor folklore throughout Black America. The examples already given should, by and large, suffice to indicate the importance of this phenomenon, and the wide area, geographically speaking, which it covers. My necessarily brief survey does not, however, ignore the trend which encouraged a process of 'creolisation' in some of these features. Fernando Ortiz could write, wittily and with justice, of 'mulatto' drums and African drums being found side by side. This naturally leads us to our second stratum: Negro folklore.

II. *Negro Folklore*

Negro (as opposed to African) folklore has a twofold origin. In the first place, we find a gradual process of 'creolisation'. This is a spontaneous development, arising within the context of Afroamerican culture through adaptation to environment and the assimilation of European elements. Side by side with it, however, there exists a second, quite different body of folklore, deliberately created by the whites for their slaves; based, it is true, on fragments borrowed from Africa, but reinterpreted in such a way as to facilitate proselytisation among the Negroes. We shall deal with these two 'folklores' separately.

Tales of revenge or compensation have their origin in the plantations. They may still follow age-old models, and serve the same social or psychological function; yet at the same time they are wholly invented, in response to the specific new demands created by slavery. Such, for instance, are the stories of Old John (Père Jean), who, despite his apparent stupidity, succeeds in outwitting his white master, or even (a still more sacrilegious notion) in sleeping with his master's wife or daughter. The symbolic riddles no longer employ traditional symbols, but invent new ones, to express hitherto unheard-of sociological realities: slavery, *marronage*, the captain whose business it is to hunt down fugitives, and contemporary political allusions. The dances, too, have been 'creolised', with a view to fulfilling somewhat different functions. The *calenda*-type Bantu dance, for instance, has lost its original purpose, that of arousing sexual excitement. In America, at least, its role is now an exclusively sociological one – that of promoting Negro solidarity against the whites, or the old against the young (who prefer somewhat different pleasures). The *umbigada* (navel-to-navel contact) still survives, but now its aim is to strike one's dancing adversary so hard a blow with one's out-thrust belly that he falls over. Eros has been transformed into an *agon*. As for the chants, I have already remarked more than once that, though they preserve an African typology, they have changed their language, and now deal, in an improvised fashion, with the ever-changing day-to-day life of the coloured community. In short, if African folklore can be defined in structural terms, its *ad hoc* Negro equivalent looks more of a fortuitous, contingential phenomenon – whether considered from the geographical, historical, social or economic viewpoint. Here I shall restrict myself to giving two illustrations, one taken from the U.S.A. and the other from Cuba.

The slave created a plantation folklore, quite different from that of Africa, and in response to a new social situation. At the same time he continued to model his chants – in the English language – on the traditional pattern, a dialogue between soloist and choir. From now on, however, we see the choir steadily gaining ground at the expense of the soloist, with work songs, songs of revolt, and also (naturally) love songs. Later, with the development of the Protestant revivalist movement, religious songs (Negro spirituals) began to draw their inspiration from the Bible, in particular from the sufferings of the Jews in the Old Testament, as a means of expressing hope in the ultimate liberation of the Negroes. Secular songs were accompanied by clapping and stamping, spirituals by a rhythmic rocking of the head and body (swing). Today, the emergence of the Blues (note the link with depression, what the

French term *le cafard*) marks a new stage in the process of 'creolisation'. The Blues embody the individual virtuosity of inspired singers, whereas other types of Negro music are group-inspired, choral. As regards the music itself, we can observe a gradual evolution from the Congo dances of New Orleans to ragtime. This change is associated with the name of Didi Chandles, who introduced a new idea of percussion into creole dance music, jettisoned traditional African instruments in favour of those used by the whites, and at the same time 'Africanised' European dance tunes by playing them in the red-light districts (since over-noisy music was forbidden, the Negro had perforce to restrict himself to the piano and muted trumpets). Here we can see the beginning of the history of jazz (a word perhaps derived from the French *jaser*, to chatter or gossip); it is, clearly, the product of musical syncretism, which followed on as a result of the break with Africa.[24] A Negro creation undoubtedly; but despite this, there is no longer anything African about it.

Quite apart from this spontaneous folklore there exists another, more artificial variety, deliberately manufactured by Europeans – in particular by the clergy – for the benefit of their slaves, according to the formula which had worked so well with the Indians. The first step was to make a selection of Negro dances, eliminating (for instance) the erotic ones, but keeping the war-dances. Negro drama would be encouraged, with great emphasis on the old African traditions of Bantu royalty, and ambassadors between kingdoms. Advantage was taken of the Negro passion for processions, bright-coloured costumes and music. In short, all these features of African culture could, by adroit manipulation, be exploited to the glory of God and holy church.

It is true, nevertheless, that on occasion the Negroes (at least those of the *marron* communities) would modify the theatrical material provided for them by Europeans in order to express their rebellious sentiments. Thus in Panama we have a dramatic piece entitled *Juan de Dioso*, dealing with the Congo rising in the time of Simon Bolivar. This popular play embodies certain African features – e.g. the authority of the queen, who plans the revolt, is greater than that of the king, Juan de Dioso. It also reinterprets certain elements in the original

Catholic playlet: the death of the prince during the war is ascribed to his treachery – captured as a runaway slave, he betrays his own brothers to gain freedom for himself. Lastly, it turns the Devil into a symbolic image of white domination. However, the Devil is finally caught, baptised, and sold at auction.[25] At Veracruz in Mexico (another region which experienced a Negro rebellion) we find a dance known as *la danza de los Negritos*, which evokes memories of the slaves. Celebrated at Christmas, this balletic mime tells the story of a Spanish corporal who is bitten by a snake. The theme can be paralleled from popular theatre in Africa, but here it is aimed at a soldier who symbolises white power and authority.[26] Yet on the whole we do not find the slaves rejecting this folklore imposed on them by the Catholic church; they preserved its pattern with only minor modifications.

The *Congos* or *Congadas*, which are found throughout Catholic America, from Mexico to Brazil, no doubt came into being through the election of the 'Congo kings'. These dignitaries (like the 'governors' of Protestant America) were elected with a view to disciplining the behaviour of slaves, and also to act as intermediaries between masters and their servants. This was an old Hispano-Portuguese custom (though in the Iberian peninsula it served a purely religious function) practised by the Negro groups imported to Europe.[27] When, during the eighteenth century, the observance was introduced to America, we find the election taking place in the morning, to be followed later by a dramatic dance, or mime. Such dances are, broadly speaking, of three types. First there are those of a processional type, virtually a full-dress parade of the ancient African court, complete with king, queen, standard-bearer (or doll-bearer), and ladies-in-waiting. To the accompaniment of tambourines, they make their way down through the town and perform dances outside the houses of notable citizens. Such processions have different names according to the area – *congos* at Sergippe, *taiêras* or *maracatús* in Recife, *afoshé* in Bahia, *cambindas* in Parahyba, and so on.[28] Then there are the processions with ambassadors, when the Congo king and queen sit in state on the public square to receive embassies from the kings of Angola, Cassamba, Mozambique and – last but not least – from Queen Ginga.[29] In the third and last variety, some ambassador from a pagan people offers the Christian Congo king a choice between submission or war, and the Congo king chooses war. Sometimes the ambassador is omitted, and we have a sudden attack by an enemy group while the Negroes are celebrating the feast of the circumcision. At all events, a major battle takes place between two groups of dancers, and during this battle the son of the Congo king is killed. An appeal is then made to a sorcerer (*quimboto*) who brings the corpse back to life. The battle is resumed, and the pagans are finally defeated, after which they beg for Christian baptism. The festivities end with hymns to the Virgin and 'coloured' saints.[30] These *congadas* bear some resemblance to those dances known as *caboclinhos*, in which the performers are Indians rather than Negroes, but which follow the same general pattern (the death and resurrection of a princess).[31] On the other hand, they should be clearly distinguished from the so-called *mozambiques*, which, broadly speaking, are straightforward singing and dancing (with sticks), and not a dramatic performance. In the folklore hierarchy, we find the *congada* at the top, and the *mozambiques* very near the bottom.[32]

At Epiphany, the Negroes of Bahia used to go round dancing and singing from house to house, demanding food, money or brandy, and accompanied by *papier-mâché* animals – the ox and the ass from the Christmas crib. Perhaps under the influence of their former clan-totemism, they added a number of extra animals to this Christian bestiary, including the ostrich, the lion, the elephant, and others. These were known as *ranchos*. In the Alagoas region, again at Epiphany, we find a new development, starting from the ox and the hobby-horse; the dancing procession gradually evolves into a theatrical troupe. As such it performs a whole series of sketches (these may be fairy tales, like 'The Fisherman and the Siren', or burlesque, e.g. 'The Servant'), ending up with a performance of *Bumba-meu-boi*, which recounts the death and resurrection of the ox.[33] The *reisado* comes nearer to being theatre than does the *rancho*, though the latter does contain one prime dramatic element in the conflict between fisherman and fish, hunter and tiger (Brazilian panther), or whatever other animal may be mimed or carried in procession. On the other hand there is no trace, as yet, of the death-and-resurrection theme. Doubtless it could be argued that this theme was a Negro creation, and in fact we do find similar small sketches in various parts of Africa.[34] On the other hand they also turn up among the Christianised Indians of Venezuela and Colombia,[35] and indeed in Europe, where the concept is connected with vegetation cults, the death of winter, and the resurrection of plants, symbolised in Cornwall by the hobby-horse, which is 'killed' and brought back to life again, just like the *Bumba-meu-boi* ox.[36] The notion of an ox that dies and is resurrected also occurs in Mexico,[37] but this time among the Indian population. There can be no doubt that even though the Negro embraced this theme because it suited his mentality, nevertheless the theme *per se* has its roots in Europe. Sometimes, indeed, the clergy would seem to have given it a Christian flavour which it did not originally possess. At Manaos, for instance, in a mystery-play performed in honour of the Negroes' patron saint, St Benedict the Moor, we find the Saint miraculously reconstructing the body of a fisherman who had been chopped in pieces by the Devil, and then bringing him back to life.[38]

Thus, in addition to the African traditions preserved by slaves and their descendants, we find another, exclusively Negro, body of folklore, bound up with what we might term 'folk' Catholicism. The colonial period, in fact, throughout Latin America, was marked by a firm determination to make Africa Christian – though this did not entail absorbing black converts wholesale into the white man's church. Instead, a new brand of Catholicism was worked out specially for Negroes, complete with its own fraternities and festivals. Later, the church changed its policy, banning dancing and repudiating the election of kings and queens; but the custom was too firmly rooted to disappear altogether. Driven from the temple, it went on in the street and has so continued to this day.[39]

III. *Class Barriers, Levels of Culture*[40]

Throughout America, in addition to Negro or African folklore, we find an important stratum which derives from Europe. The master-slave class antithesis finds natural expression in the contrast between these two patterns of folklore. On the night of a festival, while the Congos performed traditional erotic dances outside their shanties, up in the big house ballroom, to the strains of piano and violin, Europeans too would be dancing – in their case, the waltz or the quadrille. In Brazil, the Bantus called their kings *congadas*, but the whites had their own 'Emperor of the Holy Ghost', who could only be a European. Granted such conditions, one can understand why the Negroes (in their longing for social integration and self-betterment) were so determined to infiltrate European folklore, the very symbol of social superiority. After the abolition of servile labour they succeeded in their aim, though mulattoes tended to make the grade sooner than really dark-skinned Negroes. Yet as they conquered this hitherto forbidden territory, so the whites tended to abandon it, with the object of setting up fresh caste or class barriers.

One privilege in which the ruling class took great pride was, undoubtedly, the use of the horse. The medieval tradition of tournaments, games of skill, and mounted messengers galloping hotfoot along the roads survived in Spanish and Portuguese America, under the name of *cavalhadas*. But in order to participate in it one needed a horse, and this condition automatically debarred the Negro.⁴¹ Yet he won through to the privileged enclosure, though at first it was only by the tradesmen's entrance – i.e. through the mock battles of Moors and Christians, which celebrated the reconquest of the Iberian peninsula after its long domination by Islam. Because of their colour, the Negroes were naturally cast to play the part of the Moors – though of course they had to fight on foot. Nevertheless, this was the thin end of the wedge; eventually the Negro too, got astride a horse. To begin with, his role in these dramatic interludes was that of villain or buffoon. After a while, however, the European withdrew altogether, leaving him the entire field to himself. As a result it is by no means uncommon, on some Brazilian village square, to see a galloping Charlemagne or Roland who is (to borrow the time-honoured cliché of folklore) 'as black as coal'.⁴²

Another occasion exclusively reserved for whites was the nativity festival known to the French as *les Pastorales*, and celebrated throughout Mediterranean Europe between Christmas and Epiphany. It consisted of a kind of competition between two teams of young girls, all drawn from the very best families, one team wearing red sashes, the other blue. They sang a number of songs in the character of shepherdesses going to Bethlehem to worship the infant Jesus, and interspersed these with little verse sketches (also sung) with titles like 'The Laundresses' or 'The Flight of the Butterfly'. On Epiphany Day the cribs were burnt, and the European festival came to an end. The Negroes, however, now celebrated the feast day of St Balthazar, one of the Three Kings – and of the same colour as themselves. As part of the fun they were allowed to go round from house to house and farm to farm, singing, dancing, and demanding money or food. Here, at the earliest possible moment, the Negroes contrived to encroach on forbidden territory. They organised amateur troupes to perform the *'pastorales'*, not in the drawing-room, but in barns or coach-houses. These performances may have been somewhat idiosyncratic, but they always involved the two teams, with their blue and red sashes. The whites, as we know from contemporary newspaper reports, took this presumptuous innovation on the part of their former slaves extremely badly. They denounced the immorality to which such occasions supposedly gave rise, talking darkly of mulatto women who profited by these performances to promote their own profession (i.e. that of prostitution). So the *'pastorales'* disappeared from European drawing-rooms – at least until our own times, which have seen an attempt (on the part of the Folklore Commission) to revive them, in their original (i.e. European) form.

The literary contests which, in Europe, had once set minstrels and troubadours in competition with one another (sometimes on religious themes, more often on problems of cosmology, history or geography), were kept up in Spanish and Portuguese America, under the name of *desafio*. (For Spanish America, see, e.g. José Hernandez's *Martin Fierro*.) Such contests brought together men with a remarkable gift for improvisation, who 'warmed up' their individual talents by shouting abuse at each other. The audience decided the winner. The Negro, who had excellent reasons for wanting to release his pent-up fury against the white man, could now do so with impunity, since the whole thing was just a game. Consequently here, too, he plunged headlong into what had hitherto been a Europeans-only contest. In Brazil, resounding battles took place between white and Negro improvisers, the results of which were printed on broadsheets and made known throughout the *sertāo*. Very often, thanks to his sense of humour, it would be the Negro who ended by triumphing over the more bad-tempered onslaughts of his white opponent. Thus one black competitor, accused of belonging to the race of Ham, at once retorted:

> It was a white man, Judas,
> Who betrayed Our Lord.

To mockery directed at his colour, one Negro replied:

> White paper is worthless in itself
> But write on it
> With black ink
> And it's worth millions.[43]

Or again, take this couplet, from Argentina, thrown off by the Negro competing with Martin Fierro:

> I too have something white about me –
> The whiteness of my teeth.

The Jesuits were not slow to realise the way in which they could manipulate these literary contests to proselytise among the Indians. They organised a kind of competitive debating system among the natives, to argue out the most fundamental questions of the Faith. Rhyme schemes and topics were both announced in advance, and the debates themselves were interspersed with dances. These purely religious contests, which opened with prayers, survived among the Brazilian half-breeds under the name of *cururú*: a sort of folk-cult, which took place at night, and during which – as though to emphasise its Catholic-based absolutism – all profane dances and other pleasures were strictly forbidden. This was something which the Negro found radically antipathetic. But with the rural exodus, the *cururú* made its way to town, where it was progressively secularised. The Negro took advantage of this to infiltrate it, little by little, and ended up playing a leading part in the proceedings. Examples could be multiplied; there is, perhaps, not a single manifestation of European folklore which has not been taken over (whether gradually or in one fell swoop) by those of African descent. The best-known case, however, is undoubtedly that of Carnival.

Carnival as such is an institution of comparatively recent origin. Its place was formerly occupied by a group of rites designed to procure rain; these included throwing bucketsful of water about, or, alternatively, eggs filled with scented water (according to whether the district was lower-class or otherwise). This ceremony was known as *Entrudo* in Portugal, and Carnival in the South of France. In the form described above it has now disappeared (confetti was substituted for water), and no longer preserves its original function, that of a rain festival – except perhaps in North Africa. It is the new-style Carnival, with its processions, masks and balls, which has emerged triumphant in the southern states of the U.S.A., throughout the Antilles and in Guiana and Brazil. Yet even to this day it still retains its dual nature. For Europeans, Carnival is a drawing-room festival, sometimes with highly selective right of entry. For the Negro, it means fun in the streets. Though black and white do mingle to some extent in the general merriment, the former master-race has contrived to set up a new barrier against any levelling tendency, based, this time, on money. The most interesting thing from our point of view is that the whole body of African folklore (now fast disappearing among the younger generation) and its Negro counterpart (such as the *congos* and *mozambiques*, originally created by the church, but now under its interdict) remains very much alive at Carnival time. We have the royal leaders of the religious fraternities, who can no longer dance outside the church, and whose processions are known as *afoshe* (Bahia) or *maracatú* (Recife). There are the *Reisados*, with their animal-totems lurking behind the ox or ass of the crib. There are the *sambas*, and the *capoeira* which has become transformed into a *frevo* (Recife), and so on. As far as Brazil is concerned, this movement has been admirably described by A. Ramos: 'Every year this collective catharsis comes rolling, avalanche-like, into June 11th Square in Rio de Janeiro (known locally as "A Praça Onze"). Here Carnival merely serves as a handy excuse . . . . What takes place here, within a very brief time-span, is the recapitulation of a whole collective way of life. Institutions crumble or melt, become fragmented; what remains of them is gathered up on the Praça Onze. The Praça Onze is a vast mixer, a gigantic mill, which refines unconscious material and prepares it for its entry into "civilisation". A whole range of activity much akin to that of dream-elaboration (*Traumarbeit*) can be observed here; ideas coalesce, acquire symbols or masks, are sublimated, hive off into fresh concepts...', The Praça Onze is the frontier between Negro and white European culture, a frontier without clear-cut lines of demarcation, where a two-way traffic of influence exists between rival institutions, where the two cultures fuse and melt.'[44] What goes for Brazil goes for America as a whole. Negro musical processions in Martinique, though banned by the governors, made themselves a safe niche in the Carnival celebrations, where they are still take place unopposed. The Haitian secret societies of witches and warlocks similarly take part in Carnival processions, thus transforming the terrifying to the merely grotesque; among them we find such groups as Les Calinda, or the *Cochons Rouges* (Red Pigs). Paulo de Carvalho Neto has recently studied the way in which the Loanga 'nation' of Uruguay was transformed into a Carnival troupe – the last avatar of Africa by the Rio de la Plata (River Plate). Everywhere the prcoess is identical.[45]

This levelling-out process does not stop the European erecting new barriers designed to guard against any encroachment on his folklore or his festivals. Yet, paradoxically, he has no qualms about accepting Negro dances – one result of his (sometimes repressed) sexual desire for black women. He does, however, introduce modifications into them, designed to emphasise the difference between *his* way of dancing and that adopted by the descendants of his erstwhile slaves. This is a well-established phenomenon; we find one instance of it as early as the eighteenth century, with a certain erotic Bantu dance which mulattoes of both sexes transformed into the *lundu* – the first attempt to 'civilise' a dance regarded as 'savage' or 'animal'. The tango performed by Buenos Aires Negroes, in a modified form which preserved no more than a faint reminiscence of the sexual act, rapidly conquered Argentina, and thence spread over the entire world. The Brazilian samba, as practised by Negroes in the big cities, soon jettisoned navel-to-navel contact, and became a special Carnival song-and-dance act, with lengthy preliminary rehearsals in the 'samba schools' of Rio de Janeiro. It was this mildly saccharine version which the whites afterwards accepted – though even so they took all the erotic excitement out of it, and turned it into a 'white' dance. There is no point in listing all those dances of African origin, such as the shimmy, the rumba, or the habanera, which have been bastardised with Western music, and 'softened up' in such a way that, despite the European's well-known weakness for 'the lower depths', a barrier is erected between Africa and Europe. This barrier is a fragile one, it is true, since Negroes are now liable to get their own back by dancing 'European style', at least in the drawing-rooms of the coloured middle classes. The result is a constant interchange between the two folklores, occasioned by this racial battle to achieve ultimate equality; a process of struggle, competition, and shifts of balance from one camp to the other, involving a fresh transformation with each new move.

REFERENCES

1. This point has been well brought out by Peter Haworth, *Rumors and Hoaxes, Classic Tales of Fraud and Deception*, 1928, as regards North America (cited by B. A. Botkin, ed., *A Treasury of American Folklore*, New York, 1944); and by Octavio da Costa Eduardo, 'O folklore duma comunidade', *Rev. Arqu. Mun. de S. Paulo*, CXLIV, 1951.

2. This aspect of the case has been fully brought out, for Brazil, by Gilberto Freyre, *Maîtres et Esclaves*, French trs., Paris, 1952, and Luis da Camara Cascudo, *Geografia dos mitos brasileiros*, Rio de Janeiro, 1947.

3. N. N. Puckett, *op. cit.*; Joël Chandler Harris, *Uncle Remus and his Friends*, Boston, 1892; etc.

4. Vicente T. Mendoza, 'Algo del folklore negro em Mexico', in *Miscellanea de estudios dedicados a F. Ortiz*, vol. II, La Habana, 1956.

5. D. A. Preston, 'Negro, Mestizo and India in an Andean Environment', *The Geographical Journal*, 131, 2, 1965.

6. P. Penaherrera de Costales and A. Costales Samaniego, 'Loangue', *Llacta*, Quito, 1959.

7. Rogerio Velasquez M., 'Cuentos de la raza negra', *Rev. Col. de Folclor*, 3, 1959, and 'Leyendas y cuentos de la raza negra', *idem*, 4, 1960.

8. Enrique Perez Arbelaez, 'El. Currulao', *idem*, 3, 1959.

9. P. B. Marizalde de Carmen, *op. cit.*

10. Carlos Restrepo Canal, *Leyes de Manumision*, Bogota, 1935; Th. Price Jr., 'Estado y necessidades . . .' *op. cit.* Cf. for Bolivia, Costa Arguedas, 'El Folklore negro em Bolivia', *Tradicion*, Cuzco, 6, 11, 1954.

11. Juan Pablo Sojo, 'Algunas supervivencias negro-culturales en

Venezuela', *Rev. Venez. de Folklore*, I, 2, 1948; Juan Liscano, *Folklore y Cultura*, Venezuela, n.d.

12. Fernando Romero, 'La Costa Zamba', *Ultra* IX, 57, 1941; 'Instrumentos negros en la costa Zamba', *Turismo*, 134, Lima, 1939; 'Ritmo negro on la costa Zamba', *idem*, 135, 1939; 'De la Zamba de Africa a la mariniera del Peru', *Estudios Afrocubanos*, IV, 1–4, 1940.

13. I. Pereda Valdes, *op. cit.*; Vicente Rossi, *Cosas de Negros*, Buenos Aires, 1944; Paulo de Carvalho Neto, *El Negro Uruguayo*, Quito, 1965; Anthology: *Los Morenos*, Buenos Aires, 1942.

14. Arthur Ramos, *O Folklore Negro do Brasil*, Rio de Janeiro, 1935; Oneyda Alvarenga, *A Musica Popular no Brasil*, Rio de Janeiro, 1950; Alceu Maynard Araujo, *Folklore National*, 3 vols., S. Paulo, 1964. Every variant type of dance or game has given rise to numerous articles. Here I will cite only two, that by M. W. Vieira da Cunha and Mario de Andrade, 'O Samba rural', *Revue do Arqu. Mun. de S. Paulo*, 41, 1937, and that by Renato Almeida on the *capoeira*, *idem*, 54, 1939. For the stories, see especially the collections assembled by Nina Rodrigues, *Os Africanos ...*, *op. cit.*, and J. da Silva Campos, the latter published by Basilio de Magalhaes, *O Folklore ao Brasil*, Rio de Janeiro, 1925.

15. Remy Bastien, 'Anthologie du Folklore haïtien', *Acta Anthropologica*, Mexico, 1946; H. Courlander, *Uncle Bouqui of Haiti*, New York, 1942; M. Hyppolite, *La littérature populaire haïtienne*, Port-au-Prince, 1950.

16. M. Lamartinière Honorat, *Les Danses folkloriques haïtiennes*, Port-au-Prince, 1955; and Katherine Dunham, *Les Danses d'Haïti*, Fasquelles, n.d.

17. These songs, at once compensatory and cathartic, are interpreted by Herskovits (with specific reference to those of Dahomey) in terms of Freudian mechanisms; see M. J. Herskovits, 'Freudian Mechanisms in Primitive Negro Psychology', in *Essays presented to C. G. Seligman*, London, 1936, pp. 75–84. We shall meet them again when discussing the former British colonies, below. Though as strictly occasional songs they may have undergone certain modifications, they always adhere to an African *pattern*. On Haitian songs in general, see Harold Courlander, *Haiti Singing*, North Carolina, 1939; Lorimer Denis, *Quelques aspects de notre folklore musical*, Port-au-Prince, 1950, and *Chants et jeux des enfants haïtiens*, Port-au-Prince, 1949.

18. L. Denis and E. C. Paul, *Essai d'Organographie haïtienne*, Port-au-Prince, n.d.

19. Lydia Cabrera, *Refranos Cubanos*, La Habana, 1956.

20. Lydia Cabrera, *Contes Nègres de Cuba*, Paris, 1936; and *Pourquoi?*, Gallimard, 1954.

21. *Op. cit.* Cf. also José L. Franco, *Folklore criollo y afrocubano*, La Habana, 1959.

22. A certain number will be found in M. J. and F. Herskovits, *Suriname Folklore*, *op. cit.*, together with African parallels. Most of the latter are Ashanti, but we also find Toucouleur, Bambara and Mossi.

23. M. W. Beckwith, 'Jamaica Anansi Stories', *Memoirs Amer. Folk. Soc.* XVII, New York, 1924; *Folk Games in Jamaica*, 1922; *Jamaica Proverbs*, 1925. Going back to an earlier date we may note the examples collected by Mrs Milne Holne, *Mama's Black Nurse Stories*, Edinburgh, 1890; P. Coleman

Smith, *Anancy Stories*, New York, 1899; and Helen H. Roberts, 'Possible survivals of African songs in Jamaica', *Musical Quarterly*, 1926.

24. J. W. Johnson, *Book of American Negro Spirituals*, New York, 1925; W. Russell and S. W. Smith, *Jazzmen*, New York, n.d.; Olivier, *Le monde des blues*, Paris, 1962.

25. Victor M. Franceschi, 'Los Negros Congos en Panamá', *Loteria* (Panama), V, 51, 1960. The occasional appearance of animals in this dramatic interlude – the tiger, the ant, the crow – may also be a (totemic?) African element, but the point remains open to argument.

26. V. T. Mendoza, *op. cit.*

27. Renato de Almeida quotes instances in his *History of Brazilian Music*, and we know that such coronations of kings and queens continued, in Portugal, as late as the decade between 1840 and 1850 (Pinto de Carvalho, *História do Fado*, Lisbon, 1903).

28. Melo Morães filho, *Festas e Tradições populares*, Rio de Janeiro, 1888; Mario de Andrade, 'A Calanga dos Maracatús', in *Estudos Afrobrasileiros*, Rio de Janeiro, 1935; Oneyda Alvarenga, *op. cit.*; A. Ramos, *op. cit.*

29. Cf. Pereira da Costa, *Folklore Pernambucano*, 1908.

30. The best description we have of these festivals, for Brazil, is that by Mario de Andrade, 'Os Congos', *Lanterna Verde*, 1935, 1. He has traced back the historical origins of the struggle portrayed, which is none other than that of the Portuguese against the kings and queens of Angola (Queen Ginga Bândi and Don Henrique). For the other countries of Latin America, see F. Ortiz, *Los cabildos afro-cubanos*, Habana, 1921; A. Ramos, *As culturas negras no Novo Mundo*, S. Paulo, 2nd ed. 1946; John E. Englerirk, 'El teatro folklorico hispano-americano', *Folklore Americas*, XVII, 1, 1957.

31. Theo Brandão, *O Auto dos Caboclinhos*, Maceió, Brazil, 1952.

32. During Negro festivals we find both congos and mozambiques, but the latter always come at the end; João Dornas filho, *A influencia social do Negro brasileiro*, Curitiba, 1943; Dante de Laytano, *As Congadas do municipio de Osório*, Rio Grande do Sul, 1945.

33. Theo Brandão, 'O Reisado Alagoano', *Rev. Arq. Munic. de S. Paulo*, CLV, 1953, for the *reisado*; and for the *ranchos*, Nina Rodriques, *Os Africanos*, p. 263.

34. Bakary Traoré, *Le théâtre négro-africain*, Paris, 1958.

35. Olga Brueño, 'Musica folklórica venezolana', *Bol. de la Union pan-americana*, Washington, 1958, 2.

36. Numerous examples in Frazer's *Golden Bough*.

37. J. Soustelle, *Mexique, terre indienne*, Paris, 1936, p. 88.

38. Sébillot, *Tour du Monde*, XLI, p. 282.

39. R. Bastide, *Religion Africaine . . ., op. cit.*, chapter on the 'two Catholic-isms'.

40. Alluding to the title of a book by E. Goblot, *La barrière et le niveau*, a study of the efforts made by the lower classes to break through the barriers set in their path by those above them, with the aim of attaining the same cultural level. I have already applied these concepts to Brazilian folklore generally in 'Sociologie du Folklore Brésilien', *Rev. de Psycho. des Peuples*, Le Havre, V, 4, 1950.

41. On the importance of the horse as a symbol of social status among Indians, Negroes, and European immigrants, see R. Bastide, *Introduction à la recherche sur l'interpénétration des civilisations* (roneo typescript), Sorbonne lecture-course, 1950.

42. On the Moors and Christians in Europe, see Garcias Figueires, *Notas sobre las fiestas de Moros y Cristianos en España*, Larache, 1940; and for Latin America, Nueves de Hoyos Sancho, 'Moros y Christianos', *Miscellanea P. Rivet*, II, Mexico, 1958. R. Ricard, in the *Journal de la Société des Américanistes*, has published what is perhaps the earliest known text (as far as Mexico is concerned) of these mock battles between Christians and Moors; it dates from 1538.

43. R. Bastide, *Psicanalise do Cafuné et ensaios de sociologia estetica brasileira*, Curitiba, 1941.

44. A. Ramos, *Folklore Negro, op. cit.*, ch. X.

45. For Haiti, see the special number of *Présence Africaine* (12, 1951), and Emmanuel C. Paul, *Panorama de Folklore Haïtien*, Port-au-Prince, 1962, ch. VI. For Montevideo, Paulo de Carvalho Neto, *op. cit.*

CHAPTER IX

NEGRO COMMUNITIES

As this book has shown, the further we get from the old *marron* societies, the fewer African survivals we encounter. Nevertheless, each ethnic group has its own special cultural focal point, around which people's interests tend to crystallise. This may be religion, as is the case with the Yoruba; for the Angolan and Congo groups it is folklore. Consequently, while some facets of native civilisation are liable to disintegrate *in toto* when transferred to a new environment, others survive, in all their rich complexity and stirring vitality. It is for this reason that we have been able, despite everything, to posit the existence of 'African' societies in the New World – those societies to which my previous chapters have been devoted. As we have seen, the collective memory tends, by and large, to store motor sequences rather than images, and sets more store by physical gestures, dance steps, or patterns of ritual than it does by any accumulation of intellectualised memories, valuable though the latter may be. If we begin listing those physical habits of African origin which still survive in the New World, we obtain a rich haul: the practice of holding a hand before one's mouth while talking, or of clapping one's hands softly to indicate pleasure at receiving a visit, or of pointing out an object with one's lips rather than one's finger, or of carrying loads on one's head, or of swaying one's body while singing – these are only a few of them.[1]

It goes without saying, however, that these African societies do not exist in total isolation; they maintain contact with other societies, those of the whites in particular. As a result, instances of acculturation are by no means rare. In these African societies, though, acculturation is selective. Borrowing tends to take one of two forms. What you acquire is either something that agrees with ancestral tradition, that is soaked in the same general (or ritual, or holiday) atmosphere; or, alternatively, something that is of practical use, and makes for more efficient adaptation to the new environment. On the island of Trinidad we find English colonists, residents of French descent, Portuguese, Syrians, Lebanese, Chinese, Hindus and Negroes all living cheek by jowl with one another. As Crowley[2] points out, the Negro sees nothing inconsistent about being, at one and the same time, black-skinned and an English citizen, Spanish by name, Catholic in religion, a devotee of the *obeah* cult and addicted to Chinese food. Similarly, a Chinese Anglican finds nothing inherently contra-dictory in going to a Hindu *pandit* or an African *obeah*-man in order to obtain a love-charm that will get him into bed with a Portuguese Presbyterian. The image that Stonequist has given us of 'marginal man', torn between two cultures which struggle within him for supremacy, may be valid for the coloured intellectual, but has no relevance to the man in the street. The latter finds no problem in occupying several distinct worlds: since these do not cover the same areas of existence (whether technical, economic, political, religious or social) they never come into conflict. This is why I have found it easy, when discussing what I term 'African societies', to isolate and describe a special sector in which traditional African features survive, without needing to bother overmuch about cases of acculturation.

In Chapter II, however, it was established that the Negro of the diaspora is torn by conflicting urges; the desire to recapture and revive his lost past, and the need to adapt him-self to the demands of a new environment. Acculturation is one of the elements in this process of adaptation, but neither the only one nor the most important. Adaptation can also take the form of seeking adequate responses to new situations; the development of original institutions, and the formation of new behaviour-patterns are, similarly, expressions of it. What we must do now, therefore, is to study these new and still-evolving societies: the Negro-American and, in particular, the Negro-African. That is the purpose of the present chapter.

I

Though we may have been struck by the degree of African influence on religion and folklore, in the sphere of social

structure, we find, this influence is negligible. Now, if acculturation processes had been the only factors involved, it would
have been natural for American Negroes to base not only their
type of family unit, but also their political organisations, clubs
and other associations on European models. How, then, are
we to explain the existence of 'Negro' societies, the antecedents
of which appear neither European nor African? Why, after
slavery had steamrollered the old ancestral African pattern
out of existence, gods, dances and all, do we find new
societies springing up in the post-Abolition period, which owed
nothing to the example of the slaves' erstwhile masters? There
is one reason, and one only: the segregation (whether by caste
or class) of the coloured population.

I say 'class' as well as 'caste' segregation (the English terminology is open to question, but has passed into general use
among scholars), since I make no distinction, on this score,
between Anglo-Saxon and Latin America. Whether or not a
formal colour-division is established, as in the U.S.A., makes
no difference; the result is just the same. Negroes live, or tend
to live, quite separately, in a world apart. They feel 'different'
from the rest; they are forced – or prefer, but from the con-
sequential angle this makes little difference – to 'keep themselves to themselves'.

From a psychological viewpoint, and as regards the formation of the personality, these differences are indeed of capital
importance; when a human being is subject to legally justified
oppression, the experience leaves its mark on him. But in
sociological terms these differences are negligible. We find the
same type of family, the same sorts of Christian churches, the
same kind of association, both in places where a formal colour-
bar exists between blacks and whites and where it does not. To
put it more precisely: in the first case, to crash this colour-bar
is difficult, if not impossible, whereas in the second case the
gate is always ajar, to a greater or lesser extent. Yet the
majority of Negroes, because of their economic position (or
plain destitution), cannot take advantage of this opening,
which for them remains theoretical rather than real, and therefore maintain their own 'folk' societies. Though it is not the
purpose of this book to examine white-black relationships in
the New World, we must nevertheless touch briefly on the

subject, if we are to understand the way in which segregation developed after the abolition of slavery.

Relationships between slaves and their masters in the U.S.A. were regulated by an appropriate protocol which, while endorsing white domination, also (at least in certain cases) allowed affective relations between the two races: the Negro who 'knew his place' presented no real threat to the European.[3] But after the men of the north had imposed their laws on those of the south, all that the plantation-owners could think about was restoring the abolished social distinctions, either through terrorism or by means of special legislation. Thus the descendants of slaves found themselves separated from the descendants of slave-owners, in schools and factories, theatres and public transport. Excluded from every parliament and trade union, indeed from every white group, they had perforce to form their own separate society. Naturally, inter-racial marriage was forbidden, and thus this society became endogamous – which is why North American sociologists used the term 'castes' when describing it.[4] The situation, in fact, actually seems to have been worse than it was before Abolition. Miscegenation was widespread, either in the form of sexual relations on the plantations between slave-owners and slaves, or else as regular concubinage, the latter being more or less recognised by contemporary *mores* in the southern towns of the U.S.A. The resultant mulattos, anxious to get themselves accepted by society at large, proceeded to adopt white customs, in particular that of the paternal family.[5] The legislation which followed emancipation relegated them to the Negro caste; and as a result miscegenation could not prevent the development of a society apart, radically alienated from that of the whites. Yet the Negro accepted this segregation. Though in some respects it cost him dear, in others it brought him far from negligible gains – in particular, greater freedom of morals, a sex-life blessedly free of the taboos which weighed so heavily on the white middle classes, and a society diametrically opposed to that savage competition for social standing which was the hall-mark of the native-born European. Having thus passed beyond all authoritative control, he was free to create his own institutions, to design himself a new programme for living. This programme we will examine in a moment. The exodus to the big northern cities did not destroy the colour-bar; it simply formed anew, a little further up the map, as though the whites were instinctively mounting their defences against the rising tide of Negroes. Segregation here most often took the form of the black ghetto, with its stalls and hovels, its taverns and churches;[6] yet such ghettos have made possible the survival of the Negro community as an entity in its own right.

When we turn from Anglo-Saxon to Latin America, instead of segregated and endogamous 'castes' we find a multi-racial society; yet because of the severe handicap which slavery imposed, the Negro, generally speaking, still occupies the lowest strata of the population. The various governments do not pursue a segregationist policy; on the contrary, they often make great efforts to speed up the process of national integration. But in areas where a high proportion of the inhabitants are coloured, the Negroes – since they feel themselves 'different' – prefer to lead their own life apart, beyond European jurisdiction. One practice, of Catholic origin, which regulates inter-racial relationships in such a way as to avoid any traumatic conflict between individuals, is that of religious sponsorship (*parrainage*). A Negro, by definition a lower-class person, chooses godfathers or godmothers for his children from the higher-ranking class of Europeans; and since the spiritual relationship is regarded as even more important than that of physical kinship, whites and Negroes develop affective relations with one another, providing mutual aid as and when required. On the other hand, as *parrainage* operates in accordance with hierarchical principles, such affectivity does not prevent the subordination of one colour to the other. In consequence the Negro expects nothing from the white man except services. He does not imitate his way of life, or attempt to infiltrate his group; he prefers to 'keep himself to himself'. By so doing he avoids any frustration or disappointment, since, in effect, he is refusing to compete. A feast day will bring all colours and ethnic groups together in the sense that they share a common sense of joyous celebration, but physically, each remains separate. In religious processions, Negro fraternities go first, and white ones follow on behind with the municipal authorities. Europeans dance in drawing-rooms,

Negroes out on the streets. The colours are not so much blended, in any true sense, as juxtaposed. Thus in Latin (as opposed to Anglo-Saxon) America, though the Negroes are on friendly terms with other racial groups, as regards their private familial and day-to-day life they keep themselves very much apart.[7] Emancipation gave the Negro freedom, but still left him at a severe disadvantage. He fled the plantations and sought refuge in the cities, but without having learnt the craft or trade which would have enabled him to adapt to urban conditions. As a result he felt he had been abandoned. He and his fellows lived in collections of primitive shacks – the modern *bidonville* or shanty-town – as a large foreign community. After an initial period characterised by deceit, alcoholism, sponging and vagrancy, he was forced to forge himself a new social framework. The keynote of this structure, now, was no longer integration but separatism. The Negro stood outside the newly-emergent class-system altogether; he formed a sort of *Lumpenproletariat*, strictly marginal to the community as a whole.

The situation here outlined – that of the emancipated Negro who needs to, and does, create his own standards of conduct, equally remote from African and from European models – is on the way out. We may say that the rise of the coloured man, in both North and South America, is conditioned by the degree to which he genuinely absorbs or assimilates white patterns. In the U.S.A. the Negro caste is divided into three classes. The lowest (and still the most important) is that descended from liberated ex-slaves. Then comes the middle class; and above it, a very small upper class, composed of those who can claim descent from *free* Negroes or mulattos. What defines the middle class is not so much its income as the acceptance of white middle-class values: moral puritanism, a passion for respectability, good manners, the importance attached to children's education and upbringing. Broadly speaking, we can isolate certain special features which characterise this 'Europeanising' process. In the domestic sphere, there is the transition from a maternalistic to a paternalistic type of family. In matters of religion, we find a swing from revivalist to fundamentalist churches. There is ecclesiastical no less than social mobility, and we can watch it at work in the progression from prophetic and Pentecostal sects to that of the Baptists, from which it is a short step to Methodism and, finally, to the Anglican Church. Socially speaking, each step here is upward, from an inferior to a superior class. Finally, there is the institution of marriage, which progresses from a common-law union to civil and religious ceremonies, from conjugal desertion to legal divorce. This evolution is symbolised by the choice of partner (e.g. an ultra-dark but well-educated man who marries a woman of lighter skin than himself in order to have children of a colour nearer to that of the whites with whom he hopes to achieve integration).[8] In Latin America, the process of integrating the Negro into society at large is also accomplished by the acceptance of white standards. To win acceptance, the Negro must become a 'black who thinks white', to borrow a phrase current in both Portuguese and Spanish America.[9]

But this trend, as yet, applies only to *élite* groups. Negro communities still survive, especially in areas where there is a strong official colour-bar, specially designed to keep Negro aspirations in check. They are also found in the country, either on the great capitalist-type plantations, with their rigidly hierarchical organisation, or on big landed estates, where the social system is as near to feudalism as makes no difference. In either case they are remote from the main centres of civilisation, and thus from the general progressive trend apparent elsewhere. Lastly, we find similar groups (though in this case Africanised) when we turn to Negro republics such as Haiti. These Negro communities have their own original culture and institutions, which are described below.

II

I have already discussed, in Chapter II, the various rival theories on the subject of the Negro family, and their attempts to interpret such phenomena as common-law marriage, matrifocality, or successive polygny. I do not intend to return to this topic here. At the same time, the family as such is an integral element of these Negro communities, and it will be advisable to bring some of its more characteristic features to the reader's attention. While it is true that one particular type of family predominates (and has caught the interest of sociologists, who label it 'maternal' or 'matriarchal'), nevertheless in these communities we find, not one, but several different varieties. To begin with, there is the nuclear family, composed of a husband, his wife, and their children. Then we have the extended family, with uncles, aunts and married children all living in the same large compound. Lastly, there is the incomplete family, consisting of mother (or father) and children; these two varieties can be either ordinary or extended. Consider the following three communities on Trinidad:[10]

Note: m=marriage		Sugartown		Orange Grove		Mocca	
c=concubinage		M	C	M	C	M	C
All figures are percentages							
Family (simple)		12	35	25	8	14	27
Family (extended)		10	8	31	5	12	18
Family (incomplete, maternal)		2	7	3	5	2	6
Family (incomplete, paternal)		1	9	1	15	1	11
Simple		11	4			3	4
Extended		2		6		2	
Marriages		21		56		26	
Cases of concubinage[11]		62		14		45	

We see, then, that there are two conflicting types of family pattern in existence. One is the new-style Negro model, which (as we have seen) can be identified by its matrifocality and the practice of common-law marriage, and operates in close liaison with the social and economic organisation of the black community as a whole. The other follows the European pattern – a paternal-type family, legalised and sanctified by marriage. This latter model remains the 'ideal' one, even in Africanised Negro republics such as Haiti. However, since it comes expensive, it is hard to achieve. Consequently a trial-and-error series of preliminary experimental unions is necessary, in order to find a woman who will really suit you; and even then there is a further waiting period until the couple save up enough money. Finally the marriage is celebrated (with both civil and religious ceremonies) and followed by a great wedding feast. But for the majority, especially the day-labourers, moving from plantation to plantation, it is impossible to put by enough for such a step; hence successive polygyny and the preponderance of common-law marriages. Others who suffer in this respect are smallholders working exhausted land. This conflict between two patterns produces a dichotomy in the role of the two parents, which reverses their usual functions, with the mother acting as a father, and the father showing little concern for his children (though from time to time he sends his abandoned sons presents). At the same time, though the mother, or the maternal grandmother, take good care of the children, it is in fact the male members of a 'maternal' family – which more often than not means the mother's brothers – who become responsible for their 'social upbringing' or 'education'.[12] In any case, as studies of neuroses and psychoses in this field make clear, the child suffers from the conflict between the 'ideal' pattern and that actually followed. He develops an ambivalent attitude towards his mother, and when he grows up reacts to his anxiety by lapsing into Don Juanism – the effect of which is to boost the practice of successive polygyny which has caused him so much suffering,[13] and thus to perpetuate precisely what he would like to see abolished.

The Negro family, then, knows nothing of romantic love – or, to be more accurate, romantic love, as far as such people are concerned, is no more than a kind of mythical image, borrowed from white folklore. We should beware of being misled by the lyrics of American blues or Brazilian sambas, or by the love songs, to a guitar accompaniment, which one can hear at night in rural Negro communities; what they express is not reality, but a vague yearning after the European ideal. A couple pair off when the man's sexual, and the woman's economic, interests happen to coincide. The union develops from a functional exchange of services between them, and is broken off when, for one reason or another (e.g. the woman getting too old, or the man being out of work) this exchange ceases to be profitable to one of the two partners. This should not, on the other hand, lead us to talk about promiscuity and social decadence, or claim that 'civilisation' is sinking or reverting to 'a state of nature'. In fact, if marriage and the family, in these Negro communities, lack the importance attached to them by whites, there are several good reasons for such an attitude. First, as the part played by a woman's brothers in the upbringing of her children has already given us cause to infer, ties of blood are much stronger than those of marriage.[14] It is just possible that there may be some faint survival of African influence here, a blurred memory of the importance attaching to linear relationships, the preservation of female independence – this last, as we know, being a feature of most African matrimonial systems. Secondly, the Negro of the 'folk' communities, whether in North or South America, regards social life as something more essential than family life. North American sociologists have demonstrated the important part played in Negro society by in-groups or clubs; and while those of the upper and middle classes may be based on European models, those of the lower classes, far from aping the customs of their former masters, rather express group-solidarity in action.[15] Latin American sociologists, for their part, have emphasised what they term the 'associative character' of the Negro. This takes innumerable forms; coloured religious fraternities and traditional 'folk' groups in the country, voluntary associations for anything from the defence of 'the race' to the organisation of Negro balls in the cities.[16] In short, the hub of these communities is formed not by matrimonial so much as by social relationships. The latter may take many forms: neighbourhood associations, work-groups, holiday or mutual aid clubs and, lastly, religious societies. Communal considerations outweigh domestic ones, private life is less important than public activities, and 'up-beat' occasions such as religious festivals rate above the 'down-beat' ordinariness of daily life.

I would like, having mentioned them, to say something further on the subject of religious societies, since religion (Catholic or Protestant, according to area) is the main agent for solidarity in these Negro communities, the cement that keeps them cohesive. This applies rather more to Protestant than to Catholic groups, since Catholicism does not countenance any distinction of race at the communion table; but it is true of some Catholics, even so, in so far as Catholicism in South America (to borrow Gilberto Freyre's terminology) is 'social' rather than 'mystical'.[17]

Conversion of the American Negro to Christianity was, originally, reserved for house-slaves, but gradually spread until, soon after the Declaration of Independence – a period which coincided with the great epoch of religious revivalism – it had reached the bulk of the black population. That is why the religion of the Negro community is a revivalist creed, affective rather than moral or rational. Worshippers want external evidence of being 'saved' – visions, dreams, trances; and emotion is cultivated at the exepnse of reason. Some scholars, such as Herskovits, convinced themselves that this moving religion was a reinterpretation, in Christian terms, of an old African cult. But African religion is not 'affective'; it is *practical*, and characterised by specific practices. The ecstatic trance is certainly cultivated there, but apart from marginal areas, in contact with other civilisations,[18] its purpose is ritual, i.e. as a gesture rather than for affective ends.[19] If the lower-class American Negro's religion tends to be affective, this is not in consequence of some African survival, but rather because the slave – restricted, dominated, exploited, rejected – channelled his need for security and compensation into Christianity, which he adapted as a means of coping with harsh oppression. We find a similar phenomenon in Africa, during the country's conversion to Christianity; affective religion develops in the transitional period between the abandonment of an old traditional cult and the entry into a new church.[20] In short, affective religion operates in functional liaison with the social and economic programme of the black community, and is not to be explained in terms of any 'African heritage'. It is a response, not a museum-piece.

Nevertheless, the slave-owner regarded evangelisation as a useful instrument of control, which sidetracked the Negro's frustrations with hope of recompense in paradise. The Negroes themselves (e.g. men like Richard Allen or Absalom Jones) reacted by creating their own church, where they would escape observation by Europeans and, at last, be 'on their own', free to express whatever sentiments they pleased. This movement snowballed after the Civil War. Between 1866 and 1880, membership in the African Methodist Episcopal Church rose from 50,000 to 390,000. In 1866 the African Methodist Episcopal Church of Zion had 27,000 members; ten years later the figure stood at 172,000. In the period between 1890 and 1936, over-all membership of the dissident Negro churches (mainly Methodist and Baptist) rose from 2,675,000 to 5,661,000. There are certain observable differences, in the south, between rural and urban churches (whether Baptist or Methodist), but these are not fundamental. What Negroes demanded of a church was that it should not only provide a headquarters for their religious group, but also function as the central hub of their entire social life. In other words, the church must 'structure' a black community around itself. The most important thing the church had, and still has, to offer was the opportunity for free self-expression, untrammelled by white authoritariansim. In addition, however, it came to provide a number of social services, together with various associations (for men, women, and young people) where members could meet to discuss their problems – and attain a prestige which compensated for the harshness of their daily life. Not only did the community tend to group itself around its church; the minister himself tended to become the community's leader, educator and spokesman.

When the Negro went up north, the church did not, on that account, cease to perform its basic 'structural' task *vis-à-vis* the migrant community – though its various metamorphoses did, nevertheless, reflect the changes of situation, both social and economic, against which Negroes were forced to pit themselves. The preacher thus came to take a greater interest in the material welfare of his flock, and to deal with problems which were, in the last resort, political rather than religious. In order to save young people from the temptations of life on the streets, the church devoted more time to organising their leisure activities. It set up agencies to find work for the jobless. It spearheaded the Negro's defence against social discrimination of any sort. Yet it was in the northern towns, rather than the rural areas of the south, where the countless problems attached to urban life brought about a proliferation of prophetic sects or movements. The Negro, feeling himself adrift in a hostile world, sought refuge in the smaller Pentecostal groups, where he rediscovered a sense of community with his brethren. A sick Negro lacked the resources necessary to pay for medical treatment; but the laying-on of hands and miraculous prayer provided him with a free source of 'healing'. Religion, in fact, whether under the auspices of an established church, or as a messianic creed directly inspired by the Holy Ghost, always retained one constant function, that of tightening up and consolidating the coloured communities. This task it pursued in various ways. It battled with the material difficulties of its members, such as high rents or lack of work. It concerned itself with the body no less than the soul (blessing and healing sick persons). It provided a series of more or less adequate answers to a whole range of problems posed by changing economic conditions. It also improved the social standing of its adherents. At present the function of the black churches is undergoing considerable change. Separatism has lost ground; the aim now is the integration of the Negro into society at large. In the rural south, however, its traditional functions, as described above, will, I am convinced, survive for a long while yet.[21]

In Central and South America the Catholic Church predominates. (Except, that is, for the British Antilles, where we find phenomena similar to those prevailing in the U.S.A. – affective religion, prophetic or revivalist sects – together with one new feature, participation by Negroes in several churches simultaneously. Many, for instance, attend the Anglican service on Sunday, while patronising one of the Pentecostal-type sects during the week. The latter offer a somewhat more theatrical atmosphere, which gives them an additional appeal as entertainment.)[22] A number of qualifications, however, need to be made at this point. To begin with, the Catholic church is powerless, except in the towns, to carry out its pastoral mission effectively. In proportion to the population, the number of priests is minute. Furthermore, the population itself is spread out over a vast area, so that some parishes are, literally, as large as Belgium. In such circumstances Catholicism cannot fulfil the same integrating role for the black communities as Protestantism does elsewhere. Secondly, the town-dwelling Negro does not appear to possess so intensely felt a faith – or, to put it more accurately, his belief outruns his inclination for religious observance. He is far more ready to take part in great collective festivals and spectacular processions than he is to attend mass or communion. As a result, Catholicism here serves neither to break down racial barriers, nor to promote a sense of national unity. As was stated earlier, during the colonial period we find a kind of dual Catholicism developing, to a greater or lesser extent, everywhere in America; one – socially exclusive – version for Europeans, and another for those of Negro or Indian ancestry, with its own fraternities and folklore (*congadas*, *mozambiques*, etc.). It is this 'folk' Catholicism, rather than the Roman church proper, which acts as a catalysing agent for the coloured communities of Latin America. The church's contemporary campaign against all such folk-oriented phenomena (which it regards as indecent) serves to illustrate this dichotomy; the Negro reacts violently to official interference, launches into an all-out battle with his priest, stages a kind of religious strike and (at least in the smaller towns) generally comes out on top. All of which goes to show that, just as in North America, religion for the Negro is not so much any sort of spiritual creed as a social institution, the central core sustaining his sense of racial group solidarity.[23]

In Latin America, however, it is the associations which dominate the churches, and offer facilities for Negro fraternisation. These can be divided into two types: the traditional, patronised by the proletariat, and those which we may term, by way of contrast, the modern ones, which serve the small coloured middle class. There is a complete split between these two groups. Lower-class people in general regard the 'modern' associations as conventicles for the ambitious, who are more concerned with their own interests (e.g. as regards elections) than with those of 'the Race'. Be that as it may, in Latin America it is these groups that perform the function which, for the coloured communities in the northern part of the continent, is carried out by the church as a whole. The 'traditional' associations comprise two main categories. There are the old Catholic groups which have been banned officially by the clergy, but – since they fulfil an important function absolutely necessary to the survival of the community and racial solidarity – continue to flourish regardless; these include the *maracatú*, the *reisados*, and the *congos*. There are also various new associations, which have sprung up in the shanty-towns as compensation for socially marginal conditions; amongst them we may note the 'samba schools' in Rio de Janeiro, the *comparses du Carnaval* in the Antilles, and – to some degree – Negro balls everywhere. 'Modern' associations, too, can be of two types. The first is recreational; this group also tends to lay down class-distinctions *inside* the coloured community as a whole. Minor employees or officials do not patronise Negro balls, since they are afraid of their daughters losing their virginity. As a result they tend either to create their own separate dance associations or else to seek catharsis in the theatre (in the same way that societies which remain African in outlook employ the *candomblés* or *Vaudous*). This latter movement, especially the Negro experimental theatre, also helps to reduce their feeling of inferiority. Secondly, there are the associations designed to protect Negro interests, whether social or economic – to help the battle against segregation and prejudice, to encourage a sense of human dignity in every individual. The success enjoyed by the 'Black Front' in Brazil, before its suppression by Getulio Vargas's dictatorship, is symptomatic. The massive support which this movement acquired among the Negro population was due, not so much to its role as an instrument of defence, as to the fact that it enabled Negroes to rediscover themselves as a group, and structure their community in accordance with common values and generally applicable standards of behaviour.

To sum up: the process of disintegration, the moral and sociological anarchy which followed the abolition of slavery always provoked an identical response from the Negro. His reaction may have differed in detail from one region to another, but it always tended in the same general direction – towards the establishment of a homogeneous and cohesive constitution.

III

Thus, side by side with African culture – though a certain amount of interpenetration does take place between them – we find an original Negro culture, with its own laws, which are quite different from those governing a white society. A superficial theory of acculturation cannot take this distinction into account, since for its advocates anything not African has to be white, and whatever does not derive from ancestral tradition is assumed to be borrowed from the customs of the master-race. This kind of thinking ignores the part played by adaptation, the influence which economic infrastructures can have on the creation of social superstructures, and, indeed, the whole basic process by which civilisations are formed – the mental or motor response to a highly variable range of factual situations. The example of affective religion is particularly significant in this respect. As we have seen, there is nothing African about its origins (except in cases where external cultural contact can be proved, it is not an African characteristic to seek emotional satisfaction from the state of possession); nor, on the other hand, is it a mere copy of white revivalism, since its affectivity lies in the solid reaction of a whole group striving for communion together, rather than in individual attempts to achieve salvation (a feature which characterises white prayer meetings).

At the same time these two cultures (not inevitably opposed to one another) are by no means static or immobile, except as regards what we have labelled 'preserved religions'. They are living realities, which change in accordance with any modifications to the infrastructure, or any new problems posed by the over-all societies within which they exist – problems that must be resolved, and resolved in accordance with certain specific directions. Other factors which are liable to modify either values or institutions include (1) the various pressures to which African and Negro cultures are subject; (2) any alterations in individual needs or desires that may emerge, especially as a result of educational progress; and (3) changes in environment (e.g. from a rural to an urban area). We need only study the lyrics of Negro folk songs over the years to see how the Negro's aspirations were transformed – and to witness the slow emergence of a new ethnic self-awareness among people who hitherto had either been relegated to the outer fringes of society, or else (where no real colour-bar was in operation) simply left to their own devices. The movement is one from conformism to revolt, from escapist fantasy to an organised struggle for better living conditions. Similarly, we need only investigate a 'live' African religion, like that of Haiti, to see that while Voodoo's development has followed a basic African pattern, it has also been obliged to invent new 'creole' deities and a number of new myths. The former are necessary to provide some embodiment for the island's new national aspirations, the latter to replace old myths now fast disappearing. It is very likely that the transformation currently taking place in Haiti's economic and social structure will produce still further changes; but since all such modifications occur spontaneously, as the expression of public feeling rather than the decision of some *élite* group, they are quite impossible to predict. Any attempt to rationalise the various Negro societies – e.g. the idea of transforming the Haitian *combite* into a modern co-operative – has proved a clear failure. Such ideological notions, so dear to the hearts of intellectuals, here achieve scant contact with reality.

One last question remains to be answered. How valid is the distinction between African and Negro cultures – the one produced by the pressure of the past on the present, the other by that of a new environment on an isolated community? In previous studies I have, in fact, posited two distinct types of acculturation. The first I proposed to call 'material', because it was concerned with the contents of cultures in contact, and the second 'formal', because it affected the mind, and embodied a change of mentality.[24] If we are determined, at all costs, to find some link between Negro and African culture, it is, I would suggest, through these two concepts that we should work, rather than Herskovits' concept of 're-interpretation'. On the face of it there might appear to be little difference between them, since the concept of 're-interpretation' remains very close to that of 'material acculturation'; however its actual significance may have changed, the datum is still a cultural trait, whether European or African. What we are specially concerned with, on the other hand, is the mental pattern of individuals, and hence of the group. We find this formal acculturation operating at the level of both African and Negro cultures. As we shall see in the next chapter, certain intellectuals have re-thought Voodoo in such a way as to extract a philosophy from it, but the mentality they bring to their task is shaped by Western concepts. (In other words, they have combed it for an 'African philosophy' of the sort known to us from the works of Griaule, Mme Dieterlen or Fr. Tempels[25] – but through the medium of Euro-Asiatic philosophy.) Similarly with the Negro cultures we have studied in this chapter; their content is, undoubtedly, a response of one sort or another to a new environment, but such responses are filtered through a mentality which in many if not all respects (e.g. the passion for brotherhood associations or acts of collective communion) is still shaped by the old traditions of African culture.

REFERENCES

1. Herskovits, *The Myth* . . ., *op. cit.*; Thomas J. Price Jr., 'Estado y necessidades actuales de las investigaciones afro-colombianos', *Rev. Colomb. de Antrop.* II, 2, 1954, etc.

2. Daniel J. Crowley, 'Plural and Differential Acculturation in Trinidad', *Amer. Anthrop.* 59, 5, 1957.

3. Bertram Wilbur Doyle, *The Etiquette of Race Relations in the South*, Chicago, 1937.

4. Edgar T. Thompson (ed.), *Race Relations and the Race Problem*, North Carolina, 1939; Charles S. Johnson, *Patterns of Negro Segregation*, New York, 1943; Hortense Powdermaker, *After Freedom*, New York, 1939; John Dollard, *Caste and Class in a Southern Town*, Yale Univ. Press, 1937.

5. Edward Byron Reuter, *Race Mixture: Studies in Intermarriage and Miscegenation*, New York, 1931.

6. St Clair Dake and H. R. Cayton, *Black Metropolis*, New York, 1945. The most famous of these black ghettos is Harlem which has given rise to several important studies: in English, that by E. Franklin Frazier (*Amer. Journ. of Sociol.* 43, 1937), and in French, that by Vladimir Pozner ('Esclaves et dieux d'Harlem,' *Europe*, Aug. 1937, pp. 471–500). For the effects of this segregation on the development of urban Negro communities and the Negro character, see W. Lloyd Warner, Buford H. Junker and Walter A. Adams, *Color and Human Nature, Negro Personality Development in a Northern City*, Washington, 1941.

7. Charles Wagley (ed.), *Races et Classes dans le Brésil rural*, U.N.E.S.C.O., n.d.; Nancie L. Solien, 'West Indian Characteristics of the Black Carib', *South. Journ. of Anthrop.* XV, 3, 1959; etc.

8. Apart from the books by Dollard, Frazier and others already cited, see Allison Davis, Barleigh B. Gardner and Mary R. Gardner, *Deep South: A Social Anthropological study of Caste and Class*, Chicago, 1941; Franklin Frazier, *Black Bourgeoisie*, Glencoe, Ill., 1957; Horace Mann Bond, *The Education of the Negro in the American Social Order*, New York, 1934; etc.

9. See the books of F. Fernandes, H. Cardoso and O. Ianni already cited.

10. H. Edith Clark, *My Mother who Fathered Me*, London, 1917.

11. On Haiti, in the Marbial Valley (and despite strong Catholic propaganda against concubinage among parishioners) Métraux found only 1,821 married couples, as against 3,275 *placés*. Obviously it is the preponderance of 'common-law marriages' which explains the large numbers of infants described as 'illegitimate' in the statistics of these Negro communities (e.g. 71 per cent in Jamaica), and the importance attached to adoption; but illegitimate or adopted children are treated exactly the same as the others.

12. Moriss Freilich, 'Serial Polygyny . . .', *op. cit.*

13. Madeline Kerr, *Personality and Conflict* . . ., *op. cit.*

14. This point has been especially clearly brought out by Nancie L. Solien, 'West Indian Characteristics . . .', *op. cit.*

15. See, in particular, Davis, Gardner and Gardner, *op. cit.*, ch. IX.

16. Arthur Ramos, *A aculturação negra no Brasil*, S. Paulo, 1942, pp. 117–44; L. A. da Costa Pinto, *O Negro no Rio de Janeiro*, S. Paulo, 1953, chs. VII

and VIII; Roger Bastide and Florestan Fernandes, *Brancos e Negros em São Paulo*, S. Paulo, 1959.

17. Gilberto Freyre, *Maîtres et Esclaves*, *op. cit.*

18. Contact, that is, between African, Muslim and Western cultures. Cf. Rouch's excellent film, *Les Dieux Fous*, or Leiris's book, *La possession et ses aspects théâtraux chez les Ethiopiens de Gondar*, Paris, 1958.

19. Roger Bastide, *Le candomblé . . .*, *op. cit.*

20. Raoul Allier, *La psychologie de la conversion chez les peuples non civilisés*, Paris 1925.

21. The most important book on these black churches, which provides an excellent synthesis of all previous work on the subject, is undoubtedly that by E. Franklin Frazier, *The Negro Church in America*, Liverpool, 1964. Cf. also Carter C. Woodson, *The History of the Negro Church*, 2nd ed., Washington, 1921; Edward Nelson Palmer, 'The Religious Acculturation of the Negro', *Phylon* V, 3, 1944, pp. 260–5; Myrdal, *op. cit.*, chs. 40 and 43; Arthur Huff Fauset, *Black Gods of the Metropolis*, Philadelphia, 1944.

22. Madeline Kerr, *op. cit.*, ch. XII.

23. R. Bastide, *Religions africaines . . .*, *op. cit.* (chapter dealing with Negro Catholicism).

24. R. Bastide, 'L'acculturation formelle', *America Latina*, Rio de Janeiro, VII, 3, 1963.

25. Cf. Marcel Griaule, *Dieu d'Eau*, Paris, 1948; Germaine Dieterlen, *Essai sur la réligion bambara*, Paris, 1951; R. P. Tempels, *La Philosophie bantoue* (trs. from the Dutch), Paris, 1949.

CHAPTER X

PATTERNS OF NÉGRITUDE

The more the Negro tends to abandon his peasant-type communities for factory life in the big city – and the further he gets up the social ladder – the closer integrated he will become with society as a whole, so that his own distinctive characteristics begin to vanish. It is true that for him, as for the Indian, there may be a period of transition, during which he lives on the fringes of the big city, in *bidonvilles* or hovels built on the ruins of abandoned residential areas. In such circumstances he may preserve a certain number of individual cultural characteristics: the 'samba schools' of Rio de Janeiro (mentioned in a previous chapter) and the development in lower-class suburban areas of syncretistic cults both furnish evidence for such a trend. Nevertheless, from now on Negro society is of more interest to the sociologist than the ethnologist. The coloured middle classes, for instance, have entirely assimilated the values and standards of the general society within which they live. If some traces of their African past still survive, these manifest themselves, not in their day-to-day existence, but rather when the individual closes his eyes and drifts off into the nocturnal world of dreams.[1] I propose to leave my analysis of the topic there, since to make a sociological study of coloured minorities in America does not fall within the scope of this book.

There is one other point I should mention, and which, though not highlighted, must certainly have struck the reader. It is impossible to form a just appreciation of the various Negro communities unless we take into account the fact that these communities exist in a world that is governed and controlled by whites. Even when they form a numerical majority, New World Negroes always remain – culturally, economically, politically – a minority group. In chapter after chapter we have seen the shadow of the European clearly silhouetted; and the cultural attitudes we have been led to examine – resistance, retention of ancestral traditions, adaptation or re-interpretation – are all responses to a case of inter-racial co-existence based on inequality. Despite everything, we have not studied (nor shall we in this book) the problem of relations between different races and colours. Here, again, the ethnologist must yield to the sociologist. I shall limit myself to one very generalised comment. The fact is that in America there exist two separate patterns of behaviour. One is the paternalistic, which tends to prevail when the Negro accepts his inferior status, his position on the bottom rung of the social and economic ladder – a position which may win him certain affective (or erotic) compensations from the European. The other is the competitive, which occurs when the Negro finds his road to social advancement blocked by the establishment of a caste system or officially sanctioned measures to enforce segregation. Against these barriers, the object of which is forcibly to keep the Negro in his place (i.e. under the European), the coloured man rises in revolt, and the upshot is racial conflict.[2] By a seeming paradox, which in fact contains a certain implicit logic, it is under a competitive régime that we find the Negro abandoning his African heritage and 'going Western', in order to win the same rights – whether economic, political or social – as a white. It is no accident that of all the rural communities described above, those with the closest affinities to Africa are located in Latin America – that is, in the area where paternalism has prevailed. Yet even here (at least in the capital cities) industrialisation has intensified competition on the labour market, and the Negro has been forced to abandon Africa and become a citizen-at-large like anyone else.[3] It is clear that with the triumph of what has been termed 'developmental policy', the competitive régime will finally win out against the paternalist.

But here there enters a new factor. Just as the slave régime was balanced by the phenomenon of *marronage*, so the competitive system (and the frustrations to which it gives rise, since the European still remains in ultimate control, and knows how to use his authority to stop coloured men getting on) produces its own ideological version of *marronage* – the *négritude* myth. At the very moment when, faced by white refusal to accept him on an equal footing, the Negro abandons Africa in order to achieve fuller integration, he finds himself driven back to the continent of his ancestors. But since in cultures there is no 'unconscious collective' or heredity factor, but only what is inherited by apprenticeship, this Africa can be no more than an imaginary concept floating in the void – unless, that is (as we shall have occasion to observe) it becomes a subtle form of betrayal. Our starting-point in this book was African survivals; now we have reached our last Africa – the mythical version. Our wheel has come full circle.

In the United States the Negroes, being segregated from the whites through the latter's decision, reacted by hammering out a series of ideological programmes; the order in which these appeared reflected each new turn in the struggle by the oppressed race. Booker T. Washington called on his fellow Negroes to accept the subordinate status thrust on them, in the south, at the end of the Reconstruction period, in the hope that by so doing they might disarm the whites. Such tactics, he thought, would bring about a period of interracial peace, from which the Negro could benefit by improving his educational standards, especially in technical subjects; the long-term result would be economic and social advancement. His hopes, however, were doomed to disappointment. The Negro, it was true, did experience some amelioration of his lot: between 1890 and 1910 the number of coloured smallholders doubled, while Negroes acquired their own co-operative enterprises, benevolent societies, banks and universities. On the other hand, the whites maintained their dominating position by means of riots, lynchings and increasingly severe segregationist measures. It was now that another ideology came to the fore, that of Washington's opponent DuBois. This was the so-called 'Niagara Movement', a fighting programme pledged to obtain total equality for the coloured American, and full recognition of his rights. But DuBois also failed, since it was now that the southerners began their mass emigration north; and the whites of the northern states, faced with a Negro invasion of their cities, reacted as violently as the whites in the south – perhaps even more so. It followed that radicalism brought the Negro no greater benefits than acceptance of the *status quo*. Since integration into European society was clearly out of the question, all that remained was integration into the African community.

With Garvey, who preached this new crusade, we have the first real step in the direction of *négritude*. Garvey dreamed of a great community uniting American and African Negroes; this community would become economically self-supporting by the creation of a Negro merchant marine (the Black Star Line). Though he was himself a cradle-Catholic, he attempted to cement the unity of his projected group by founding a Negro religion, with a black God – the African Orthodox Church. Garvey also accepted certain white ideas, such as those of non-miscegenation and racial purity (with the paradoxical result that he got backing for his campaign from the Ku Klux Klan), not to mention a scheme for running the African continent with a top-level cadre of U.S. Negroes; this won him the further support of American imperialists, who saw in Garvey's theory the instrument by which Africa might be deflected from the European to the Yankee colonial orbit. So in addition to the ideologies of conformism and resistance there emerged a third, advocating flight; but since the vast majority of American Negroes now regarded themselves, both emotionally and intellectually, as Americans rather than Africans, this inevitably came to nothing.[4]

Though the movement collapsed, it still left some eddies in its wake. Negro intellectuals had opted for assimilation ever since the days of slavery; Phyllis Wheatley the poet is a good example. Laurence Dubard was the first person to express the aspirations of the Negro community, but in order to get his ideas accepted, he had to wear a mask. The only way he could achieve success with his dialect poetry was by identifying himself with the 'Nigger Minstrels', whose appearances on the boards of provincial theatres projected the image of the Negro as a buffoon. But after Garvey we see writers beginning to drop the mask; with the 'Negro Renaissance' and the Harlem Movement the anti-white revolution came out into the open. In this connection we may mention the names of such figures as James Weldon Johnson, Claude McKay, Countee Cullen, Langston Hughes, Jean Toomer, and – rather nearer our own day – Richard Wright, all of whom have achieved wide recognition.[9] But when we study this literature we find nothing

'African' about it. It may be possible to speak of *négritude* in the sense of 'pride in colour'; but this runs directly counter to the idea of *négritude* as we find it in a poet like Aimé Césaire, where it embodies the desire to 'belong to Africa'. In one well-known poem Langston Hughes wrote:

> I too sing of America,
> I am the Negro brother –

which more or less typifies the ideological attitude adopted by these Harlem writers.

It was left to the common people to discover true *négritude*; and since, as I have said, the common people's reactions are invariably channelled through their religion – from the church as security to the messianism of Father Divine – it is in the sphere of religion, again, that we must seek the way back to Africa. In sharp contrast to the old-fashioned pattern of the Pentecostal-type sects, or the cults of ecstatic possession, the Muslim churches seek to emphasise Negro racialism – and with integration an impossibility, what other stand could they adopt? The Muslim church, in fact, has burnt its bridges with the American community at large, and symbolises this break by a rejection of Christianity; what it wants is to identify itself with Black Islam. But alas – and it is not the first time we have had occasion to note this – just when we appear to be closest to Africa is precisely the moment when we are furthest away from it, for the underlying idea here is that the Negro, far from being an African, is an Asiatic, with roots in the Prophet's Arabia rather than south of the Sahara. His sacred scriptures, moreover, once he has rejected the Bible, are still represented by an imported work, the Koran (though we should note that the Koran used by this church has nothing to do with the real Koran, but is an 'inspired book', written by Timothy Drew, the founder of the sect, and kept strictly secret). The Negro has not dared to push matters to their logical conclusion, i.e. by re-embracing animism or polytheism. Even in his most deeply rebellious moments, he reveals one ingrained white prejudice which he has absorbed – the belief that all African religions are a mere tissue of superstitious nonsense. Thus instead of putting down roots in eternal Africa, as we might have expected, he becomes a naturalised Asiatic. It is all a far cry from the Cuban *santeria*, the Brazilian *candomblé*, or Haitian Voodoo – which today remain the only genuine lines of approach to '*Africanitude*'.[6]

When we turn from the U.S.A. to the Antilles, we find an abundance of parallel phenomena. We have seen how, in Jamaica, the transition from 'Myelism' to the 'angel-men' was marked by an eruption of various religious manifestations, both prophetic and spiritualist. But the solid European resistance to any real political or economic advancement on the part of the Negroes made such phenomena seem illusory, a mere distraction from the real struggle that was going on elsewhere. Thus messianism changed in character: its centre of representation shifted from the Negro rural worker to the coloured *Lumpenproletariat*, where it found expression in the Ras Tafari movement.[7] Political claims were, it is true, still presented within a context of sectarian religion; but this time the emphasis lay on action rather than catharsis. The Negro is destined to rule the world, and must from now on prepare against the coming of the millennium, which will be marked by the overthrow of the racial hierarchy at present established. Ras Tafari – in other words Haile Selassie, King of Kings and Emperor of Ethiopia, with whom these Jamaicans have had no kind of contact or correspondence – has been chosen by the angels as this millennium's new messiah. He is invincible, and he alone can control the atomic bomb. Thus he has been chosen as the object of a cult which looks forward to the moment when all whites will become the servants of the blacks, and the blacks will inherit the earth. It is true that here we come closer to Africa than does the Muslim church, since the messianic centre is the Empire of Ethiopia; yet nevertheless, in spite of everything, betrayal creeps in. The Negroes, it transpires, are in fact Jews, a reincarnation of the ancient Hebrews, born in the Antilles as a punishment for former transgressions,[8] which, however, are now forgiven.

Voodoo itself has not been wholly exempt from such distortions. Since it was a peasants' religion, middle-class mulattos and Negroes (whose cultural bias lay towards France) for long repudiated it with some contempt. Later, however, the North American occupation led to an upsurge of nationalist feeling among writers, which in turn produced a sense of solidarity between the *élite* and the rural masses, both of them uniting against the foreigner in their midst. With the appearance of *Les Griots* (a now defunct review), and above all with the publication of Price Mars' brilliant studies of Voodoo, writers began to recover a measure of pride in their African heritage.[9] This was the starting-point for a whole new movement, no longer centred on the idea of revolt, but rather working towards the creation of a new culture, peculiar to West Indian Negroes, which J. S. Alexis aptly entitled 'supernatural realism'. Since Haitian literature follows the Marxist line, its aim is to be 'realistic'; but since reality on Haiti is shot through and through with elements of mystery, fantasy, and plain witchcraft, 'realism' tends to be magical as well. Here too, unfortunately, the risks of betrayal are all too apparent. One dangerous moment is when the intellectual, in his efforts to defend Voodoo against European criticisms, begins reinterpreting it in terms of white concepts and prejudices. On the other hand his claim that Voodoo embodies a philosophy (and one that will stand comparison with those of the West) is perfectly justified. Marcel Griaule was a pioneer in this field, and a few pages of Mercier suffice to demonstrate the metaphysical profundity of Fon thinking.[10]

The point at which the process of betrayal begins is when, rather than search through Voodoo *internally* for a genuine African philosophy, one reinterprets it with the aid of theosophy, 'psychic research', and other theories which have nothing African about them, but are supposed to make the whole thing more 'serious'.[11] The Brazilian mulatto puts his black mother's picture in the kitchen, but hangs his white father's portrait in a place of honour in the drawing-room. The Haitian intellectual carries this one step further. He puts his black mother in the drawing-room too – but dressed in European clothes, and wearing cheap jewellery rather than her own splendid cowrie-shell necklaces.[12] There is far more authenticity (to use a currently modish term) about the 'supernatural realism' of J. S. Alexis, or, in Cuba, the poetry of Nicolas Guillem. The latter gives marvellous expression to Africa as a living entity – but living on the enchanted islands of Amercia, blending an African vocabulary and African onomatopoeic phrases with gutter-slang or creolised Spanish, and the sonorous Yoruba drum-rhythms with voluptuous melodies that originated among the Caribs.

The intellectuals of the Antilles and French Guiana have taken a similar path, and encountered the same temptation to betray their origins. But in their case the temptation takes a different form. At first writers in these parts tried to show what good Frenchmen they were; but they came to feel, as one of their number, René Ménil, afterwards wrote, that this imitative literature was the consequence of 'repressing the (African) spirit in a slave's conscious mind, and replacing it with a characteristically white-oriented outlook, which became rooted in the collective subconscious, and indeed watched over it as a garrison watches over a conquered town'. Their first task, then, was to get rid of this imposed outlook; and the charge of dynamite which blew the French superego sky-high was provided by surrealism. In this way they might indeed have rediscovered Africa – or at least the only Africa which has any reality in America, that of the American Negro peasants. Aimé Césaire, however, took a diametrically opposite line, and in his poetry began to advocate a brand of *négritude* which was conceived as 'a return to one's native roots', i.e. to Africa. The only trouble was that, since all culture has to be acquired (indeed, it cannot otherwise exist), the poet's Africa inevitably emerged as a product of the imagination (a magnificent one, be it noted: Césaire's poetry is among the finest being written today), put together from books by ethnologists, who do not, unfortunately, always give a very precise picture of the facts. His *négritude* is thus more of a quasi-political manifestation than a return to the only genuine Africa, so faithfully preserved by the Afroamerican lower orders. Sinder is well aware of this; he willingly accepts the ambiguities inherent in an Africa which, bastardised or not, is in any case the only version with an objective existence for Americans (as opposed to a mere 'image' projected by some intellectual), and he uses them as a source of fresh beauty.

We should not, however, restrict our criticisms to intellectuals alone. The common man who gets on in society is equally liable – depending on how far he has absorbed white prejudices against those of slave descent – to succumb to identical temptations. We have already seen one example in the Muslim churches of the urbanised Negro population in the U.S.A. Brazil offers a similar phenomenon, the so-called 'spiritualism of Umbanda'. I have already described, in my chapter on syncretism, the way in which the *macumba*, itself of Bantu origin, was transformed into this type of spiritualism, which, like the Muslim church or the church of Ras Tafari, is at heart a protest-movement directed against white prejudices. That is why it supports a number of those African beliefs or customs which are widespread among the coloured masses. The existence of the *Orisha* is admitted. There is a priesthood under the direction of the *babalaõ*. Against Allan Kardec, the possibility of a special Negro spiritualism is envisaged, in which contact is made with the spirits of former slaves, who return to earth, via their mediums, to do good, in spite of the past, to the descendants of those who enslaved them. But since, at the same time, Africa is conceived of very much in the same way as the whites saw it, i.e. as a land of 'barbarism', such people are liable to invent a whole mass of myths and ideologies which, while pretending to revivify the African heritage, in fact tend to betray it. *Umbanda*, in fact a Kimbundo word, is equipped with a fantastic etymological derivation from Sanskrit. The African continent becomes a mere way-station for an esoteric science which supposedly originated in India, and made its way thence to the coloured population of Brazil. The African theory of reincarnation is identified with the Indian theory of *karma;* the cult of the *orishas* is based on certain passages in Annie Besant; and so on. Thus for these people the 'return to Africa' is really a *rejection* of Africa as their mother-country (the contemptuous image created by the whites still lingers on) in order the better to claim affinity with Asia, cradle of world civilisation, and already at the top of the cultural ladder while Europeans were still a mass of savages.[13]

Side by side with this religious movement among the small coloured middle class, we also find Brazilian intellectuals, both Negro and mulatto (e.g. Guerreiro Ramos), expounding their own theory of *négritude*. This theory is in sharp contrast to that of Césaire, because it springs from a quite different ideology, one invented by the whites, after the abolition of slave-labour, in order to keep race relations under better control; the 'whitening' of 'aryanisation' of the Negro. What it comes down to is an apologia for miscegenation which, by progressively diluting the black element in a predominantly white population, leads eventually to its total disappearance.[14] Obviously, this desire for a systematic elimination of all negroid features from the inhabitants of Brazil arouses a sense of inferiority and alienation among the Negroes themselves. *Négritude* sets out to provide an escape from this ideology. It does, indeed, also accept miscegenation (an integral part of the country's *mores*, to oppose which would be so much labour lost); but the conclusion drawn from this is that every Brazilian worthy of the name has at least a drop or two of Negro blood in his veins, and that Brazil should be regarded as a Negro rather than a white country. What is more, this should be a matter for pride, since black is a more beautiful colour than white.[15] *Négritude*, then, is not a 'return to Africa', nor even the means used to justify an African or Afroamerican culture – something these Brazilian intellectuals regard as 'savage' or riddled with superstition. It is, quite simply, a justification for Negroes as such, whether from the viewpoint of colour or race.

This quick survey of the evidence, despite its brevity, nevertheless gives us a clear picture of the metamorphosis now taking place. At first Africa survived in America as a physical reality, mingling lovingly with other cultures, of which the Negro, as opposed to the white, gave it a fresh lease of life and vitality. Later, however, this reality began to dissolve into a mass of ambiguous, contradictory images: ideologies for the intellectuals, messianism for the masses, and more politics than mysticism. Now like every superstructure, these transformations are the expression of an objective reality. They mirror the Negro's transition from 'community' to 'society', from rural to urban life; they also hint at the pressure which industrial capitalist society exercises on the coloured masses, through its need for an ever larger and more highly qualified labour force. The Negro is thus obliged to emerge from his state of 'marginalism', and find a place in the general class-structure. On 'preserved' African culture, however, on isolated folklore traditions, even on Negro cultures, these structural changes tend to have an effect much like that of a steamroller, which flattens everything in its path. Yet Africa obstinately refuses to die, and still clings on – at least, as an ideal dream. This phenomenon has a certain political value, but its very fragility shows that any authentic cultural heritage is quite dead.

Such a conclusion may seem pessimistic. It would, however, be a mistake to consider only the negative elements of change now operative in New World societies. To begin with, we have studied only one aspect of Césaire's *négritude* – the way he has built up his own polemical vision of Africa, rather than base himself on Afro-Antillean reality, which, for a West Indian, constitutes the only living, objective reality he knows. But there is a more positive side to the matter, which we should not neglect. Césaire's poetry expresses such things as the shrinking of global distances and the consequent development of inter-continental contacts – through radio, television, improved sea and air transport, and the resultant accumulation, in the heart of America, of messages and information from the other side of the Atlantic. From this point of view, it seems to me, we are coming back to a new version of the old 'three-cornered voyages', with close contact between Africa's civilisations and their Afroamerican offshoots. In houses in Bahia I have seen cuttings from Nigerian newspapers pasted up on the walls. *Candomblé* priestesses make air trips to visit their Yoruba 'cousins'. Teachers from Nigeria come over to Brazilian universities and reinstruct the 'sons and daughters of the gods' in their long-forgotten ancestral tongue.[16] Thus the develop-ment of higher learning, far from destroying native values and replacing them with those borrowed from the West, may instead act as a departure-point for fruitful trans-oceanic *rapprochements*.

The worst mistake our sociology makes is that of concerning itself exclusively with the Promethean side of our civilisation; working as it does from a certain specific view of the effects created by urbanisation, it sees only the social-gregarious, rational or self-interested sides of human relationships. In its struggle against organicism, it forgot that societies and cultures constituted living, organic realities, reacting to external environments, absorbing them, and in due course evolving fresh values. Planning is a fact of life, but it has its limitations. Infatuation with our own thaumaturgic will makes us prone to forget that communities often react to our plans in a quite unpredictable fashion. Life has its reasons, which reason does not know. Let us return, then, to our examination of industrial, capitalist, densely-populated urban society. If it destroys, it also creates. In the first place, though it may change castes into classes and create new openings for social mobility, the fact remains that it still rests on a stratification which in America, by and large, divides up according to colour. Secondly, though it caters better to man's material needs, the way it cuts him off from nature (imprisoning him in a concrete wilderness, destroying the affective relationships which prevailed in the old communities, secularising the religious-minded) tends to create a spiritual void. Thus it arouses needs, reactions and compensatory urges which may form a starting-point for new cultural creations. Jazz, as we saw above, derives from one of two sources. Either it comes from the music of the *calenda*, reinterpreted with Western musical instruments (as it is forbidden to make too much noise in a built-up area); or else from European dance music, which the Negro, with his natural musical inventiveness, broke up and modified. In either case it was an urban invention. Blues, on the other hand, took very well to being transplanted from country farms to railroad gangs, and thence to factories up north. The blues, in fact, *became* an urban phenomenon. The typical Cuban orchestra is the result of a hybridising process, also found in the towns on the island, between African musical instruments with mulatto modifications, and European ones that have been 'Africanised'. The Cuban *santeria*, the Brazilian *candomblé*, and the Voodoo (*Vaudou*) of Haiti are now moving towards new and original types of ballet, to unfamiliar dances, and perhaps, in the future, a theatre that will conquer the world.

Negro culture, then, has not been destroyed by urbanisation and industrialisation; on the contrary, it is responding to new needs which the city *per se* could not satisfy.

But there is another point to be considered. That spiritual void which the city creates at the heart of each human individual is resented, naturally, just as much by the European as by the Negro. As a result, the European turns increasingly to Africa or Black America for the satisfaction of those vital needs which industrial society can no longer answer. While discussing Césaire above, I postulated a return – though in a new form, for history never repeats itself – to the 'three-cornered voyage'. What we have here is, similarly, a reversion (though in an equally new form, adapted to new social patterns) to something that happened under the slave-owning régime. While the Negro was shedding his African heritage, the European, *per contra*, began to 'go African', supplementing his own civilisation with new cookery recipes, art forms, and super-stitions.[17] The current popularity of books such as J. Jahn's *Muntu* or Sartre's *Orphée Noir* (*Black Orpheus*) bears witness to this 'Africanising' passion among Europeans. We may also recall the way in which Negro dances were converted into white ballroom dances, and with what striking success, first in America and afterwards in Europe. These dances answer a need bred of urbanisation. They take one of two forms, which correspond respectively to the two sociological patterns in which they evolved – that is, paternalism, or interracial com-petition. Those dances which come from the big cities of the U.S.A. suggest a régime in which the white society controls and censors the black one. That is why they are more 'Negro' than 'African', and tend to sanction just those gestures that are firmly repressed in everyday life, but can at last burst out during the evening, in a riot of jazz and a joyous upsurge of motor activity – a rhythmic frenzy, working off anti-white aggression by jerking and leaping, with plenty of motor violence. On the plantations of Latin America, on the other hand, paternalist models still prevail; and dances there, as F. Ortiz accurately notes, even when they reach the European drawing-room, continue to imitate 'the vicissitudes of amorous seduction, right up to its climax in orgasm'. Now urban whites, like Negroes, are slaves to their jobs, bound by a number of taboos which keep various groups – young and old, men and women, workers and employers – apart from one another, and sunk in the grey drabness of day-to-day life. As a counter to all these controls, to the mechanical actions dictated by a factory job, to the suppression of aggressive instincts that cannot be released, to the anonymity of social controls, we have such things as swing, jitter-bugging, the Big Apple or boogie-woogie. These facilitate motor release, and produce a physical frenzy which in some cases (as I have evidence to prove) can go so far that it creates a modern version of the old sacred ritual.

The city does, it is true, offer another road to freedom and release, through sex. It is no accident that this should develop at the same time as industrialisation and urbanisation; its function is compensatory – with the special advantage of presenting no particular danger to capitalism or to the government. Yet while the city cultivates eroticism, it also destroys its potential by reducing the sexual relationship to a simple animal act, and thus doing away with the long preliminary period of courtship which formerly led up to it. As a result, the orgasm has lost its truly liberating function. Dances such as the tango or samba constitute an attempt to reintroduce these old approaches, to make the road of desire long and difficult once more, to create a new swing away from pure eroticism, which is always disillusioning, towards true passion.

I believe, then, that the Afroamerican cultures, far from being dead, are in fact spreading, and being absorbed by Europeans. Tomorrow, in this ceaselessly changing world, they may well put out yet other new flowers, and feed, with their honey or pimentoes, the promise of further fruit to come.

REFERENCES

1. John Dollard, *Caste and Class in a Southern Town*, Yale Univ. Press, 1937

2. See the chapters by R. Bastide, Dr L. E. Braithwaite, Munro S. Edmonson and Ray Marshall in *Industrialisation and Race Relations* (ed. Guy Hunter), Oxford, 1965. Van den Berghe, in the United States, has placed considerable emphasis on this bi-polarity in race relations.

3. Cf. R. Bastide, 'The Development of Race Relations in Brazil', in *Industrialisation and Race Relations*, Oxford, 1965, pp. 9–29. One point which calls for special notice is that in Negro periodicals, such as *A Frente Negra*, the Negroes refuse to regard themselves as Africans – a term which they regard as synonymous with 'savages'.

4. In addition to E. Franklin Frazier's book, referred to in my introduction, see G. Myrdal, *An American Dilemma*, vol. II, New York, 1944, chs. 34–37; Roy Ottley, *New World a-Coming* (Portuguese trs.) Rio, 1945.

5. The most sociologically orientated study on this literature yet published is that by Robert Ezra Park, *Race and Culture*, Glencoe, Ill., 1950. See also Jean Wagner, *Les poètes Nègres des Etats-Unis*, Paris, 1963.

6. On the Negro Jewish and Muslim churches in the U.S.A. see Frazier, *The Negro Church in America*, Liverpool, 1964, pp. 63–7; A. Huff Fauset, *Black Gods of the Metropolis*, Philadelphia, 1944, ch. V; Vincent Monteil, 'La réligion des Black Muslims', *Esprit*, Oct. 1964, pp. 601–29.

7. On the Ras Tafari movement, see G. E. Simpson, 'Political Cultism in West Kingston, Jamaica', *Social and Economic Studies*, vol. IV, Jamaica;

'Jamaica Revivalist', *idem*, vol. V; 'The Ras Tafari Movement in Jamaica', *Social Forces*, 34, 2, 1953.

8. Psalms 63 and 31; Ezekiel, 36, 28.

9. R. Bastide, 'Le Dr Price Mars et le Vodou', in *Témoignages sur la vie et l'oeuvre du Dr Jean Price Mars*, Port-au-Prince, 1956, pp. 196–202.

10. P. Mercier, 'The Fon of Dahomey', in *African Worlds* (ed. D. Forde), Oxford, 1954, pp. 210–34.

11. Milo Rigaud, *La tradition vaudoo* . . ., *op. cit.*

12. R. Bastide, 'Le mythe de l'Afrique noire et la société de classe multi-raciale', *Esprit*, Oct. 1958, pp. 401–13.

13. R. Bastide, *Religions Africaines* . . ., *op. cit.*

14. On this ideology, see F. H. Cardoso and O. Ianni, *Côr e Mobilidade social em Florianopólis*, S. Paulo, 1960; F. A. Cardoso, *Capitalismo e Escravidão*, S. Paulo, 1962; F. Fernandes, *A Integração do Negro à Sociedade de Classes*, S. Paulo, 1964.

15. R. Bastide, 'Variations sur la négritude', *Présence Africaine*, 1st quarter, 1961, pp. 7–17.

16. Musicologists point out the way in which African music, imported to the U.S.A. on records, has influenced contemporary jazz, de-Westernising it and reintroducing many African features.

17. I am not using the word 'superstition' here in its pejorative sense, but as a scientific term to denote fragments of ritual or taboo which have become detached from their pattern or institution, and survive as elements in isolation.

INDEX

72 73 74   12 11 10 9 8 7 6 5 4 3 2 1